ASPECTS
OF THE
PRESENT

Feingold Studios

MARGARET MEAD

ASPECTS OF THE PRESENT

Margaret Mead
and
Rhoda Metraux

Preface by Sey Chassler

"I speak out of the experience of my own lifetime of seeing past and future as aspects of the present."
—MARGARET MEAD,
Blackberry Winter

William Morrow and Company, Inc.
in conjunction with *Redbook* magazine
New York 1980

Library of Congress Cataloging in Publication Data

Mead, Margaret, 1901-1978
    Aspects of the present.

    1. Women—United States—Social conditions.
2. Family—United States.   3. Children—United States.
4. Human ecology.   5. Ethnology—United States.
I. Metraux, Rhoda Bubenday, (date)   joint author.
II. Title.
HQ1426.M4   305.4   79-26688
ISBN 0-688-03629-5

Printed in the United States of America

First Edition

1   2   3   4   5   6   7   8   9   10

Book Design by Michael Mauceri

Preface

What was she like, Margaret Mead? What was she like to work with? People have asked me that since she died. And they had always asked all of us here at *Redbook* that question while she was working with us. She worked with us for something like seventeen years, and so we had a chance to know what she was like.

She was a complete professional. When she was with *Redbook*'s editors, with me and with Robert Levin (our Articles Editor who died before she did) and with Helene Pleasants, who edited her copy and now has worked on this book, and with Silvia Koner, our current Articles Editor, she was herself an editor. She and Rhoda Metraux would come to our offices three or four times a year and meet with us over lunch (she always enjoyed good food) to discuss subject matter. She talked well and tossed out ideas at a rapid rate, but occasionally the rush of her thoughts and the mass of her information would tangle, and what had started out as a specific idea for a column would end as an abstraction. At those times she was always willing and even eager to talk through the ideas again in order to clarify. She was concerned with clarity whether it was for prose or thought or the functions of life or the relationships of people. Clarity and sanity were her goals.

During our meetings and luncheons we would talk about young women because that is the business of *Redbook*—publishing a magazine for young women—and because they were the people she felt it was most important to speak to. We would talk about children and about men, about the passage of time and the ordering of society. About nurturing and the threats that human beings were constructing against their own lives. We talked about the pollution of the air, the earth, the waters. We talked about the dangers of a nuclear holocaust and of radiation destroying us in silence. And we talked about peace. Peace was Margaret Mead's passion.

Every three or four years we would bring a small group of our readers to our offices to meet with Margaret and Rhoda. They would talk about what it is to be a woman, to be married, to have children, or to be unmarried and to have no children. They would talk about the potential that women have and how to use that potential.

These meetings always seemed to refresh Margaret and to exhilarate her. The last one was only a few months before her dying. She was not well, but in her accustomed way she moved and inspired the group and helped them to articulate their thoughts and to examine their lives. At these meetings, as in our more private editorial meetings, we chatted about the food served at the luncheons and about how business was going and about politics. On everything Margaret Mead had opinions, and she expressed them with high enthusiasm and, most of the time, with great eloquence.

Like the rest of us, when she was full of energy she was at her best. But there were, of course, days when she would come to meet with us after a series of lectures and much travel, and she would be tired. While fatigue sometimes took the bounce away, it never took her mind away or her heart or her soul.

Margaret Mead loved to laugh. Margaret Mead loved to explain things to people. Margaret Mead reached out beyond herself.

She could be outrageous. I have heard her get into arguments concerning subject matter relative to publishing in which she was absolutely wrong and misinformed. I heard her once defend her position for twenty minutes before settling for a draw. When she did that sort of thing she was not only a marvel to hear but a marvel to contemplate, because as she went down fighting she was picking up information from her opponents and assimilating it into her being. One never had the feeling that she took knowledge into her brain only. She seemed to take it into herself. It became part of her and it joined with all of the knowledge she had accumulated in the past, becoming part of a network of knowledge, information, intelligence and opinion that she had with her always. She drew from that network constantly, and, drawing from it, she always knew where she was in the world, and, knowing where she was, she was able to tell you where you were. As she spoke, she navigated. And as you listened, you knew where you were. She drew you in.

Much of the writing she and Rhoda Metraux did for us has a similar effect, as the reader will find in this collection of *Redbook* columns. The writing is clear and straightforward and very rich. It provides nourishment.

Margaret Mead didn't reserve herself for her working colleagues alone or for her readers. She reached out in much the same way to strangers who would come to speak to her in restaurants, on planes, on the street. It was easy for the world to recognize her. Her figure, short, and somehow in the later years chunky yet elegant, was dominating. She walked strongly and forcefully and with purpose. Carrying her five-foot thumbstick, waving it at taxicabs and friends, leading the way with it, she was known everywhere, in Kansas, in Athens, in New Guinea, everywhere. And everywhere she was willing to spend time, to share her time, with strangers. I have sat with her in public places when people came to pay their respects to her. She greeted them always as friends and made them feel known and recognized.

And yet, having seen Margaret Mead in all of these ways, I have seen only a small part of her vast and varied life. I did not know her as a scientist or as a traveler or as a friend (except through our working together), as a leader in her own profession of anthropology, as an adviser to Presidents and to governments or as a teacher. I did not know her socially. I did not know her as her staff knew her or as those who shared her religious experiences knew her. There were so many Margaret Meads that only a very few people could have shared her fully.

But whatever we had of her at *Redbook* we had in full measure. She took criticism and editing with grace and acceptance. She was a co-worker and worked with us; she never asked to be more than that. She wrote twelve columns for us every year for more than seventeen years and never missed a deadline. We saw her four or five times a year. We spoke to her perhaps once a month or so. She was with us the full time, as she must have been with the dozens of other people in her busy life. She was "on staff." And we are all grateful for that.

We were happy to be working with her, even when she growled at us for being what she thought was not quite as smart as we should be, or could be.

Margaret Mead was not ambiguous. She gave you herself. She let you be, and expected you to be, yourself.

Margaret Mead loved to be loved. While she was living, I had looked forward to writing this preface as a tribute to her, making it something we could share, making it a gift to her. It is a gift to her still.

And finally she wanted you to know how she felt about you. Not long before her illness, we had a long talk in her office about an article she was writing for us. During the talk, she somehow felt she had hurt my feelings or that somehow I was angry with her. I was not. When the meeting was finished, I said good-bye and started down the stairs from her office in the American Museum of Natural History. Halfway down, I heard her call me: "Sey." I turned. "Are you angry with me?" she asked. "No. Why do you ask?" "You didn't kiss me good-bye," she said. I ran back up the stairs and kissed her good-bye.

Joyfully, then.

Sadly, now.

Remembering the joy.

SEY CHASSLER
Editor-in-Chief
Redbook magazine

New York, N.Y.
1980

Foreword

These essays, written for publication in *Redbook* magazine over a ten-year period, 1969–1979, are one outcome of a continuing dialogue about American culture and the concerns of anthropology in the contemporary world that had its origins long ago in the exigencies of World War II.

This was the setting in which Margaret Mead and I met and began to work together. She came to Washington early in 1942 to become the Executive Secretary of the Committee on Food Habits in the National Research Council, a role that demanded great skill in interpreting American culture to Americans. By then she already had the experience of long, intensive and innovative fieldwork in six South Seas cultures, beginning in 1925—the research that provided the foundation for all her later work in the field and in the world at large. I myself was a very new anthropologist. I had recently come back from a short, exploratory field trip to Haiti, and the year I spent as Margaret Mead's research assistant was my first experience as a professional anthropologist. In a word, I had everything to learn. It was difficult, but it was also exhilarating because so much was new to both of us as we experimented and I tried to devise means of getting at the right questions—questions that might lead us in the direction of useful answers. For this was applied research, directed very immediately toward action here at home and eventually abroad when the time came that we had to take into account the needs of other peoples.

From the first we recognized that we shared a long-term commitment to understand American culture, but our background and approach were quite unlike. Margaret was old-American, fully aware of her family's place in this country.

I was a third-generation American in a family that had strong living ties in Europe. She came of age in the explosive, innovative postwar years of the 1920s, and the problems she took to the field or that emerged from her fieldwork were relevant to some of the most heated discussions in Western societies in that period. Thirteen years younger, I came of age in the somber, increasingly desperate and violent years of the 1930s, when every discussion of politics, social issues and the possibility of a general world war had conflicting ideological overtones. I was an unpublished writer and active in a union of publishing workers.

However, I believe that the special kind of awareness that very early made each of us an observing participant in our culture goes back much further. We had a long-time perspective that certainly derived from our relationship to grandparents. Margaret's first, perhaps most influential teacher was her grandmother; mine was my grandfather in whose home I grew up and from whom I learned to distinguish politics from political issues. We were also readers and, after a fashion, writers of poetry from an early age, a discipline that made us continually aware of the metaphors of our daily life.

This excursion into the past cannot of itself "explain" how or why we became students of American culture; but it may suggest the seriousness of the quest. We Americans are renowned the world over for our eagerness to tell one another how well or how badly we are doing, as well as for our willingness to listen to the impressions of strangers, outsiders. This was not Margaret's way, although her response to the ongoing scene was vividly immediate. As a disciplined student of our culture, she continually worked on the kinds of problems about which she lectured, taught and wrote.

The invitation to write a monthly column for *Redbook* came in 1962, following the publication of a delightful interview between Margaret Mead and Margaret Truman. Earlier there had been some talk of a newspaper column, modeled on that written for many years by Eleanor Roosevelt. *Redbook* offered a much more interesting and viable plan. Responsibility for a monthly article left Margaret relatively free to lecture (in itself a source of subject matter), travel, even go to the field for short periods. Having a schoolboy son, I wanted to remain closer to home and could do background research and some of the writing as a part-time activity. It was a form of collaboration we both enjoyed, perhaps for the very reason that it kept us hotly arguing, time after time, as we had to work our way through our differences to clarity.

The editors of *Redbook* accord equal dignity to their authors and audience. In seventeen years I cannot remember being asked to drop an idea or to modify a statement that might be displeasing, but only—and this very often—to make clear what had seemed obvious to us, but strange to others. Over the years only one column was not published—an early one on grandmothers at a time in the 1960s when relationships of the young to the elderly were unintelligible. The omission was redeemed later, when Margaret wrote about herself as a new grandmother.

Our problem was never that of finding subjects on which we could agree, but often that of narrowing down the choice. During the ten years covered by this volume it became the custom to meet from time to time at lunch to exchange ideas for columns, occasionally for a series, some entirely topical, others with a longer range, sometimes suggested by the late Robert Levin, *Redbook*'s Articles Editor for eleven years, more recently by *Redbook* Editor-in-Chief Sey Chassler. During these years we also had the great good fortune to have as a mentor and copy editor Helene Pleasants, whose professional life was contemporary with ours, so that she understood what we were saying and made sure that we said what we meant to say. Most recently she has worked with me on this book.

Most of the different kinds of columns we wrote are represented in this volume, not in sequence in time, but clustered in terms of some of our larger preoccupations. Every one, however, is dated so that it is possible to relate the subject to the events that gave it significance. Some are very specific to the American scene, as Margaret reflected on American responses to our bicentennial celebrations and to our current attitudes toward adoption and crime and the death penalty. She was stirred by the hope that Congress would pass legislation for a more humane and responsible welfare program; I have let her statement stand even though no action of the kind has been taken. She wrote at length, as she spoke frequently and at length, about the state of our family life.

In these years she also became increasingly concerned about ecological dangers that threaten all civilization and the survival of future generations; not only the nuclear dangers that are an obvious threat, but also the dangers that are inherent in our willful disregard of the rights of many peoples to good air and clean water. She saw it both as a danger and as a hopeful possibility that we shall overcome our ancient beliefs about boundaries when we recognize that water and air are the common necessities of all peoples everywhere and cannot be contained. However, her overriding concern was for the earth's children. She was to have been on the National Commission for the International Year of the Child, and the last column to which she gave her attention was intended to quicken our faltering awareness of how much must be done to protect the future through children.

In *Blackberry Winter*, Margaret Mead wrote: "I speak out of the experience of my own lifetime of seeing past and future as aspects of the present." The experience of her lifetime included co-operative research and interpretation of research with many individuals and working groups that permitted her to expand greatly her understanding of the present. She had the rare gift of being able to take from others and to make what she had taken her own without in any way diminishing the individuality or worth of those who worked with her.

There can be no further volume of her work. But because of the continuity of her presence, there can be continuity in our understanding.

RHODA METRAUX

New York
October 1979

Contents

I
Looking Back and Ahead

What Have We Learned?
Where Are We Going?

OCTOBER 1971

For more than 50 years pessimists have loudly proclaimed that while technology has rushed ahead, our thinking about social institutions, customs and beliefs, our willingness to use technology to meet human needs and our ability to translate concern for human life into actuality—all have lagged far behind.

We are told that modern man, battered and buffeted by multiplying complexities, simply swings back and forth between well-known and equally unsatisfactory ways of trying to solve the real problems of human living. Around the world men swing from tyranny to rebellion and revolution and back to tyranny in forms more devastating than before because of new controls made possible by advancing technology; from preoccupation with war and the uses of aggression to preoccupation with peace and often ineffectual efforts to outlaw aggression; from puritanical prudery to counterpuritanical exhibitionism; from strict and heartless discipline of the young to foolish permissiveness and license; from unfounded idealism to despairing cynicism about man's ability to create a livable world.

It is said that while our technological capacities have steadily advanced, so that we could—if we would—build a world community, our ideas about human living, swinging back and forth like a pendulum, have never really advanced at all. We have created no improved image of man that was not set forth long ago in some philosophy or religious creed. We have not developed an ethic that unites instead of dividing human groups. So deeply has this pessimistic view permeated

19

contemporary thinking that few people stop to question whether it is true.

Is it true, for example, that no new relationships between the sexes are possible? Are there only four possible sex relationships: one man and one woman, one man and several women, one woman and several men, many men and many women? Is the only alternative to sex contrast, as we know it, unisex—in which both men and women lose out? Is it true only men can run the world's affairs?

Is it true that we can never rid the world of the danger of witches and witch hunts? That fears of witchcraft merely will take new forms, so that time and again in the future, as in the past, thousands of misunderstood, accused—and self-accused—men and women will be doomed to be burned or drowned, run down by mobs or condemned by due processes of law?

Is it true that human beings are necessarily at the mercy of their unconscious impulses and their equally unconscious self-punishing efforts to control their fantasies? Are taboos a necessary aspect of social control?

Is it true that human identity is threatened by the technology men have invented in their search for power over nature? Must human beings sacrifice themselves to an unending search for power over the natural world?

Are the old incapable of learning? Incapable of putting their experience at the service of change and the future? Are children condemned to imperfect comprehension and years of waiting to become adults, only to find themselves bound by the strait jacket of convention?

I do not think any of these things are necessarily so.

My experience as an anthropologist has led me to think that as we have come to understand more about the laws of the physical universe in which we live, we have also—significantly in the very recent past—acquired a kind of knowledge that gives us choices human beings never before have had. This is our knowledge about our own humanity—our newly emerging understanding about the nature of human nature.

The growth of technology has been spectacular. Much more quietly, and for the most part in slow, stumbling steps, we have also gained insight and a new perspective on our human selves—who we are and what we may become.

Two major difficulties, among many others, long stood in the way of this kind of enlightenment. One is a belief that must be as ancient as human life—the belief that the people of one's own social group represent all that human nature is capable of. This belief has always divided people into contrasting entities: "we" who are fully human and "they" who, being different from us, must be more or less (and, most often, less) than fully human. This belief was based, as it still is, on isolation and failure of communication, involuntary or imposed. A simplistic belief, yes, but one that is built into much of what we think and feel about ourselves and other peoples.

The second difficulty, a modern one, is that people cannot be studied as whole human beings in laboratories. We cannot turn microscopes on the complex processes of individual development. We cannot turn telescopes on the cultural and social arrangements for living that human societies have developed through history. We cannot experiment or make blueprints for styles of living. We can learn only from the lifestyles different peoples have developed over many generations.

Our new knowledge is the measure of how far we have come. For we know now, as no one could have known in the past, that all human beings belong to one species. What distinguishes human groups one from another is not inborn; it is the way in which each has organized and perpetuated experience and the access each has had to other living traditions. had. This is our knowledge about our own humanity—our Great civilizations have developed out of rich and continual cross-cultural contacts; simple, "primitive" cultures have survived through the accidents of isolation.

The realization that we can study human behavior only as it actually happens—in the real situations of real cultures—is in large part the contribution of anthropologists. Through their work, especially with small societies the world over, they have learned to look, however imperfectly, at vastly different patterns for living and to treat them all as equally valid expressions of human nature. What this has meant is that we now, as never in the past, can see ourselves and other peoples within a framework that includes all of us and in which our own way of life is but one version among many.

In the past Americans accepted as an article of faith the idea that people can change their way of life in their own lifetime. This was intrinsic to our belief that immigrants from the most diverse backgrounds could become Americans. Today we know that this capacity for culture change is not peculiar to our kind of society. Wherever new lines of communication have opened up, wherever ideas new to a people have taken hold of their imagination, people have been able to change.

But as we have also become aware, in a more sophisticated way, of the strength and continuity of older traditions in molding people's thoughts and feelings—just as we have come to see ourselves as a pluralistic society and also as a people who have incorporated much of our diversified past into our present—we have become doubtful. We have become pessimistic about our capacity to live with all this diversity.

But I believe that what we are really struggling with is not loss of faith in old beliefs. Rather, we are struggling with new insights that at present are being expressed in many strange and bizarre ways. We are in deep conflict between accepting new responsibilities and retreating to old explanations. Like the explorers of an unknown land, we look back and ahead, hesitating to explore the world that is opening up to us.

But I do not think the choices resulting from growing self-knowledge all lie in the future. We are already well along in the process of translating what we understand—even what we so far only dimly perceive—into new convictions, new practices, new institutions.

The current explosion of arguments about the relationships of men and women is, I believe, one example of how far we have progressed. For I do not see the activities of all the different women's liberation groups as the sudden expression of a heavily tyrannized group—a group that includes half, or more than half, of the world's population. The foundations for new life-styles for women have been laid throughout modern society.

We are well aware today that the disabilities attributed to women are social disabilities, different in different cultures. We know that the isolation in which so many women live in the modern world is socially imposed. But we also know, from the experience of women who are making their own way, that women are fully capable of the kinds of accomplishment that men have developed and value.

I see the present liberation movement not as the first rumbling sound of a revolution but as a form of self-assertion through which women are heartening themselves and one another to act on what they already feel and know. We are witnessing not the first but very likely the climactic act of the drama.

There are, however, two things that are genuinely new in the present situation. One is the dawning recognition that if women are to be freed to become full human beings, then men must be freed to become full human beings too. Belatedly we are discovering that men's domination over women, as long as it has been accepted by men and women, has prevented men from recognizing in themselves (and women from recognizing in their fathers and sons, their lovers and husbands, their brothers and friends) human needs that grow out of dependence, especially trust in the strength of persons with whom they can only partly identify. We are discovering that men, to the extent they have treated women as sex objects, have bound themselves to conceptions of masculinity that cramp their own talents and imagination. We are learning that men exclude from their own consciousness the qualities they attribute to women—qualities they believe must be denied and fought within themselves.

We know that what constitutes "masculinity" and "femininity" varies extraordinarily the world over. What human beings have done in most societies over most of time is to dichotomize human capacities; what is feminine is also not-masculine; what is masculine is also not-feminine. So boys and girls have grown up accepting within themselves the qualities they are expected to have but denying those they are expected not to have, whether or not this fits their temperamental bents and talents. Belatedly we are discovering that in those situations in which girls and boys, men and women, are free to share opportunities, they also are free to develop as individuals.

The other thing that is genuinely new is the idea of choice about parenthood. In every culture some women and some men, whether out of choice or necessity, have been refused or have denied themselves parental roles. Neither abortion nor contraception, however practiced, are new ideas. But the requirement that the social group perpetuate itself has been so strong throughout human history that very few could avoid the social pressures to procreate, bear and rear children.

As long as this was so, most of women's talents, strength and capacity for devotion were necessarily bound up with the care of children. Equally, of course, men's activities, however diversified, were largely bound up with providing what they conceived to be an environment in which their women and children could survive and, if possible, flourish and multiply.

But today we are concerned with a kind of human living that goes far beyond survival, just when we have learned, in fact, that survival itself depends on limiting our population to the number of human beings our planet can support. And with growing self-knowledge we are coming to understand that awareness and freedom of choice are the basis of both individual development and a society that values human dignity. In such a society, being parents out of choice and being a chosen child are equally necessary.

We are living in a time of transition. Old traditions die hard and we cannot predict how new ones will develop over generations. We can divest ourselves of stereotype beliefs about differences between men and women. But we cannot know what special gifts women—and men—may have until a life-style is developed in which all people can function as full human beings, sharing responsibility for one another in as yet unforeseen ways.

The Fear of Witches

For the diorama of Bali in the Hall of the Peoples of the Pacific in the American Museum of Natural History,* I chose the climactic scene in a favorite Balinese ritual drama: the confrontation of the Dragon and the Witch, theatrical figures at the center of Balinese life that symbolize safety and danger, life and death and, at a much deeper level, father and mother.

In earlier scenes of the play the witch appeared as an old hag who instructed her child-witch disciples how to spread plague, death and destruction across the land. The dragon in mortal form appeared as the king of the devastated country (or sometimes only his emissary) who had insulted the witch and failed in combat against her.

But now, at the climax, the supernatural witch, a masked, terrifying figure with hideous, hairy breasts, long, sharp-pointed fingernails, teeth like tusks and a tongue that shoots forth flames, confronts the masked supernatural dragon, a huge, rollicking, lovable, puppyish creature into whose harmless, gaping jaws human beings can thrust their heads for safety and protection from the witch. Attacked by the dragon's disciples, the witch sends them into a trance during which they turn their daggerlike krises on themselves. But in the end the witch collapses and the dragon restores his followers to normal life.

* The Hall of the Peoples of the Pacific formally opened on May 18, 1971. In 1975, owing to a major reorganization of the Museum's exhibition space, the hall was temporarily closed. The relocated hall, the designs for which Margaret Mead herself approved, is scheduled to open in 1981.

The theatrical image of the witch, who fails but is never wholly destroyed, gives the Balinese a tingling sense of terror in which they delight and which enhances the low emotional tone of everyday life. They would not do without her for anything. Once a foreign painter persuaded a theatrical company to perform the Javanese version of the play, in which the witch is killed. The Balinese audience refused to go home until the witch was resuscitated so that, on some other day, she could perform her terrifying pantomime of destruction.

The witch in Bali epitomizes both the fearsome and fear itself; she is the woman a man may marry believing he is marrying a beautiful young girl, a stranger, who turns out instead to be a witch. She is the menacing creature that lurks unseen at a childbirth, ready to kill the newborn infant. She may be the neighbor who comes to call and strokes a child's throat—and the next day the child is dead.

But the attraction of the witch figure, which grips the imagination of the Balinese, lies in the fact that, fearsome as she is, she is herself afraid. It is this that explains her immense and enduring appeal as she dances at the height of her power, hideous and frightening—and pathetically alone in her own fear.

Fascination with the combination of menace and fear—a sense of horror that attracts, an attraction that must be denied—is characteristic of witch figures and of attitudes toward the uncanny powers of witches almost everywhere such figures appear around the world. The witch is and is not what she seems. As in so many medieval representations, the young witch, dazzling in her enchanting beauty, stands in front of the haglike old witch who is bereft of all feminine charm, ugly and grim.

Sometimes witches are pictured only in hideous forms, as among the Trobrianders, who believe in supernatural witches that flit in the treetops and haunt new gravesites. Or, as in Haiti, the witch appears as a solitary—a poor, feeble old woman living utterly alone who offers sweetmeats to children in a simulated gesture of friendliness in order to poison them. But the duality of the witch expressed in the power of transformation—the ability to disguise herself as a harmless or delightful person and suddenly to change herself into a nightmare creature—is an enduring characteristic.

Almost everywhere, witchcraft works with reversals. The witch who appears to be beautiful is a hag. Witches do not dress up for their secret rites; they go naked or even take off their human skin. They hold their meetings not at midday but at midnight. On their journeys they do not walk but fly, riding on peeled rods or similar objects, or ride facing backward on an animal such as a goat.

It is true that witchcraft is not confined to women. Especially where it is believed that the powers of the witch are inherited, there are also male witches. In Bali an occasional man, the only child of a witch mother, may be credited with being a witch by inheritance. And the leader of a "coven" (the English name for an assembly of witches) often is believed to be a male. Sometimes he is human, sometimes supernatural. In Europe he may be considered to be Satan himself, the personification of evil.

Nevertheless, witchcraft is most closely associated with things that are feared about a woman: the delusive quality of beauty and charm; the belief that the woman who yields in a man's arms has only lent herself to him for her own dangerous purposes or that the woman sleeping by a man's side is really somewhere else in mind and spirit, leaving behind only an empty shell; the fear that the midwife may snatch away the newborn or cause it to die or that a woman's hand, stretched out in apparent compassion, may do a deadly injury.

Witches may know spells or make brews and philters, and old women who cure with herbs may be treated like witches. But witches are not the same as magicians or sorcerers who have learned the magic arts of controlling the world, even the supernatural world. The central point about witches is that their power is *innate*. They do their harm through sheer in-born malignancy. They may even work evil in spite of themselves. Whether they will or no, their touch sours milk; their glance makes lambs and foals and children die.

It is this belief that witchcraft is innate—that a woman may be a witch unknowingly or, knowing it, may be unable to quell the power of evil in her—that infuses witchcraft with its special sense of the uncanny. The witch's fear of this power, sometimes her wicked delight in it, is complementary to the male fear that the woman he loves may be, after all a witch.

In a recent study in rural Ghana, M. G. Field, an ethno-psychiatrist, worked with middle-aged women who believed that they must be witches because they had lost so many children. In many ways their anxieties resembled the guilt-ridden fears of older women Field had treated in a hospital in England, women who believed that against their own will and without knowing how or why, they had done damage to members of their own families whom they loved.

The extraordinary thing is that the image of the witch is remarkably constant all over the world. In one place and time the idea may be like a simple sketch while elsewhere—as in 16th- and 17th-century Europe—it may be tremendously elaborated. This indicates that the essential conception of the witch is one that is very, very old in human history or, alternatively, that it is a conception that can very readily spring up among both men and women.

There is no real way of knowing whether witch-fear was invented many thousands of years ago or whether it arises again and again from some patterned regularity in human experience. In either case, the idea of the witch is carried by language and figures of speech, by folk tales and the fright figures used to make children behave. It is there, ready to be used and elaborated upon. Once in a Sepik village in New Guinea, among a people who had no representations of witches, only folk tales about them, I came upon a little girl, a child nurse, who had set her baby brother down in a hole she had been digging and was dancing over him with gleeful, witchlike gestures.

A belief in witches and dread of witchcraft comes and goes, but it is recurrently brought back to terribly vivid life by fears that, in turn, can lead to panic and attacks against almost any group in a community. Epidemics, earthquakes, hurricanes, a succession of inexplicable disasters—any of these may drive a primitive people to try to embody their fear and rage in other human beings and then to exterminate the human agents they believe to be responsible for their misfortunes. Or a people may attempt to project on some group the emotions by which they are shaken in a period of very deep culture change when the foundations of the universe as they know it appear to be crumbling.

We have seen upsurging accusations of witchcraft in primitive societies when a people felt overwhelmed by the experiences of contact with a Western culture. And in the 16th and 17th centuries Europe was shaken by a deep sense of impending evil and disaster, which led some men to construct utopias through which they hoped to save human souls and led other men to a preoccupation with evil that resulted in a protracted and drastic witch hunt in which thousands of witches, many of them self-confessed, were mercilessly tortured and burned alive. In the American colonies witchcraft was feared and punished, and 20 persons were hanged as witches in Salem, Massachusetts, in 1692.

Witchcraft, then, must be regarded, as an ever-present cultural potentiality, present as fear and as fright in those who are feared. Where are we to look for the source of this belief, focusing on women, that postulates an innate power for evil that is as frightening to those believed to be possessed by it as it is to those against whom the power is believed to be directed?

I think we must look for the source in the very early mutual relationship of the mother and the infant—in the experience of the very little child wholly dependent for its survival on an all-powerful mother and the experience of the mother wholly responsible for the care of a helpless child. This is the relationship that Erik Erikson has called "basic trust," which is built in the first months of life.

The reverse—basic *mistrust*—may have as one element fear of the mother, who appears to be so powerful and who incomprehensibly thwarts the child's unformulated wishes and needs. But there is also, I believe, another element—the unrecognized and unreconciled wishes of women, their own unmet needs as persons, that are aroused in response to the helplessness of the children in their care.

Throughout human history most women have had to channel their desires to be a person and to do something in life into their care for their families. Most women, identifying with their own mothers and grandmothers, have learned to accept their tasks responsibly and to carry them out with warmth and tenderness. But not all of them and not always— as also most, but not all, infants—can respond adequately to the warmth and tenderness offered them.

In some cases and perhaps at some moments in all mother-child relationships there is a mutual response of fear. It is not only the child who longs for and at the same time repudiates and fears the all-powerful mother. It is also the mother herself who, in response to the child, yearns for and fears a power she does not have but in her fantasy might have. This is, I believe, the recurrent source of witch-fear: the male's fear that all women, like his image of his mother, may be too powerful, as well as the female's fear that she may grow up to become, like her image of her mother, powerful and destructive.

Is there a way out of this ancient, recurrent danger of fear and panic? It is not enough, I think, to reassure ourselves that we no longer believe in witches, in innate evil or in supernatural powers. Significantly, some groups working in the women's liberation movement are playing with the image of witches, and one writer, commenting on the revival of the idea of the witch, remarked: "There is one in every house—a woman."

I do not know whether the idea of the witch can ever be wholly wiped out—as the witch is never really killed in Bali. But there are steps we can take that will protect most children.

One we have been experimenting with in our culture. This is the involvement of the father in the care of his very young children. This would alter the balance, as the infant would have, from the beginning, two persons to depend on and to turn to as a resource in the long process of identification and differentiation.

The other is only now, for the first time in human history, really possible. Today having a child and caring for a child—one's own or an adopted child—is an open choice, one among all the different choices a woman can make as a way of living years of her life. We are hardly conscious of this as yet. But parents can rear their daughters as well as their sons with the expectation of an open future, building on that expectation instead of on fantasies that must be repressed.

These two things, taken together, can mean that a generation of men and women can emerge who are not frightened of women or, in the case of girls, afraid of being adult women. But this will come about only if we do not, like the Balinese, cherish the image of the witch and continue to hold on to her as a figure who not only terrifies us but also delights us with her fear.

Can We Live without Taboos?

DECEMBER 1971

Is it true that only primitive people have taboos—prohibitions that are charged with a dangerous power to punish anyone who dares to break them? Or do civilized people also have taboos? Are all taboos bad, or only some of them? What makes a taboo good or bad? Is it the emotional power of taboos that we object to? Should we—indeed, can we—rid ourselves of taboos?

Anthropologists often are asked questions of this kind. Some people, of course, ask simply out of curiosity about strange customs in distant parts of the world. But many others, it seems to me, ask in the expectation, or at least the hope, that what anthropologists have learned about human experience in cultures very different from our own can help us see our own perplexing problems in a fresh perspective, and so, perhaps, find more workable solutions.

Taboos—and all peoples have some taboos—are especially puzzling. The whole process is so mysterious. Rationalization and professed disbelief alike often have little effect on the working of a taboo. Some are so lightly held—such as the taboo against reading even an open post card addressed to another person—that breaking them may cause only a quiver of discomfort. But others have an unconscious hold that is extraordinarily strong and deep.

Many young Jews brought up in Orthodox homes, for instance, took sick when they were inducted into the armed services and for the first time had to eat nonkosher foods. Similarly, the American taboo against even the discussion of sex in the presence of young children has been so strong that we have the greatest difficulty in devising—let alone putting into practice—forms of sex education that would protect children from the dangers of accidental exposure to harmful experiences.

Most people think of a taboo merely as a stringent prohibition against something. But in fact it involves several things. It always identifies and sets boundaries around the thing tabooed. In effect it declares that this person, this place, this object, this act, this idea or belief, is inviolable. It also poses a threat: Whoever crosses the boundary—that is, breaks the taboo—arbitrarily and inevitably will be punished. A taboo works like a trap. Break the taboo and you spring the trap. No other agency of punishment is needed.

Taboos are socially shared beliefs that are perpetuated by consensus. But each person protects and enforces them through his or her own fear and anxiety, the involuntary sense that there is no escape from the anguish and guilt that breaking a taboo arouses. This means that, by and large, people steer clear of examining what a taboo is about, why it came into being—as if the very thought might jeopardize one's safety and peace of mind. It is these aspects or taboos that give them their enduring strength.

Some peoples have enormously elaborated the use of taboos as the means of carrying on the rules of conduct in their society. A few taboos, such as the taboos on incest and murder, are, as far as we know, universal.

Perhaps the strongest and most ancient of all taboos is that against incest—the taboo prohibiting sex relations between any members of a family except the husband and wife. Usually it is not phrased in this way. People think of the incest taboo as forbidding sex relations between father and daughter, mother and son, brother and sister. But there would be no family within which to forbid sex relations if the parents were not there to produce, through one set of accepted sex relations, other persons with whom sex relations were forbidden.

Sex relations forbidden between certain persons arise from sex permitted, even required, of other persons.

In a great many societies the world over, the primary incest taboo extends far beyond the immediate family to include a whole series of relatives, real or fictive. Here again we find that what is forbidden on the one hand is permitted or required on the other. The two systems, in fact, interlock and reinforce each other. For example, among the Trobriand Islanders of Melanesia, Father's sister's daughter is the proper wife. From earliest childhood (and whether or not he actually marries her) a boy calls this cousin by a term that marks her as a potential wife. But Mother's sister's daughter is likened to the boys' own sisters and, like them, this cousin is taboo.

In a small community this kind of social ordering means that everyone knows who are and who are not potential sexual partners—in whose presence, for instance, someone can tell sexy jokes and in whose presence one must always behave with decent respect and propriety. Equally important, it means that a whole group of young people, protected by the taboo, can grow up safely on terms of affection and mutual dependence without too much worry about sex.

There have been many attempts to explain the primary incest taboo, but most explanations do not amount to much. Essentially the incest taboo does only one thing—it protects the integrity of the family.

It means that while they are growing up children can be given and can express a deep affection that does not include sex. It means that they are safe from molestation and, equally, that adults are protected from the seductive attractiveness of the young. The taboo protects children by carrying them through their early—and largely unconscious—struggles with their own emotions so that later they can turn outside the family safely for other kinds of love relationships. It protects all the members of the family from inappropriate behavior that could lead to devastating competition and allows them to form ties of intimacy and affection that need never be broken.

In the United States we have attempted to rationalize the incest taboo by placing a tremendous emphasis upon the dangers of inbreeding as the principal reason for forbidding incestuous sex relations and incestuous marriages. Many people firmly believe that children born of incestuous unions are destined to be feeble-minded or to suffer from some other devastating incapacity. Those who accept this pseudoscientific explanation—as almost everyone does—do not realize that they are also accepting the ancient taboo, the idea of automatic punishment—a punishment visited upon the children.

The taboo as we phrase it works well enough to protect the members of a biologically related (what we still call a "blood-related") family. But it provides no real protection for the kind of family in which great numbers of Americans now live—a family in which only some of the members are true kin.

Stepfathers and stepdaughters, stepmothers and stepsons, stepsisters and stepbrothers are not "blood-related" kin, but they live together in one household as if they were. The incest taboo as we have explained it to ourselves does not apply to them. Living in closest intimacy, they are outside the boundaries of the automatic protection provided by the taboo, the deeply felt sense of the inviolability of primary family relationships in which sex is forbidden. Yet prohibitions remain necessary—perhaps become even more important as a protection against the stresses of complex relationships.

Once in a while a feeling of true kinship may spring up quite spontaneously. Recently a young girl said to me: "Now that my mother and my stepfather have a baby girl of their own, I feel as if my stepbrother were a real relative. Because after all, the baby is his sister and my sister too."

Such an individual solution, reciprocally accepted, can protect a particular family. But we cannot count on every family's finding a viable solution to the problem of how to live together in a home whose members are very differently related—or not at all related—to one another as kin.

What we need is a way of defining and protecting our complex family relationships that is shared by the whole community and to which each individual is deeply committed.

This is just what taboos—the deeply held taboos about incest and murder—succeeded in doing. It is true, of course, that they never worked perfectly in any society. No taboo is so dreadful that some do not break it and dare the consequences. No taboo is so carefully guarded that some, like Oedipus, do not break it unknowingly. But in small societies and in very slowly changing ones, in which everyone shares most of the same kinds of experience, taboos have worked well enough so that, quite unexamined, they have provided the protections that keep individuals safe and the community functioning.

Many taboos that grew out of religious injunctions, for instance, embodied practical folk wisdom. The practice of eating only food that was ritually clean, or kosher, protected people living in the hot climate of the Mideast from the serious illness that could be caused by unsanitary butchering or the inexpert preparation of food. The dietary taboo on pork, observed by Jews and Moslems alike, prevented people from eating an easily spoiled meat at a time when refrigeration was unknown. These taboos are still widely observed even when the practical reasons for them are largely forgotten.

In fact, if we really examine how most taboos work, we find that usually there is a good reason for them. We come to realize that a taboo such as the one on incest is both a social protection and the basis for an ethical code. A taboo forbids. But as I pointed out, by defining what is forbidden, it also defines what is permitted or required.

The heavy negative emphasis of a taboo, as we can better understand today, derives from the fact that the content of a taboo is built into a very archaic part of the human conscience. Taboos provide a kind of primitive ethical code or a practical protection embedded in concrete practices that people can follow without awareness, knowing only that they have no choice.

But today we live in a society that seeks to make people free by making them aware of what they are doing and why they are doing it. Taboos do the opposite. What we need instead are ethical rules that we can think about and adapt to the real and changing needs of our complex society.

How can we begin to move in this direction?

We must begin, I think, by recognizing the fact that the current "scientific" interpretation of the incest taboo, for example, is only a rationalization—just that and nothing more. Only then can we begin to think about and work out the rules of a responsible ethical code, rules that will accomplish in a positive sense what a taboo could do only through prohibitions: that is, create a viable home in which everyone can live in safe intimacy. Knowing that our ethical nature is part of his humanity, we can expect that in time such a consciously accepted ethic—replacing the mysterious taboo—will be built into the deeper levels of personality.

Taking these steps is important today in a world in which marriages are very fragile and the relationships of those who live together are very vulnerable—a world in which taboos often are dismissed as outdated. The development of a new ethic of this kind is likely to become even more important in the communal designs for living with which the young are experimenting. For in the future, in an extremely crowded world, people may become almost entirely dependent for true intimacy and companionship on the living arrangements of small clusters of people of different ages, only a few of whom are related to one another by kinship or even marriage.

Taboos of all kinds worked well enough as long as people lived—and expected to live—the same kind of life generation after generation. They worked as long as parents could teach children concretely, through practice, what they could expect to do and be as adults in a family and a community.

They do not work—as they are not now working—very well in a society in which people believe that they can plan for a future that is different from the past and can bring up children to make choices—new choices based on understanding what their aims are.

I do not think human beings will ever live wholly free of taboos. But we can construct ethical systems that will embody the positive and protective aspects of taboos, making them part of our conscious thought.

UFOs: Visitors from Outer Space?

SEPTEMBER 1974

"Do you believe in UFOs?"

Again and again over the years, I have been asked this extraordinary question, at times by people everywhere I go, at other times only by the few people whose passionate curiosity is sustained even when no new spectacular sightings are publicly reported in the press, in popular books or by serious scientists gathered at a meeting to discuss the problem.

Interest in unidentified flying objects always fluctuates as the number of reports of sightings rises and falls. But few people realize that in recent years masses of sightings seem to have come in waves, now in one part of the world and now in another—from the Far North to Antarctica, from North and South America, from Europe to the Orient, even from remote Papua New Guinea. In 1939 and 1946 Scandinavia seemed to be a center of UFO activity. In 1947, 1950 and again in 1952 the largest number of reports were made in the United States. In 1954 a wave spread from France across Western Europe and into Africa. The next wave, in 1957, began in South America and appeared to spread all over the world, reaching a climax of sightings in the United States.

Then there was a pause. News stories died down, flying saucer jokes faded away and people forgot—until 1967, when the waves of sightings began again and continued, now here and now there, almost up to the present.

In spite of all this, people still ask each other: "Do you believe in UFOs?"

I think this is a silly question, born of confusion. Belief has to do with matters of faith. It has nothing to do with the kind

40

of knowledge that is based on scientific inquiry. We should not bracket UFOs with angels and archangels, devils and demons. But this is just what we are doing when we ask whether people "believe" in UFOs—as if their existence were an article of faith. Do people believe in the sun or the moon or the changing seasons or the chairs they are sitting on?

When we want to understand something strange, something previously unknown to anyone, we have to begin with an entirely different set of questions: What is it? How does it work? Are there recurrent regularities?

Beginning in this way with an open mind, people can take a hard look at all the evidence. They sift out the vague rumors, the tall tales, the obvious mistaken judgments, the fanciful embroidery of detail, the hoaxes and the distortions introduced both by those who are overeager to believe and by those who are determined to discredit everything.

Beginning in this way we can answer the question most people really have in mind: Yes, there are unidentified flying objects. There are phenomena that, even after the most cautious and painstaking investigations, cannot be explained away. This much, at least, we must accept.

Thousands of sightings have been reported, and not only by individuals faced, alone at night, by the terrifying spectacle of a shining disk hovering soundlessly over the trees or apparently coming at them as they are driving down a road or touching the ground and then suddenly taking off vertically in a tremendous burst of speed. Pilots have continually reported sightings, and sometimes several planes have given chase—always unsuccessfully. Persons unknown to one another have described the same phenomenon seen in the same night—or daytime—sky.

Occasionally many people have watched, stunned, the same UFO event. In 1954, during the great wave of sightings in Europe, thousands of people in Rome watched while a cigar-shaped object—which simultaneously was tracked on the airport radar—performed acrobatic feats over the city for more than an hour. Radar tracings are not uncommon, and very occasionally fleeting views have been captured by cameras.

Sightings seem to become more numerous at those times when we on earth are taking a forward step into space. In 1897, four years before the first dirigible was successfully flown in France, sightings of phantom airships—never satisfactorily explained—raised excitement to fever pitch in America in the 20 states where they occurred. Late in World War II, crews of bomber squadrons in several war theaters described disturbing "blobs of light," which came to be known as "foo fighters." Intelligence services, ours and others', conjectured that they must be secret devices invented by the enemy; when it turned out that this was not the case, no new explanation was forthcoming.

Again there was the world-wide wave of sightings in 1957 when Russia and the United States launched the first satellites. And most recently, in the autumn of 1973, just before the unmanned U.S. spacecraft Pioneer Ten was to fly past Jupiter and out of our solar system, a new wave of sightings began.

Many explanations are possible. The simplest—and the most likely—explanation of the coincidence of sightings and events on earth is our own growing awareness. With each increase in expectation of what human beings could invent to lift themselves off the surface of the earth, more people accepted the evidence of their own eyes when they saw unidentifiable objects crossing the sky. And quite reasonably some of them related what they saw to objects they had heard or read about—airships at the turn of the century and, in 1957, satellites that might one day carry men to the moon or even, by a great stretch of the imagination, beyond our Milky Way galaxy to the Andromeda galaxy hundreds of thousands of light-years away. And what one man saw, others could accept with their own eyes.

That there are waves of "visits" by UFOs seems incontestable. But that sightings are much more massive just when we are entering some new phase of space exploration may be due to our own heightened interest in and greater sophistication about what is possible.

The late Carl Jung, in his book *Flying Saucers*, published in 1959, added another dimension. He neither rejected nor accepted the reality of UFOs. What he suggested was that there is also a psychological component—what he called a living myth or a visionary rumor that is potentially shared by all human beings in a period of great change and deep anxiety about the future. UFOs, he speculated, might be a world-wide visualized projection of this uneasy psychic state. But he also speculated that the two unknowns—UFOs and our human visualized projections—may simply "coincide in a meaningful manner."

A very different explanation is that UFOs, in spite of world-wide sightings, are no more than a gigantic hoax. Not long ago a huge crowd watched a "UFO" float over a stadium. This was indeed a hoax—a balloon lighted by a candle. So it has been argued that if one sighting is a hoax, all sightings must be hoaxes.

In this view all the accumulated supporting evidence is denied. It has often been reported that UFO sightings have been accompanied by interference with and sometimes the temporary failure of car and airplane motors, communication devices and power lines. But if a great, luminous object speeding across the sky can be simulated, can't some device for bringing about electromagnetic disturbances be part of the hoax?

Arguments of this kind directed against UFOs are no more valid than the hoax arguments intended to demolish the evidence of psychic phenomena. Just because fake mediums sitting in darkened rooms can induce gullible dupes to shake hands with cold, sand-filled rubber gloves, there is no reason to deny the reality of psychic phenomena we cannot yet explain.

Undeniably, such arguments have a seductive power. The temptation to produce hoaxes and the temptation to believe that what is strange and not understood must be a hoax are equally human vulnerabilities. And so in exactly those fields in which human beings are exploring possibilities that boggle the mind it is most likely that some people will perpetrate hoaxes and that others, as one way of protecting themselves from anxiety, will suspect that they are being hoodwinked. But this does not mean that the whole thing is a hoax. It means only that one recurrent response to fear of the unknown is insistence that it's all some kind of trick.

Certainly a great many people are frightened by the idea that somewhere in outer space (we once thought somewhere in our own solar system) there are beings who are technologically more advanced than we are. Today, apparently, it is precisely those who are best informed about our technological capabilities—some government officials, scientists and members of the armed forces—who are most disturbed by the idea that technologically superior beings from some other, unknown planet are taking an interest—an unexplained interest—in our planet Earth.

Consequently, from time to time we have official reports from groups such as Project Grudge, Project Blue Book, or the Colorado UFO project headed by Dr. Edward Condon that play down the evidence. UFO sightings are said to be really fireballs, lightning, flights of geese, the evening or the morning star, weather inversions that cause strange reflections, artificial satellites, hoaxes, the visions of disturbed individuals, and so on. These are, or may be, the explanations of many sightings. But in the end even such reports—usually based on samples of sightings from only a few areas, so that information about world-wide regularities is lost—always come to the same conclusion: There *are* unidentified flying objects. That is, there is a hard core of cases—perhaps 20 to 30 per cent in different studies—for which there is no explanation.

Yet the denials continue. While some scientists are probing space for evidence of extraterrestrial intelligence, others deny that any creature could build a vehicle that could arrive here from anywhere in space. But a little quiet thought ought to convince us that, knowing what we now know about space technology, the capability of reaching Earth from somewhere else depends only on others having taken further steps into the unknown that are beyond our present ability.

Of course, there have always been those who have insisted that nothing further is possible. Trains, cars, airplanes, voyages to the moon . . . But other scientists and inventors have gone ahead and made feasible what once had been demonstrably impossible.

The next questions are the most fascinating ones. If UFOs —the genuinely unexplained, unidentified but well-authenticated ones—are in fact vehicles that have come from a great distance, with or without intelligent life aboard, *What are they doing? Why don't they declare themselves?*

These questions introduce a suspense element that is almost unbearable to us. If these creatures—whoever they are—have been coming here or have been sending unmanned vehicles here for a hundred years (or, as some investigators claim, for thousands of years), what are they doing it for? There is, of course, not the slightest evidence that "they" have ever done anything. There is some possible evidence of occasional landings. There is a giant crater in the Soviet Union that cannot be explained by any existing meteorological or geological knowledge. And there are unexplained accounts of brief landings. But that is all.

For the rest we can only imagine what purpose lies behind the activities of these quiet, harmlessly cruising objects that time and again approach the earth. The most likely explanation, it seems to me, is that they are simply watching what we are up to—that a responsible society outside our solar system is keeping an eye on us to see that we don't set in motion a chain reaction that might have repercussions far outside our solar system. This is a plausible way of thinking to attribute to such living extraterrestrial creatures—as plausible as any that we ourselves at present are capable of imagining.

But there is no evidence one way or the other, I think, whether or not UFOs have intelligent life aboard. They may well be unmanned vehicles controlled from elsewhere in space. We ourselves are learning very rapidly how to control and how to obtain increasingly sophisticated information from space probes.

And there is one UFO that we know about in the greatest detail. Pioneer Ten, which is forging its way into deep space, will, after all, someday be an unidentified flying object to the intelligent beings on some other planet in some other solar system.

On the Edge of the Unknown

How do *you* define the occult?

I asked a group of my students that question not long ago. Their answers were both knowledgeable and puzzling—and very different from what they would have been only a few years ago.

All of them—somewhat to my surprise—said correctly that the occult has to do with things kept "secret" or "hidden" from those not initiated, and with the mysterious and perhaps the supernatural. But their examples encompassed the ancient and the modern, the East and the West; they included subjects nowadays studied by scientists, and other subjects believed to be beyond the reach of empirical science as we understand it today. They ranged from astrology and alchemy to witchcraft, from medieval cabalism to modern Theosophy, from Taoism to Yoga, from geomancy to numerology, from palm reading and fortunetelling with tarot cards to clairvoyance and telekinesis and telepathy, from the magical to the mystical. Altogether it was an extraordinary mélange of ideas, beliefs, practices and forms of both prescientific and scientific exploration and explanation, held together by the idea of mystery and of some relationship to what we call the supernatural.

None of the students rejected the idea of the occult out of hand, and the diversity of the subjects mentioned suggests the paths on which their curiosity had taken them and, further, the extent to which the idea of the occult has captured the imagination not just of these students but of so many of their generation.

Why should this be? How is it that so many of our young

people are fascinated by forms of wisdom that originated long ago in Babylonia and ancient Egypt, by conceptions of life and arts developed in the distant past in China and India, by beliefs and practices known in Europe in the Middle Ages and earlier?

It is certainly strange and unexpected that in a generation that belongs by birth to the space age, so many young people have turned away from the sciences that have made possible the world they live in and the extraordinary expansion of our knowledge about our universe. Instead there are, all around the world, very large numbers of young people who spend long, solitary hours in silent meditation; others who gather in groups to chant mystical syllables in monotonous, dream-like repetition; others who concentrate on learning complex and difficult body disciplines; and still others who scan numbers minutely to work out the relationship between the day and the hour of their birth and the astrological potentialities of a day on which they propose to make a journey or marry or take an examination.

How can we explain all this?

It is useful, I think, to bear in mind that since the earliest times and in the simplest cultures of which we have any knowledge, members of human societies have tried to understand the past—where they came from and who they are and how the world came to be as it is—and to discover how to predict the future so as to order their lives more safely. And as far as we know, this kind of striving often has been a compound of two very different things: careful, accurate observations of the part of the world in which a people lived, and imaginative explanations of *why* and *how* that often were closer to dreams than anything we think of as science.

People have observed the movements of the sun and the moon, the configurations of the fixed stars, the motions of the visible planets, the changing seasons, the migrations of birds or whales or salmon or the monthly appearance of fish over the reef. They have mused on the way sleepers seem to leave their inert bodies and travel to far places, and on the way a person's shadow grows and shrinks and dances in the flickering firelight; and they have concluded that there must be some part—perhaps more than one part—of the self that is separable from the body and may have existed before birth and may endure after death. And some peoples have solved, with a belief in an endlessly turning circle of reincarnation, the problem of life and death in which past and future are linked. But however differently human beings have tried to explain what they could observe, thinking about our relationship to the cosmos has been a distinctive, universal human activity.

Through long ages, workable knowledge slowly accumulated and was passed from one people to another—as, for instance, the idea of zero treated as a number passed from Hindu to Arabian and finally to European mathematicians in the later Middle Ages, making modern mathematics possible. But almost invariably ancient wisdom was embedded in magical, religious or ideological systems. Such systems enfolded the knowledge that made it possible, for instance, for the ancient Egyptians to work out quite accurately the length of the solar year or, using simple geometric principles, to measure land accurately and design great structures such as the pyramids.

Sometimes an element has escaped from its magical matrix, but without losing a kind of aura of the mysterious, the marvelous. There is, for example, the number 7. This was the number of the luminaries in the sky (the sun, the moon and the five visible planets) that were observed in their courses by the ancient Babylonians and were believed to control the fate of all human beings. So 7 became embedded as a key number in astrology, but it also broke free of its matrix and time and again has been associated in a marvelous way with great things. So we have Rome built on seven hills; we have the seven seas and the Seven Wonders of the World, the seven ages of man, the seven deadly sins, the seventh heaven, where, according to Islamic belief and the Cabala, God and the most exalted angels live. There is also the seventh son (or the seventh son of the seventh son), variously believed to be gifted with healing powers or to be clairvoyant or telepathic or simply lucky, and among Gypsies the seventh daughter, who always tells true fortunes.

People can get into a fine state of confusion over beliefs like those that relate numbers to the events of life. And their belief that there is a real relationship can easily affect their expectations and their acts, and so the outcome of events. The belief that 13 is an unlucky number, a number that foreshadows disaster, is still potent enough to cause a hand to slip, a bolt to be left unfastened, a mission to fail on the 13th day. Yet the Thirteen Colonies stood together against England to form a new country.

When people go back through degraded superstition and the veils of religious symbolism to trace a magic number or a whole number system to its oldest matrix, there is a very good chance that they will feel they are finding out something secret and wonderful, something that puts them in touch with the deep wisdom of the ancients, something that can give them power too. And they may begin to think that numbers matter—like the Pythagoreans, who built a kind of religion on the belief that the essence of all things is number and that the most complex ideas could be expressed as relations between numbers.

Tracing back such a philosophical conception of how the universe is constructed and how human beings are related to the universe and one another, people may easily come to endow numbers (or, equally, some other set of emotionally highly charged symbols) with extraordinary powers. And when they find that there is working knowledge embedded in such a matrix (for the Pythagoreans were innovative mathematicians as well as philosophers and religious cultists), they may well take it as proof that the special view of the universe, the religious belief, also is "true."

This is, it seems to me, one important ingredient in the current fascination with the occult. And because so many of these old beliefs have been superseded as obsolete, outlawed religiously or politically (sometimes 1,000 or more years ago), driven underground and carried through generations by tiny groups or carried in writings buried in obscure libraries and rediscovered by accident, there is also the fascination of secretly resuscitating and secretly joining with others in practices known only to an initiated few. This identifies the practitioner at one and the same time as an individual who is different and as someone who belongs to a group with a unique identity. In a world in which individuals continually see themselves classified anonymously as one in a category of thousands—or millions—the search for personal identity can become crucial to survival.

But there is another aspect to the search that guides modern young people in their choices of what to look for in ancient beliefs and practices. Modern science and its application —for example in medicine—has become increasingly impersonal and detached from the problems that beset individuals as they grow and mature, suffer disappointment and loss and try to find satisfaction and happiness—or simply health and quiet. So in their search for some alternative life-style a great many young people turn to those occult beliefs and disciplines in other cultures—Chinese or Indian, Japanese or Persian in origin—that promise both a greater understanding of one's own self and some sense of unity between one's private, personal self and the infinite, impersonal universe. In the predicament in which these young people find themselves, the familiar disciplines of Christianity and Judaism have become bonds to be cast off and only the unfamiliar disciplines of Zen or Yoga or one of the new cultist groups have the imaginative power to give them access to their own minds and bodies and a sense of participation in some larger, spiritual whole.

This is, I think, a use of the occult that is quite different from anything in the past, for it is a specific response to needs unmet in our very troubled present. For many it has great fascination; for some it is a way out of the present.

However, there are also points of real contact between certain ideas of great importance in the occult—telepathy, for example—and the thinking of scientists whose experiments have taken these ideas to the very edge of science. Here the extraordinary engineering capacities of scientific instruments are being brought to bear in more and more refined ways to explore and characterize the infinitely small and the vastly distant, the extremely delicate and the extremely complex. With the use of infrared photography and under certain conditions, today we can take a picture of a car that was parked in a parking place yesterday; we can "look" at the land surface of Mars; we can "see" with the radio telescope unimagined distances into the universe. And on this growing edge of knowledge, scientists are devising experiments that may—almost certainly *will*—give us, in time, new insight into the powers attributed to seers and clairvoyants, to those who have the power to "see" auras, to communicate with plants, to dream or visualize events outside the bounds of time.

Instead of a world in which scientists, who have been by definition unbelievers in all that the great religions have ever claimed, are divided by a deep, unbridgeable gulf from blind believers, who insistently reject all that science has learned, we are in the process of discovering a middle ground. Here the most open-minded scientists and the most open-minded believers in occultism can meet to plan and carry out experiments in an atmosphere of expectant, skeptical but also meticulously careful exploration. We are living on the edge of the unknown not only in terms of possible communication with other intelligences somewhere in the universe but also with renewed and greatly expanded knowledge of our own human sensibilities and capacities.

It can be said that in some sense we have come full circle. And it may be that among those young people who seem to be lost in some unreal relationship to the magical thinking or the miraculous beliefs of the past, there will be some who will shake themselves loose of inappropriate beliefs, past and present, and will help to shape a world society in which women and men know what human beings in the past could see only through a glass darkly, know only in part.

II
Women in Today's World

Women: A House Divided

MAY 1970

How far ahead are you thinking?

As the demands for immediate changes in women's lives become more strident and angry, this is a question every woman must ask herself and try to answer honestly. For the time span within which change is projected will make a great difference. Concentration on the very near future—a decade or two—will certainly bring about some very necessary reforms, but it will also obscure the basic issue—how women will face living in a world in which homemaking and childbearing are no longer the single central focus of their lives. Change in our time can be only a step toward preparing our daughters and our daughters' daughters to think and act in new ways.

There are other questions as well.

Married or single, working or not working today, women must begin to think in terms of a basic choice: Public role and private role—which is the more important? In an emergency which would you sacrifice? If your child was sick or unhappy, would you leave him in someone else's care, as a man must do? If your husband's job took him to another country, would you give up a promising career to go with him? Would you go far away from friends and relatives for your career?

However important, responsible and fulfilling a woman's work may be, the answer is quite predictable. Most women will put their families first. And few will think them wrong. This is the choice women have been brought up to make and men have been taught to expect. It is the unusual woman, the woman wholly committed to her career or an impersonal goal, on whom criticism descends.

Up to the present the dilemma is one most women have managed to avoid. One way of doing it has been by defining their work as an adjunct to their personal lives. Even today, in 1970, when over one third of the women living in husband-wife homes—about 15 million married women—are working, this remains true. The kinds of positions women hold and the money they are paid are, at least in part, a reflection of women's own definitions of the place of work in their lives and of the reciprocal belief among men that giving a woman a career job is a high risk.

Only a change in viewpoint will enable women to take full advantage of the opportunities they now are so ardently seeking.

Looking ahead, another question each woman must ask herself is: How do you feel about other women?

Two generations ago the few women who chose work over a home cared a great deal about feminine solidarity. Set apart from the women who stayed home and the men among whom they worked, they had need to count on one another. Today, I think, women place far less reliance on other women for friendship or companionship. The picture most women have of a wider world outside the home is one in which they will spend their days together with men. But will they?

Women students complain—and rightly so—that women are far underrepresented at the upper level of the academic, the professional and the business world. A principal demand of every feminist group is that women be given equal opportunity with men to rise to the top. But are they prepared for a world in which women are active at every level?

Given the choice of a man or a woman, how many girls today would elect to study under a woman? How many women in business would choose to work for another woman? How many wives today willingly trust another woman with the care of their children? How many women enthusiastically accept another woman as a companion for recreation?

Perhaps the most valuable aspect of the new women's protest groups is the rediscovery that women can think and work together and find common ground for action. However, the continual fracturing of these groups suggests that women as a group do not easily achieve working solidarity.

The point is not that we have to look forward to some new division of the sexes in social life or in the working world. The point is rather that women as individuals want to be treated as people—as full human beings. For the present men are the principal target; it is they who are accused of treating women as second-class citizens. For some they are "the enemy." But we shall become full human beings, I think, only when we ourselves can treat one another as full human beings, worthy of other women's trust and respect.

This must include, as well, a new regard for women's traditional occupations within and outside the home. Otherwise there is a very real danger that we shall lose what is most precious in human life—the ability to give devoted and cherishing care to other human beings—just at the time in human history when it is most imperative that we learn how to expand our capacity for caring and to translate it into ways of protecting the earth itself.

Women are in a peculiar position today. On the one hand they downgrade the things they know best how to do. But on the other hand they are extremely unwilling to share with others the tasks they do in their homes. The truth is, women are trapped in their present conception of a home as a very private place from which everyone but their husbands and children are excluded. How much of a trap it is comes out in the only solution to conflict between home and work many wives and mothers have to offer: Why can't my husband stay home in an emergency? Take care of a sick child for a day? Wait for the plumber? It doesn't occur to them that this is no solution. It would only put a man, instead of a woman, in the position of relinquishing outside responsibilities.

Such a solution looks only to the past. As long as a woman's care for her family represented her major social responsibility, her greatest opportunity for achieving a measure of independence and self-expression lay in having a home in which she was the chief executive. This we have achieved. In most American homes there are no mothers-in-law, no daughters-in-law, no maiden aunts or dependent sisters. Even daughters often leave home as soon as they are grown. There are no servants with status. At most there may be a cleaning woman with her own (usually mistaken) ideas of where to set down the ashtrays or how to arrange a bouquet. And now wives and mothers, though they reign supreme, look down on homemaking tasks.

By denigrating the tasks that women have done for their families we also have demeaned all those who could replace us in our homes. On this crucial point women's freedom to choose what they will do and women's view of other women are joined.

Looking to the future, beyond the day when women long to leave their homes out of discontent, we can find a way to reverse this trend. For then making a home for one's own family or for the family of a woman who has made a different choice will also be a matter of choice. Some women will choose to become engineers and doctors and lawyers and physicists and biochemists. And some will prefer to care for homes and little children. Whether this is a possibility that can be realized depends essentially on women's attitudes *now* toward women's roles as homemakers and caretakers of people. Will a woman biochemist, for instance, learn a new willingness to share her homemaking role with another woman who is professionally trained as a homemaker?

As women's sense of their freedom to make choices grows, the importance of what women have done and been in the past will acquire a new visibility. For this reason women have a special responsibility to accord dignity to women's work, to recognize the fact that the fields of women's traditional activities involve high-level skills, not only drudgery, and to prize those who, given a chance to do so, learn them as professionals.

Some forms of so-called women's work, of course, already are highly professionalized. The time has come when homemaking too should move in this direction. It is quite possible that just as today young men are choosing to be teachers of small children—with the greatest future benefit to early-childhood education—so also eventually some men will choose other, formerly feminine, caretaking roles as a profession. In another generation it may well be that people will speak not only of "mothering" but also of "fathering" and "parenting" as special talents to be sought out and developed in many individuals.

Women's attitudes toward other women are no less important in the redefinition of women's relationships to men, in the development of new styles of work and in the openness each may have to the other's interpretations of phenomena. In the past, distrusting their own abilities and viewpoints, women have been overeager to accept men's judgments or they have been overresistant to any modification of their own judgments about social legislation, the handling of crime, priorities in national goals or the uses made of the earth's resources.

But in time, as men and women begin to work together as intellectual equals on the multiple problems of public life, women will have new insights to offer and new solutions to propose. Then the feminine preference for persons, for caretaking and conservation, for intimacy of understanding *combined with* the masculine preference for working with things, for mastery and exploitation, for rational objectivity, can enrich our perceptions of the world. For women this will involve a change of scale; for men, a greater trust in intuitive—subjective—processes.

No one can possibly predict how long it will take for partnerships of this kind to come to fruition. Nor can one begin to guess what new viewpoints about human behavior and the nature of civilization will grow out of such new associations of men and women.

But I think it is safe to say that the outcome depends on women's willingness to work for immediate change within a framework of more than one generation. What women have to give is not heritable in the sense that it is built into the female organism. It is, instead, learning that has been passed on from mother to child for hundreds of generations. It can be lost by women who deny their past. It can be distorted by women who deny the realities of a changing world. It can be safely learned and modified by daughters who sense their mothers are moving imaginatively in the direction their children—sons and daughters—will take in making a new social reality, given time.

Women with a Drinking Problem

FEBRUARY 1975

Almost every one of us nowadays knows someone who is a very heavy drinker, or even an alcoholic—a person who can't take one drink without taking far too many. But if that friend or relative is another woman, we do hate to admit it, even to ourselves. Yet heavy drinking, especially among young women, is on the increase, and it is believed that about one third of some 10 million people who have severe alcohol problems in our country are women.

Social drinking on almost every kind of occasion and relaxed drinking at home—a cocktail before dinner, wine with a meal, a cold beer on a hot evening—have long been an acceptable part of life for the majority of Americans in most parts of the country. In many social circles, and within some occupations, having a drink is as common as eating, and people expect and accept a drink as readily as they do food.

Almost no one today raises an eyebrow because a girl on a date drinks with her male companion or a wife sits down with her husband for a restful drink or a woman takes a cocktail in public with friends or colleagues, men or women. And many parents, anxious about drug problems, much prefer to offer their college-age—or even high-school—children some kind of alcoholic drink if only they will stay away from marijuana or more dangerous, addictive drugs.

But alcohol too is a drug. Fortunately, for most people it is safe most of the time. But for some people, under some circumstances, it can become an extremely dangerous drug that can lead to a very serious illness—alcoholism.

There was a time not long ago when many people thought

of the alcoholic's self-destructive, irresponsible drinking as sinful and the alcoholic person as someone who lacked moral fiber. Depraved persons, people who lived in dismal slums, the men who had descended to Skid Row and, among women, prostitutes and the most miserable drudges—these were the people we believed were most likely to become alcoholics.

It was reformed alcoholics—men like those who founded Alcoholics Anonymous to support others in need of help and who pressed for research on the problem—who took the lead in changing our views. Now we recognize the fact that alcoholism is a disease that deeply affects the lives of men and women in every part of our society. And as we have removed our moral blinders we have come to realize that this disease, with its multitude of victims, is a growing national problem. In response, Congress in 1970 passed the Comprehensive Alcohol Abuse and Alcoholism Prevention, Treatment, and Rehabilitation Act and established a National Institute of Alcohol Abuse and Alcoholism to further research and develop methods of treatment.

This was an immense step forward. But we have a long way to go in changing our social lives in accordance with what we know to protect those who may become alcoholics and to support those who are making the long, hard effort to recover. In particular, women need to take the initiative in helping women.

As a disease, alcoholism has certain peculiarities. It is, for one thing, an *end* state that can be diagnosed only after an individual has become an alcoholic. With many diseases it is possible to indicate those who are vulnerable to them because of inheritance or some previous illness or the individual's response to various kinds of tests. But vulnerability to alcoholism has been established only statistically in terms of very rough social criteria—coming from a family of heavy drinkers, working in one of the occupations in which heavy drinking is expected, living in certain areas of the country or belonging to certain ethnic groups.

It is also thought that some individuals have a high addictive capacity. Some people who become alcoholics take drugs as well or smoke addictively, and some alcoholics who stop drinking become compulsive smokers or eaters. But except for an extreme allergylike sensitivity to alcohol, any trait that is characteristic of some group of alcoholics also is characteristic of others who are not alcoholics.

There are, in fact, no definite early warning signals, such as there are for some kinds of cancer or heart disease. And the very fact that some heavy drinkers become alcoholics while others do not, although they may seem to be almost identical in temperament and behavior, makes it all the more difficult to warn one's friends or take heed oneself. Indeed, the greatest danger lies in that fixed belief, "I am not an alcoholic. I can take liquor or leave it alone." It is a belief an individual may cling to long after having started down the road that will end for her in the illness of alcoholism perhaps months, perhaps years, later.

As far as we know, there is no single cause of alcoholism. But the alcoholic is someone for whom alcohol is both irresistible and progressively poisonous. The need of such a person for alcohol may increase under circumstances of strain or suffering until she, or he, must be taken to an institution to be detoxified, only to begin the process over again with the next opportunity to drink. Nor do we know of any cure as yet. At best, the victim learns never again to take a drink.

Up to a point we are beginning to face the realities of the problem. But only up to a point. For in spite of changed attitudes, we still are excessively secretive when it comes to a woman's drinking problem. Most research focuses on male alcoholism, while women generally are either ignored or treated as if their problems were the same as men's.

As I see it, nothing could be less true. In the modern American world, women live under conditions different from men's, suffer from different frustrations and face very different problems. It should be obvious, then, that the situations in which women become vulnerable to the disease of alcoholism are in large measure peculiar to women and that they have special needs that must be met if they are to find their way back to normal, healthy living.

Some things we do know.

Nowadays it is young women in their 20s who begin to drink heavily—women who are still groping for a satisfying life-style or who are frustrated in their efforts to find themselves. Possibly women are less able than men to adapt themselves to heavy drinking, since once a woman begins to drink heavily she is likely to progress more rapidly than a man toward alcoholism.

Having a job is less protective for a drinking woman than for a drinking man. Until men become so deteriorated that they can no longer function, exacting job requirements may hold them in place. Doctors, for example, may survive years of alcoholism before they crack. But nurses (one of the few women's professional groups that have been studied in relation to drinking) are less monitored by society and slip down from job to job. Typically, an alcoholic nurse may end up as a night nurse in a nursing home for the aged—a "low visibility" job for her that also may be disastrous for her patients.

For women there is the special danger of starting to drink —out of boredom or loneliness or fatigue—when they are at home with no one to interrupt or divert them and no one to correct their judgment about whether or not they have overstepped a safe boundary. It is a danger that affects almost equally the young housewife and the single girl left alone for a weekend.

The young mother pulls herself together for the arrival of her children from school—perhaps for a long time before she stops trying to pull herself together at all. The single girl pulls herself together on Monday morning to go to her job, dull as it may be, but there is always the prospect of another week-end that may be as lonely as the last. Or in desperation she may take herself to a singles bar and drink in the hope that this may make sex with a stranger more possible. Most difficult of all is the situation of the young widow, divorcée or wife separated from her husband who has to carry the burden of caring for a home and children and earning a living.

But for all lonely women—women who want to be out in the world, women who want companionship, women who carry too heavy a burden to enjoy living—drinking is a temptation as a means of escape; and solitary, unmonitored drinking, often in secret, increases the possibility of their becoming a victim of alcoholism. But there is danger in drinking in public places too, especially for the woman who drinks to oblivion. The crowning possibility of utter degradation—to find oneself pregnant and to have no memory of how it happened—is the kind of extreme circumstance that makes women fear their drinking even as they drink, and makes men shudder at the task of protecting an alcoholic wife or mother or daughter.

Then there is the problem of recovery and rehabilitation.

Initially, for advanced alcoholics, what is most essential is a long period of treatment in an institution in which physical therapy, a careful diet and a judicious use of drugs is combined with strong, supportive group therapy. Later, couple therapy or family therapy may help the recovering alcoholic regain confidence in the people closest to her. But in the beginning sharing her struggles with others who are facing the same harsh reality may give a woman greater courage and so greater support.

Some communities are establishing halfway houses for alcoholics, but as one might expect there are few especially designed for women. So it is hard to get a woman accepted in a halfway house and, particularly if she has a husband and children, harder to keep her there unless she feels sure of its benefits.

At best such temporary homes are located in quiet, relatively affluent neighborhoods where women are protected from the importunities of men and from the near presence of bars and brothels. There is such a halfway house in Germantown, Pennsylvania, called Interim House, which has a high record of recovery. The women who live there for several months—Black and white, poor and well-to-do—do not drive cars or spill over into the neighborhood. Living in this kind of protective environment is one of the things that gives back to women some sense of being worthy of care, of being trusted and capable of trust.

But always, in just such a neighborhood, a halfway house rouses anxiety and sometimes real hostility. Neighbors fear that any institution, located there, may lower the value of their property or upset any good integration they may have achieved. So the few halfway houses we have for women alcoholics, designed with their needs in mind, always are in danger.

Yet I believe that women who are concerned for women's place in our society can express a sense of responsible solidarity by working to establish and support halfway houses in which women can recover from illness and begin to find themselves. It is certainly one way by which women, happy in comfortable, unthreatened homes, may learn enough to keep their own homes—and other homes—unthreatened and children safer.

This is one thing concerned women can work on effectively.

There are also common-sense ways in which you yourself —and every woman—can take initiative in preventing the kinds of excessive drinking that lead so many people to alcoholism. All of us can help in developing new and safer styles of handling drinking. For example, it is a good idea to serve food, not just fattening party tidbits, with drinks. It is not necessary to urge another drink and another on guests.

And you can be watchful about those cocktails before dinner when your husband comes home tired and hungry and you yourself are tired and tense from a long day. You can keep your home supply of beer, wine and liquor small, and lock the liquor closet during the years when you have preteens or teen-agers who sometimes may be at home alone. You can join with other parents in setting styles for teen-age parties. Together with the men in your family, you can discourage irresponsible back-and-forth "treating" at club meetings and at other social occasions. These are all ways in which we, as women, can protect those who are vulnerable or heedless for themselves.

But above all, I believe that women can help other women who are troubled and getting into difficulties with alcohol. Women today must, I think, be willing to admit frankly that some of their friends—or even they themselves—may have a drinking problem. Women, knowing best what the problems of loneliness and frustration are for women, can talk straightforwardly with each other and help one another work out some better solutions—solutions that may involve willingness to seek professional help.

Once we face the problem honestly—with concern and in friendship—we can understand the hazards and the high stakes that are involved both for ourselves and, looking ahead, for our growing daughters.

Abortions: The Need for a New Ethic

SEPTEMBER 1973

The whole situation regarding abortion in this country has changed dramatically since the beginning of this year of 1973.

The Supreme Court in its momentous decisions last January clearly placed the right of a woman to obtain an abortion in the area of individual freedom, to which this country has always been explicitly dedicated. By overruling state laws that restricted or prohibited a woman's right to make her own decision about having an abortion, the Supreme Court brought to a standstill the fierce battle raging between those who were fighting for and against "liberalized" abortion laws. The basis of the court's decisions was the recognition of a "right of personal privacy" free of government restriction.

However, the Supreme Court did not leave the country without guidelines for the future. For the first three months of pregnancy, the court ruled, a woman's decision should be wholly free of legal interference. During the last six months states are permitted to "regulate the abortion procedure in ways that are reasonably related to maternal health"; that is, states may pass legislation to protect the well-being of the woman who decides to terminate a pregnancy. And finally, during the last ten weeks of pregnancy, when it is assumed that the child-to-be "has the capability of meaningful life outside the mother's womb," abortions may be legally prohibited except to protect the life or health of the mother.

Thus freedom of decision by the individual woman is guaranteed but it is not absolute. In the later stages of pregnancy the well-being of the mother and, in the end, the well-being of a new, viable human being both are given protection.

70

The great thing is that we have arrived at this point—after bitter and emotion-laden battles—without coercion of anyone. No state is obliged to decide through legislation whether abortion is a "good" or a "bad" practice. No religious group in the country has been permitted to impose its particular beliefs—its own conceptions of morality—on any other group. But at the same time, no individual conscience need be compromised. Those who believe that abortion is equivalent to the murder of a living being with a God-given soul are wholly free to follow their own beliefs and to win others to these beliefs; those who believe that the termination of pregnancy can be a protective and beneficent act can now legally seek—and legally provide for—such a termination.

This is as it should be in a pluralistic society like ours, in which men and women of very different faiths and ethical convictions live together in the same communities.

But, of course, the struggle is not ended, although there has been a lull in the past few months. The toning down of emotion as the immediate conflict was brought to a close, the relaxation of anxiety about the development of commercial abortion mills in states with comparatively liberal laws and, above all, the relief at sweeping away illegal practices that degraded everyone involved have contributed to the sense of quiet after a storm. But we cannot rest with this.

Individual freedom to act without an ethic to support that freedom is not enough. The immediate battle for freedom of conscience is over. But this means only that we have arrived at a new stage. Now, I believe, we must decide how we are to use this freedom with good conscience by developing practices that are consistent with the value we set on individual life and interpersonal relations in families and in the whole community.

So Americans have a new set of tasks: how to make abortion as dignified, as humane and as constructive as possible. In addition, I think we must work toward a definite policy on which both sides of the religious controversy will be able to agree frankly and honestly—a policy of reducing the need for abortion to the absolute minimum.

How can we best accomplish these aims?

There is no simple answer. But I think we can begin with the fact that the decision to terminate a pregnancy, for whatever reason, is always deeply personal. And the truth is that at present we do not know very much about the ways in which different American women respond to elective abortion. In the past so much depended on secrecy and concealment, the dangers were so great and the cost so prohibitive, that these factors themselves led to tangled emotional situations. Now we can work toward clarification.

Of course the causes for which women choose abortion as a solution are themselves extremely varied—rape, discovered hereditary defect, the failure of contraceptives, illness during pregnancy, inadvertent use of a drug that endangers normal development of the fetus, the dissolution of a relationship on which the mother counted to provide a father for her child, economic hardship or the choice against parenthood at any time. Any of these, and many other reasons, may lie behind a woman's decision, and each may affect her state of mind differently.

But there are also very fundamental, temperamentally based differences among women. There are women who, believing strongly that a child is a human being from the moment of conception, feel even more strongly that every infant deserves to be wellborn. For such women, elective abortion may mean that they cannot mourn for the child who might have been as they would have mourned for a baby who was born dead.

Mourning is a significant and necessary part of all human behavior in response to tragedy, and its absence may produce a peculiar effect—the necessity to repeat the unfinished experience. Psychiatrists in South America, where most persons are reared in the Catholic faith, have found that it is not uncommon for women to repeat unwanted pregnancies ending in abortion, and in addition, to fail to complete other tasks, the very tasks for which they originally thought it was desirable to postpone motherhood. Women who respond in this way, with deep conflict, need special help to succeed in determining that abortion is an experience they can put behind them and need never repeat.

At the other extreme there are women who have no deep feeling about a just-conceived child. These are women who may welcome as important individuals the children they bear, but their imagination simply does not penetrate their own bodies and participate in the processes of pregnancy.

There are also today some women for whom having an elective abortion is in a sense a declaration of rights—a statement that they are in control of their own bodies and their own destiny. This is very understandable in this period in which women are struggling in many different ways to find themselves as persons. But there is a danger in it—a danger that abortion, treated in this way, may become an end in itself. And this eventuality, I believe, must somehow be avoided.

So one of our tasks—immediately—is to find out much more about women's responses to abortion and how to meet their different needs.

This means that we must work to provide the kinds of settings for abortion procedures to which any woman anywhere can go and in which she will be treated as a person with an ongoing life.

We are already seeing a new kind of "business" develop around abortions. Clinics and hospitals in our society, like doctors, cannot advertise. But commercial agencies that specialize in the referral of women to selected clinics and hospitals not only can but do advertise. Such agencies flourished in the situation that developed when legal abortions were available in only a few places. Now I think we must do everything we can to prevent this kind of commercialization of abortion, with its emphasis not on persons but on profit.

The alternative is the development of local, nonprofit clinics that are known and respected and to which women, on their own initiative as well as on referral by their doctors, can go for the termination of pregnancy. What is needed is a kind of clinic in which every woman who enters will be assured of being met and surrounded by people who share her anxiety, assure her of good medical care and can give her hope that this will never happen to her again. In clinics of this sort we can learn what women's needs are and how to meet them in a variety of ways. Model clinics already exist in some communities. I think we should support them, work to develop others like them but adapted to the expectations of the particular women who go to them, and integrate them into the community itself.

At an international conference I attended in Sweden last year, it was proposed that there be centers called "Centers for Love and Life," to which both men and women could go for help in solving problems concerned with their relations with each other, with their possible future children, with their responsible choice not to have a particular child or with their decision to have no children at all.

Certainly one way of integrating a new type of clinic within the community—as well as of meeting the very considerable financial burden and so keeping costs within reasonable limits —would be to bring together within one complex premarital, planned-parenthood and family counseling; abortion and postabortion counseling; facilities for childbirth; sterilization facilities and sterility counseling. In this way a single center would represent responsible and cherishing care for children, their mothers and fathers and the men and women who were making alternate choices. An innovation of this kind would not be easy to achieve, but it would be an ideal worth working for by the women—and the men—of any community. And a plan that included, instead of excluding, husbands and fathers would have a much better chance of success.

But there are other steps too that must be taken.

There is every likelihood that the battle to make abortion difficult will be renewed as state legislatures begin to consider new measures. People must therefore be ready to work with national voluntary agencies for a common set of standards for the whole country for the licensing of clinics and other protective laws. Such regulations are necessary for reasons of safe care. But it is also very necessary to see to it that the measures taken really fulfill the purposes for which they are intended, and do not entangle us instead in a new web of restrictions, different in each state.

Beyond this, we must not emphasize abortion as a method of population control. Instead, we must encourage and support research on safe contraceptives for men as well as for women. It is only in this way that men too may gain greater freedom of choice and join with women in the responsibility of decisions about having or not having a child. Abortion on demand is now a woman's recognized right. But contraception, available by choice to both sexes, makes it possible for husband and wife together to defend the wife and mother's right to her own body.

The whole battle over abortion, I think, has diminished our awareness of the real change that is taking place in our thinking. Having a child, in fact, no longer is regarded as an inevitable accompaniment to adulthood and marriage, but as a serious and considered *choice*. In keeping with this, we may well come to think of the just-conceived fetus as an individual. There are already societies to advocate the rights of the unborn. It is but a further step to consider the rights of children not yet conceived. These children, planned and expected long before their conception by couples who choose to be parents, will be born into a world that their parents had a part in creating for them.

Once this comes about, it will be difficult for the most unimaginative woman not to feel concern for the individual she is sheltering in her body. And as this sense of the individuality and rights of the unconceived and the newly conceived increases, we may expect the use of abortion to diminish and become rare. This is what we have to work for even while we work to make abortion safe and an experience that women can bear without losing the ability to cherish life.

Women as Priests—a Challenge

JUNE 1975

On July 29, 1974, in Philadelphia, 11 Episcopalian women were ordained as priests. The ceremony was unprecedented. It was also illegal. Had the candidates been men, there would have been no problem. The 11 women were ordained deacons in good standing; that is, they had fulfilled all the requirements demanded of candidates for ordination. But the Protestant Episcopal Church did not recognize the right of women to become priests.

The event made headlines here and abroad, particularly when two weeks later the House of Bishops of the Episcopal Church, in a hastily convened session, passed a resolution declaring the ordination to be not merely irregular (as everyone knew it was) but also invalid. And there the matter rests —very uneasily. The decision has been strongly contested, but as yet the issue remains unresolved.*

Participation in this ordination was an act of faith. It was also an act of courage—on the part of the 11 women, who decided that they would no longer wait for the governing body of the Church to be won over; on the part of the three bishops who performed the ceremony and the many priests who joined in the traditional laying on of hands; and not least on the part of the liberal-minded, largely Black congregation of the Church of the Advocate, which offered its parish church for the occasion.

A large number of women's groups as well as a great many

* In September, 1976, at its General Convention, the Protestant Episcopal Church of the United States approved the ordination of women and accepted the 11 women ordained in Philadelphia as priests.

individual members of the women's liberation movement have hailed this particular set of events as a breakthrough. They have treated the ordination as a unique event over which every woman—and every man who cares about the status of women—should rejoice.

I greatly respect the courage of the women who took this step.

But, it seems to me, there are questions that should be asked. Was this event really a milestone in the history of women's liberation? Is ordination, in fact, a wholly new role for women? And most immediately, does it make a difference whether this irregular ordination of women in the Protestant Episcopal Church was a *first* step in a long campaign to give women a new role in religion or, on the contrary, a *final* step before the capitulation of a citadel of prejudice?

I think it does make a difference.

In fact, the participation of remarkable women in the religious life of the United States is by no means new. It goes back to our very beginnings—to the courageous stand taken in 1637 by Anne Hutchinson, when the Puritan ministers and civil authorities of the Massachusetts Bay Colony banished her as a heretic and an advocate of the right of private judgment in religious matters.

Over the years, whether we look at the history of the individual women who became ministers in churches of various denominations or at the different religious groups that have admitted women to the ministry, the record is impressive. Three women in particular come to my mind, all of whom in their lifetime were known throughout our growing country as ministers and as passionate advocates of social reform.

One was Antoinette Brown Blackwell, born in 1825, who was one of the first college-educated women and the first ordained woman minister in any church in this country. She was a graduate of Oberlin College and Oberlin Theological Seminary, and in 1853 began her ministry in the Congregational

Church. Later, like so many Congregationalists of her generation, she became a Unitarian.

The second was Olympia Brown, who was born in 1835 in
a log cabin in Prairie Ronde, Michigan. When the University
of Michigan refused to accept her as a student, she went to
Antioch College, in Ohio, and later to the Theological School
of St. Lawrence University, in Canton, New York. In 1863,
when she was 28, she was ordained in the Universalist Church,
that most liberal and most American of all Protestant denominations, existing almost entirely within the United States.
After she married she kept her maiden name—possibly the
first American woman to do so—and throughout her long life
as a famous public figure was known as the Reverend Olympia
Brown.

The third was English-born Anna Howard Shaw, who during her girlhood also lived in a log cabin in a remote part of
Michigan. At 15 she was teaching school, and at 24, while she
was a student at Albion College, in Michigan, and battling for
the rights of women students, she was granted a license to
preach by the general conference of the Methodist Church.
Eight years later, when she had completed her studies for the
ministry and was already the pastor of a church, she sought ordination so that she could administer the sacraments, baptize
and receive members into the Church. The Methodist Episcopal Church twice refused her, but in 1880, when she was
33, the Methodist Protestant Church accepted her as an ordained minister.

These pioneering churchwomen—and many others whose
names and lives are unknown to most women in today's liberation movement—wanted to preach in order to spread the good
word. They fiercely attacked the fortresses of special privilege
—the men's colleges, seminaries and medical schools that
would not admit women, the congregations that would not
listen to women, the political bodies that would not respond
to women's demands. Exclusion limited the opportunities of

women to work for the things they deeply believed in.

They came to know the leading secular feminists of their period and, like them, worked devotedly on the major social issues—the abolition of slavery, general education, temperance and, above all, women's suffrage, a right for which these long-lived pioneers fought for 50 years and more. They worked too for peace and international order; in 1919, in the last months of her life, Anna Shaw lectured across the country in a vain effort to win American popular support for the new League of Nations.

Significantly, the churches in which women for a long time —some for a century or more—have played active, responsible roles, often as ordained ministers, are those that have rejected an elaborate hierarchy. They also have emphasized the equality of all human beings and espoused the cause of the humble, the poor and the disfranchised. Although the denominations differ from one another in some particulars, they share the Protestant belief in a direct, unmediated relationship between human beings and God.

They include the Congregationalists, whose beginnings in America go back 350 years to the Pilgrims; their offshoot, the Unitarians, who emphasized the unity of God and mankind; the Universalists, who rebelled against the dour Calvinist belief that a loving God would condemn any of his children to eternal punishment; the Society of Friends—the Quakers— who, rejecting all hierarchy, believe in the full equality of men and women; the Methodists, who began their ministry among the laboring poor in England; and more recently (1879) the Christian Scientists, whose founder was a woman. Among them also are the religious groups that have been consciously moving into and along with the contemporary world. In Reform Judaism the first woman rabbi was ordained in 1973.

Nevertheless, after the pioneering generation there was a hiatus. Women moved only slowly and sporadically toward greater responsibility in churches, so sporadically that there appear to be no connecting links between the pioneer church-women and today's liberationists. And the question of what to do about women in the church frequently has played an important part in the splintering of denominations. Anna Shaw was ordained by the Methodist Protestant Church when the Methodist Episcopal Church turned her away.

The solutions have been contradictory too. For example, in the Methodist Church women for a long time have been licensed to preach and have been ordained, but they were accepted as full members of the governing body, the general conference, only in 1956. In the same year, in the Presbyterian Church women were permitted for the first time to assume priestly functions, although they had served for a long time in responsible lay positions as elders and deacons.

One thing, however, is clear. Recently it has been mainly the religious denominations associated, directly or indirectly, with very ancient traditions—Orthodox Judaism, Roman Catholicism, and the Protestant Episcopal Church in the United States—that have most adamantly resisted the inclusion of women in fully responsible religious roles.

But it is against the wider background of women's long struggle for recognition in churches—and their successful efforts that go back at least to the middle of the 19th century, more than 100 years ago—that we must look at the episode of the ordination of the 11 Episcopalian women. Seen within this context, the ordination, unprecedented in this denomination, fits a slowly emerging pattern. By strenuous efforts it may be possible for the opposition to hold back the tide for a little time. But, I believe, a priestly role for women is now inevitable.

The only questions are when and—far more important—*how* we shall come to define the role of priest or minister or rabbi when each of these can be filled by either a man or a woman.

The earlier women, whatever their denomination, were Protestants and in an important sense applied Christians—Christians who saw the ministry as an opportunity to work for the transformation of the social order. They threw themselves passionately into causes and worked tirelessly for women's rights because they believed that women had so much to contribute as women to the creation of a world that was more in keeping with their religious beliefs and social concerns. But perhaps they hoped to accomplish too much too quickly. There were no true successors to these idealistic feminists, and certainly there was no group that looked beyond them in their aims.

Today the emphasis is far more on rights and on the ministry as an opportunity for religious fulfillment than as an opportunity to solve the pressing problems of the world. Women's liberation has become an end in itself. In the past the voices of excluded women played on the conscience of men as Christians, as believers in justice and equality, who were depriving women of the means of Christian accomplishment. Today women play upon the conscience of those who exclude them—the bishops and priests, the prominent laymen, the traditionalist theologians, the church politicians—as men who are unfairly exercising their ecclesiastical prerogatives. Women have gained enormously through those who preceded them in the struggle for feminine recognition. They no longer can be put down. But they still may fail in a deeply human sense by concentrating so intensely on what women—as women—have the right to demand.

The time has come, I believe, for women to take the next step—a step that will take them beyond feminist concerns narrowly conceived. What we now need to think about innovatively is the way we conceive of men and women in their special relationship to the roles they are coming to share in many aspects of their lives, not only in the particular setting of a religious institution. And as it is women, on the whole, who are demanding the right to new roles, it seems to me it is women who will have to be innovative, at least initially, until they capture the imagination of the men.

Our image of the priestly role has been and still is very specifically masculine. We identify the role with those who traditionally have filled it. But certainly the woman who is ordained a priest cannot become a "father" ceremonially. There are women who feel that in their hands the priestly role will become completely feminine and that in their prayers God too will become feminine. However, a simple reversal of this kind solves no problem.

What is needed instead is a new concern for what a gifted woman can contribute to the conception of the priestly role as a woman, without denying or destroying what is male and valuable. It is equally destructive for men or women today to insist on an all-or-nothing dichotomy—this or that exclusively. Our innovative aim must be to rethink the roles that men and women are coming to share in terms of how they can be enriched by the complementary gifts of both men and women.

We shall not learn how to do this overnight or develop within a short time images that many—perhaps all—of us can share. But we can begin by thinking, for example, what it means to be a *parent*, not merely a mother or a father. And then, as always happens, our thinking, our imagining, will echo from one person and one kind of relationship to another.

If the ordination of the 11 Episcopalian women touches off this kind of innovative image building, it may indeed be a kind of breakthrough for all of us. But as we reject prejudice as a last step in a process, so we must also take a first step in creating something new. The question is: Are we willing to try?

Volunteers: The Time Is Now

SEPTEMBER 1975

Yesterday was a day I shall long remember. Because yesterday I had word from the Vietnamese wife of a dear friend and I could cable to her distracted husband in Hong Kong, "Good news!"

We knew that she had left Saigon, but after that—nothing. When the weeks passed, hope turned to doubt and doubt to despair. And then suddenly a telephone call. "I have a message for you," a young woman with a warm but very tired voice told me. She spelled out a long Vietnamese name. "You do know her, don't you? She asked us to tell you that she reached Guam on May ninth and wants you to know that she is safe and well."

That telephone call, relaying a message from halfway across the world, was made by a Red Cross volunteer who had had to find out who I was, where I lived and how to reach me. She was one of hundreds of volunteers who have spent innumerable hours re-establishing the lifelines of thousands of Vietnamese refugees who are crowding the camps on Pacific islands, on the West Coast and increasingly in different parts of our country. Working day and night, these volunteers have carried out an immense emergency sorting and co-ordinating job. Scattered members of families have been located and put in touch with one another, and friends and relatives in this country and in Europe are at last able to reach out helping hands.

Soon the basic sorting process will be more or less complete. But this is only the first, and in many ways the easiest, step. Many more people will be needed—people with much

energy, time and a great variety of skills—to help the Vietnamese refugees who are settling here find their way into
American life. A very large number of those who are needed
will have to be responsible volunteers. It is the only way the
job can be done.

We live in a society that always has depended on volunteers
of different kinds—some who can give money, others who
give time and a great many who freely give their special skills,
full time or part time. If you look closely, you will see that
almost anything that really matters to us, anything that em-
bodies our deepest commitment to the way human life should
be lived and cared for, depends on some form—more often,
many forms—of volunteerism.

Our hospitals depend on boards of trustees whose members
—most of them very busy people—put their expertise to work
in the interests of health care. Most hospitals depend on do-
nors, rich and poor, who give money. And they depend on
many people without money to spare—as well as a few for
whom money is no object—who give long hours to caring
tasks.

Our schools depend on dedicated citizens who are willing
to serve on school boards and dedicated parents who give
time and money to all the extras that make a school something other than a storage place, a playpen or a prison for
small children. And schools depend on the dedication of
teachers who give their time to the PTA, to conferences with
parents, to coaching a team or producing a play or to community projects that center in their schools. Whenever such
activities cease to be voluntary and become requirements in
addition to teaching duties, resentment rises and the school
begins to fall apart.

Without dedicated volunteers we would not have the parks
where our children play, the sliding boards and seesaws and
climbing towers in playgrounds, or the museums where children can see Greek temples, dinosaurs reconstructed or In-

dians in full-feathered regalia. And there would be few libraries. People living in small communities have always known this. But now in big cities everywhere, libraries are closing for lack of tax or voluntary support, and the volunteer boards are overwhelmed by the problems of city budgets.

In fact, if we look carefully, we cannot help realizing that virtually all the activities that make a town or part of a city into a community depend in one way or another on volunteers. But during the past 25 years, when so many things have gone wrong in a world rushing pell-mell to take advantage of new inventions without stopping to fit them together with older, valuable ways of doing things, our thinking about volunteerism has suffered from destructive change.

As more and more socially oriented tasks have been fully professionalized and taken over by men and women as their major, money-earning occupations, the image of the volunteer has been debased. Thirty years ago a forceful, elderly woman could argue in favor of first-class higher education for women because, in her words, "after all, women must man the boards"—that is, take on responsible volunteer work. Today a great many people picture women volunteers as well-to-do, well-intentioned but poorly informed ladies with time on their hands, and male volunteers as retired men who drive clinic patients to hospitals or support the activities of the well-intentioned ladies.

The activities of many public-relations firms also have contributed to a debased picture of voluntary efforts. The time and energy given to good causes by prominent people no longer is seen as genuine public service. Instead it is often —and too often correctly—defined as a device for advancing some individual's social, political or professional ambitions. In addition, lists of those who have given to good causes are sold from one good cause to another, and today even the most modestly charitable individuals have their mailboxes jammed with appeals—their names misspelled and five appeals from the same good cause. Some appeals are completely genuine—appeals to feed the hungry in a country shattered by famine or to save some valuable piece of the environment. Others are barely concealed commercial ventures and still others are traps for unwary, kindhearted givers.

In these various ways both the sense of responsible public service by men and women who actually have given thousands of hours of hard work on committees and boards and the spontaneity of individuals who have given a few hard-earned dollars to a cause they care about deeply and personally have been largely destroyed. Volunteerism has been grossly commercialized, mechanized and deprived of the formerly generous motives of dedicated citizenship in communities that nevertheless continue to depend on volunteers for more than mere survival.

Most recently, as a *coup de grâce* to the whole idea of ever doing anything except for money, certain groups within the women's liberation movement have branded volunteer work other than political work as a rip-off—just one more way of keeping women from being recognized as professional persons and from being paid adequately for work performed.

It seems to be touch and go whether volunteerism can survive.

But during this very period in which the old picture of the volunteer has been distorted and all but destroyed, new forms of voluntary action have come into being, and the number of volunteers—men and women with many skills to back their commitment—has been growing steadily. According to one recent estimate, some 37 million Americans are engaged in voluntary activities.

Many of them are new volunteers—people who were not involved earlier. Over the last decade and more, these new volunteers have been especially active in the rapidly developing, controversial movements and programs that are the precursors of new styles of living. The civil rights movement,

the upsurging movements of ethnic groups, the antiwar movement and counseling for conscientious objectors, centers for
advising women about abortion and birth control, projects
for prison reform and for the protection of consumers, all the
causes connected with the protection of the environment
and, indeed, the women's liberation movement—these have
drawn thousands, more likely millions, of devoted, committed
and hardworking volunteers. But the significant thing is that
they do not see themselves as "volunteers"; they speak of
themselves as men and women doing jobs that need to be
done.

Elsewhere, in the well-intentioned but sometimes misdi-
rected poverty programs, another new idea about the volunteer
has been developing. This has grown out of efforts to include
what is sometimes called "indigenous personnel"—which is
simply a more respectful way of saying that the poor should
be involved in their own programs. Of course, this has been
possible only to the extent that those who give their time to
work in these programs have been paid for costs they are
unable to meet while they are doing unpaid volunteer work
—that is, the cost of baby sitters or a day nursery, carfare,
lunch money and, sometimes, appropriate clothing.

In the same period a related idea has taken firm hold among
young people, mainly high-school and college students, who
have flocked to museums and laboratories and public offices,
parks and playgrounds to work during the summer. They are
not paid salaries and very few are given scholarships. Instead
they are given small sums to cover lunch and carfare, no
more. What they are giving is time and effort to hundreds of
different kinds of jobs that in many cases would not get done
without their willingness to work. Yet they do not seem to
think of themselves as "volunteers" but as individuals doing
jobs that they want to do.

These, and many others working on a great variety of
tasks, are people whose basic subsistence is guaranteed in

some way, whether they are welfare mothers, students living at home, retired women and men on small pensions or young wives and husbands with children at home. They have skills and dedication and time but no money to spare.

We had come to think of anyone with time to spare as somehow a negligible person. We are learning—or perhaps relearning—otherwise. The women and men who become responsibly involved in the poverty programs that are intended to change their lives and the lives of their children, the young student who is eager to participate in activities that may have bearing on her future lifework, the well-educated young mother who needs every penny her husband earns, the retired woman with 40 years of disciplined experience in getting a job done—every one of these people has something to offer that makes time an invaluable gift. Characteristically these new volunteers say, "It's essential. And if we don't do it, who will?" So they take on the job.

But we need to back up the new volunteers and support their view of what they are doing. And the time is now.

Everywhere essential services paid for from Federal, state and local taxes are withering away. Everywhere programs that we know are essential are being turned down because there is no money in public budgets to initiate them. Or programs are turned down because people do not realize that by law certain public funds must be matched by private gifts. But above all, services are being limited or withdrawn, programs are closing down and new projects are refused funding because so much of our thinking about volunteerism is distorted and out of date.

We need to re-establish respect between professionals and volunteers. We can go part way by realizing that time, wisely used, is an invaluable contribution. We can take another step by being aware that a job well done, whoever does it, is the measure of a person's worth, not the money she may (or may not) be paid. And we can realize that *both* experience and training enter into the expert's knowledge of how to get things done.

The volunteer has to know that her job is worthwhile. A low rate of pay would be no answer. But even minimal reimbursement for expenses can help her feel that her needs too are being considered. However, we must go much further than this. Full respect means acknowledgment that responsible work is exactly what today's younger volunteers say it is: work that needs to be done. One form of acknowledgment would be to give every serious volunteer tax credit and social-security credit as a well-earned benefit in the present and for the future. It is high time we acknowledge that volunteers should get something as well as give something. Americans never have believed wholeheartedly that virtue should be its sole—as well as its own—reward.

These are minimum aims to work for. But we cannot wait for them to happen. The need for volunteers is too pressing in every community and at every level. We must not neglect the needs of our home communities. Nor must we neglect those we have committed ourselves to helping—in particular, at present, the Vietnamese we ourselves brought into our midst.

We desperately need volunteers to get work done. But getting work done also will mean that we shall arrive at a much better understanding of our needs and our real capacities to meet them.

III
American Families Today–and Tomorrow

Can the American Family Survive?

FEBRUARY 1977

All over the United States families are in trouble. It is true that there are many contented homes where parents are living in harmony and raising their children responsibly, and with enjoyment in which the children share. Two out of three American households are homes in which a wife and husband live together, and almost seven out of ten children are born to parents living together in their first marriage.

However, though reassuring, these figures are deceptive. A great many of the married couples have already lived through one divorce. And a very large number of the children in families still intact will have to face the disruption of their parents' marriage in the future. The numbers increase every year.

It is also true that hazards are much greater for some families than for others. Very young couples, the poorly educated, those with few skills and a low income, Blacks and members of other minority groups—particularly if they live in big cities—all these are in danger of becoming high-risk families for whose children a family breakdown is disastrous.

But no group, whatever its status and resources, is exempt. This in itself poses a threat to all families, especially those with young children. For how can children feel secure when their friends in other families so like their own are conspicuously lost and unhappy? In one way or another we all are drawn into the orbit of families in trouble.

Surely it is time for us to look squarely at the problems that beset families and to ask what must be done to make family life more viable, not only for ourselves now but also in prospect for all the children growing up who will have to take responsibility for the next generation.

There are those today—as at various times in the past—who doubt that the family can survive, and some who believe it should not survive. Indeed, the contemporary picture is grim enough.

• Many young marriages entered into with love and high hopes collapse before the first baby is weaned. The very young parents, on whom the whole burden of survival rests, cannot make it entirely on their own, and they give up.

• Families that include several children break up and the children are uprooted from the only security they have known. Some children of divorce, perhaps the majority, will grow up as stepchildren in homes that, however loving, they no longer dare to trust fully. Many—far too many—will grow up in single-parent homes. Still others will be moved, rootless as rolling stones, from foster family to foster family until at last they begin a rootless life on their own.

• In some states a family with a male breadwinner cannot obtain welfare, and some fathers, unable to provide adequately for their children, desert them so that the mothers can apply for public assistance. And growing numbers of mothers, fearful of being deserted, are leaving their young families while, as they hope and believe, they still have a chance to make a different life for themselves.

• As divorce figures have soared—today the proportion of those currently divorced is more than half again as high as in 1960, and it is predicted that one in three young women in this generation will be divorced—Americans have accepted as a truism the myth that from the mistakes made in their first marriage women and men learn how to do it better the second time around. Sometimes it does work. But a large proportion of those who have resorted to divorce once choose this as the easier solution again and again. Easily dashed hopes become more easily dashed.

• At the same time, many working parents, both of whom are trying hard to care for and keep together the family they have chosen to bring into being, find that there is no place at all where their children can be cared for safely and gently and responsibly during the long hours of their own necessary absence at their jobs. They have no relatives nearby and there is neither a day-care center nor afterschool care for their active youngsters. Whatever solution they find, their children are likely to suffer.

The consequences, direct and indirect, are clear. Thousands of young couples are living together in some arrangement and are wholly dependent on their private, personal commitment to each other for the survival of their relationship. In the years from 1970 to 1975 the number of single persons in the 25-to-34-year age group has increased by half. Some couples living together have repudiated marriage as a binding social relationship and have rejected the family as an institution. Others are delaying marriage because they are not sure of themselves or each other; still others are simply responding to what they have experienced of troubled family life and the effects of divorce.

At the end of the life span there are the ever-growing numbers of women and men, especially women, who have outlived their slender family relationships. They have nowhere to turn, no one to depend on but strangers in public institutions. Unwittingly we have provided the kind of assistance that, particularly in cities, almost guarantees such isolated and helpless old people will become the prey of social vultures.

And at all stages of their adult life, demands are made increasingly on women to earn their living in the working world. Although we prefer to interpret this as an expression of women's wish to fulfill themselves, to have the rights that go with money earned and to be valued as persons, the majority of women who work outside their homes do so because they must. It is striking that ever since the 1950s a larger proportion of married women with children than of married but childless women have entered the labor force. According to recent estimates some 14 million women with children—four out of ten mothers of children under six years of age and more than half of all mothers of school-age children—are working, the great majority of them in full-time jobs.

A large proportion of these working women are the sole support of their families. Some 10 million children—more than one in six—are living with only one parent, generally with the mother. This number has doubled since 1960.

The majority of these women and their children live below the poverty level, the level at which the most minimal needs can be met. Too often the women, particularly the younger ones, having little education and few skills, are at the bottom of the paid work force. Though they and their children are in great need, they are among those least able to demand and obtain what they require merely to survive decently, in good health and with some hope for the future.

But the consequences of family trouble are most desperate as they affect children. Every year, all over the country, over 1 million adolescents, nowadays principally girls, run away from home because they have found life with their families insupportable. Some do not run very far and in the end a great many come home again, but by no means all of them. And we hear about only a handful whose terrifying experiences or whose death happens to come into public view.

In homes where there is no one to watch over them, elementary-school children are discovering the obliterating effects of alcohol; a growing number have become hard-case alcoholics in their early teens. Other young girls and boys, wanderers in the streets, have become the victims of corruption and sordid sex. The youngsters who vent their rage and desperation on others by means of violent crimes are no less social victims than are the girls and boys who are mindlessly corrupted by the adults who prey on them.

Perhaps the most alarming symptom of all is the vast increase in child abuse, which, although it goes virtually unreported in some groups, is not limited to any one group in our population. What seems to be happening is that frantic mothers and fathers, stepparents or the temporary mates of parents turn on the children they do not know how to care for, and beat them—often in a desperate, inarticulate hope that someone will hear their cries and somehow bring help. We know this, but although many organizations have been set up to help these children and their parents, many adults do not know what is needed or how to ask for assistance or from whom they may expect a response.

And finally there are the children who end their own lives in absolute despair. Suicide is now third among the causes of death for youngsters 15 to 19 years old.

In recent years, various explanations have been suggested for the breakdown of family life.

Blame has been placed on the vast movement of Americans from rural areas and small towns to the big cities and on the continual, restless surge of people from one part of the country to another, so that millions of families, living in the midst of strangers, lack any continuity in their life-style and any real support for their values and expectations.

Others have emphasized the effects of unemployment and underemployment among Blacks and other minority groups, which make their families peculiarly vulnerable in life crises that are exacerbated by economic uncertainty. This is particularly the case where the policies of welfare agencies penalize the family that is poor but intact in favor of the single-parent family.

There is also the generation gap, particularly acute today, when parents and their adolescent children experience the world in such very different ways. The world in which the parents grew up is vanishing, unknown to their children except by hearsay. The world into which adolescents are growing is in many ways unknown to both generations—and neither can help the other very much to understand it.

Then there is our obvious failure to provide for the children and young people whom we do not succeed in educating, who are in deep trouble and who may be totally abandoned. We have not come to grips with the problems of hard drugs. We allow the courts that deal with juveniles to become so overloaded that little of the social protection they were intended to provide is possible. We consistently underfund and understaff the institutions into which we cram children in need of re-education and physical and psychological rehabilitation, as if all that concerned us was to get them—and keep them—out of our sight.

Other kinds of explanations also have been offered.

There are many people who, knowing little about child development, have placed the principal blame on what they call "permissiveness"—on the relaxing of parental discipline to include the child as a small partner in the process of growing up. Those people say that children are "spoiled," that they lack "respect" for their parents or that they have not learned to obey the religious prohibitions that were taught to their parents, and that all the troubles plaguing family life have followed.

Women's liberation, too, has come in for a share of the blame. It is said that in seeking self-fulfillment, women are neglecting their homes and children and are undermining men's authority and men's sense of responsibility. The collapse of the family is seen as the inevitable consequence.

Those who attribute the difficulties of troubled families to any single cause, whether or not it is related to reality, also tend to advocate panaceas, each of which—they say—should restore stability to the traditional family or, alternatively, supplant the family. Universal day care from birth, communal living, group marriage, contract marriage and open marriage all have their advocates.

Each such proposal fastens on some trouble point in the modern family—the lack of adequate facilities to care for the children of working mothers, for example, or marital infidelity, which, it is argued, would be eliminated by being institutionalized. Others, realizing the disastrous effects of poverty on family life, have advocated bringing the income of every family up to a level at which decent living is possible. Certainly this must be one of our immediate aims. But it is wholly unrealistic to suppose that all else that has gone wrong will automatically right itself if the one—but very complex—problem of poverty is eliminated.

Is there, in fact, any viable alternative to the family as a setting in which children can be successfully reared to become capable and responsible adults, relating to one another and a new generation of children as well as to the world around them? Or should we aim at some wholly new social invention?

Revolutionaries have occasionally attempted to abolish the family, or at least to limit its strength by such measures as arranging for marriages without binding force or for rearing children in different kinds of collectives. But as far as we know, in the long run such efforts have never worked out satisfactorily.

The Soviet Union, for instance, long ago turned away from the flexible, impermanent unions and collective child-care ideals of the early revolutionary days and now heavily emphasizes the values of a stable family life. In Israel the kibbutz, with its children's house and carefully planned, limited contact between parents and children, is losing out to social forms in which the family is both stronger and more closely knit. In Scandinavian countries, where the standards of child care are very high, serious efforts have been made to provide a viable situation for unmarried mothers and the children they have chosen to bring up alone; but there are disturbing indices of trouble, expressed, for example, in widespread alcoholism and a high rate of suicide.

Experience suggests that we would do better to look in other directions. Two approaches may be rewarding. First, we can look at other kinds of societies—primitive societies, peasant societies and traditional complex but unindustrialized societies (prerevolutionary China, for example)—to discover whether there are ways in which families are organized that occur in all societies. This can give us some idea of needs that must be satisfied for families to survive and prosper.

Second, we can ask whether the problems that are besetting American families are unique or are instead characteristic of families wherever modern industrialization, a sophisticated technology and urban living are drawing people into a new kind of civilization. Placing our own difficulties within a wider context can perhaps help us to assess what our priorities must be as we attempt to develop new forms of stability in keeping with contemporary expressions of human needs.

Looking at human behavior with all that we know—and can infer—about the life of our human species from earliest times, we have to realize that the family, as an association between a man and a woman and the children she bears, has been universal. As far as we know, both primitive "group" marriage and primitive matriarchy are daydreams—or nightmares, depending on one's point of view—without basis in historical reality. On the contrary, the evidence indicates that the couple, together with their children, biological or adopted, are everywhere at the core of human societies, even though this "little family" (as the Chinese called the nuclear family) may be embedded in joint families, extended families of great size, clans, manorial systems, courts, harems or other institutions that elaborate on kin and marital relations.

Almost up to the present, women on the whole have kept close to home and domestic tasks because of the demands of pregnancy and the nursing of infants, the rearing of children and the care of the disabled and the elderly. They have been concerned primarily with the conservation of intimate values and human relations from one generation to another over immense reaches of time. In contrast, men have performed tasks that require freer movement over greater distances, more intense physical effort and exposure to greater immediate danger; and everywhere men have developed the formal institutions of public life and the values on which these are based. However differently organized, the tasks of women and men have been complementary, mutually supportive. And where either the family or the wider social institutions have broken down, the society as a whole has been endangered.

In fact, almost everywhere in the world today societies *are* endangered. The difficulties that beset families in the United States are by no means unique. Families are in trouble everywhere in a world in which change—kinds of change that in many cases we ourselves proudly initiated—has been massive and rapid, and innovations have proliferated with only the most superficial concern for their effect on human lives and the earth itself. One difference between the United States and many other countries is that, caring so much about progress, Americans have moved faster. But we may also have arrived sooner at a turning point at which it becomes crucial to redefine what we most value and where we are headed.

Looking to the past does not mean that we should return to the past or that we can undo the experiences that have brought us where we now are. The past can provide us only with a base for judging what threatens sound family life and for considering whether our social planning is realistic and inclusive enough. Looking to the past is not a way of binding ourselves but of increasing our awareness, so that we are freer to find new solutions in keeping with our deepest human needs.

So the question is not whether women should be forced

back into their homes or should have an equal say with men in the world's affairs. We urgently need to draw on the talents women have to offer. Nor is there any question whether men should be deprived of a more intimate family role. We have made a small beginning by giving men a larger share in parenting, and I believe that men and children have been enriched by it.

What we need to be sure of is that areas of caretaking associated in the past with families do not simply drop out of our awareness so that basic human needs go unmet. All the evidence indicates that this is where our greatest difficulties lie. The troubles that plague American families and families all over the industrialized world are symptomatic of the breakdown of the responsible relationship between families and the larger communities of which they are part.

For a long time we have worked hard at isolating the individual family. This has increased the mobility of individuals; and by encouraging young families to break away from the older generation and the home community, we have been able to speed up the acceptance of change and the rapid spread of innovative behavior. But at the same time we have burdened every small family with tremendous responsibilities once shared within three generations and among a large number of people—the nurturing of small children, the emergence of adolescents into adulthood, the care of the sick and disabled and the protection of the aged. What we have failed to realize is that even as we have separated the single family from the larger society, we have expected each couple to take on a range of obligations that traditionally have been shared within a larger family and a wider community.

So all over the world there are millions of families left alone, as it were, each in its own box—parents faced with the specter of what may happen if either one gets sick, children fearful that their parents may end their quarrels with divorce, and empty-handed old people without any role in the life of the next generation.

Then, having pared down to almost nothing the relationship between families and the community, when families get into trouble because they cannot accomplish the impossible we turn their problems over to impersonal social agencies, which can act only in a fragmented way because they are limited to patchwork programs that often are too late to accomplish what is most needed.

Individuals and families do get some kind of help, but what they learn and what those who work hard within the framework of social agencies convey, even as they try to help, is that families should be able to care for themselves.

Can we restore family stability? Can we establish new bonds between families and communities? Perhaps most important of all, can we move to a firm belief that living in a family is worth a great effort? Can we move to a new expectation that by making the effort, families can endure? Obviously the process is circular. Both optimism and action are needed.

We shall have to distinguish between the things that must be done at once and the relations between families and communities that can be built up only over time. We shall have to accept willingly the cost of what must be done, realizing that whatever we do ultimately will be less costly than our present sorry attempts to cope with breakdown and disaster. And we shall have to care for the failures too.

In the immediate future we shall have to support every piece of Federal legislation through which adequate help can be provided for families, both single-parent families and intact poor families, so that they can live decently and safely and prepare their children for another kind of life.

We shall have to support Federal programs for day care and afterschool care for the children of working mothers and working parents, and for facilities where in a crisis parents can safely leave their small children for brief periods; for centers where the elderly can be cared for without being isolated from the rest of the world; for housing for young families and older people in communities where they can actually interact as friendly grandparents and grandchildren might; and for a national health program that is concerned not with fleecing the Government but with health care. And we must support the plea of Vice-President Walter F. Mondale, who, as chairman of the Senate Subcommittee on Children and Youth, called for "family impact" statements requiring Government agencies to account for what a proposed policy would do for families—make them worse off or better able to take care of their needs.

Government-funded programs need not be patchwork, as likely to destroy as to save. We need to realize that problems related to family and community life—problems besetting education, housing, nutrition, health care, child care, to name just a few—are interlocked. To solve them, we need awareness of detail combined with concern for the whole, and a wise use of tax dollars to accomplish our aims.

A great deal depends on how we see what is done—whether we value it because we are paying for it and because we realize that the protection given families in need is a protection for all families, including our own. Committing ourselves to programs of care—instead of dissociating ourselves from every effort—is one step in the direction of re-establishing family ties with the community. But this will happen only if we accept the idea that each of us, as part of a community, shares in the responsibility for everyone, and thereby benefits from what is done.

The changes that are needed cannot be accomplished by Federal legislation alone. Over a longer time we must support the design and building of communities in which there is housing for three generations, for the fortunate and the unfortunate, and for people of many backgrounds. Such communities can become central in the development of the necessary support system for families. But it will take time to build such communities, and we cannot afford just to wait and hope they will happen.

Meanwhile we must act to interrupt the runaway belief that marriages must fail, that parents and children can't help but be out of communication, that the family as an institution is altogether in disarray. There still are far more marriages that succeed than ones that fail; there are more parents and children who live in trust and learn from one another than ones who are out of touch; there are more people who care about the future than we acknowledge.

What we need, I think, is nationwide discussion—in magazines, in newspapers, on television panel shows and before Congressional committees—of how people who are happily married can help those who are not, how people who are fortunate can help those who are not and how people who have too little to do can help those who are burdened by too much.

Out of such discussions can come a heightened awareness and perhaps some actual help, but above all, fresh thought about what must be done and the determination to begin to do it.

It is true that all over the United States, families are in trouble. Realizing this should not make us cynical about the family. It should start us working for a new version of the family that is appropriate to the contemporary world.

New Designs for Living

OCTOBER 1970

The development of new designs for living—this, I think, is one of our most urgent needs today.

Once the self-sufficiency of each nuclear family helped to ensure its security and independence. Today the same kind of self-sufficiency—in which each family must provide for all its own social and emotional needs—has become a heavy burden. Far from freeing people for other things, the task of maintaining a home squanders an inordinate amount of energy. What we need to develop instead is settings in which adults can experience a greater sense of community and in which children, as they grow up, can be close to adults other than their own parents.

All over the country articulate groups are working out ideas and supporting programs designed to bring about social changes they believe are necessary for our well-being, even our survival, as a people. Women's liberation groups are demanding that women be treated as whole persons—individuals who can choose to have or not have children and who are free to take part in every kind of activity and to develop their talents in all spheres of life. Economists are thinking in terms of a basic income that will guarantee to each individual a measure of security and freedom of choice. Educators and students are struggling with the problems of how to democratize teaching and learning. But it is taken for granted that these and many other kinds of change will take place around, without essentially involving, our kind of family.

It is true that almost every aspect of family living is being

106

subjected to criticism. Extreme pessimists believe that the family as it exists in our culture may be doomed. Others emphasize the urgent need to shore up our contemporary versions of marriage and family life. But very few people, except for the young who are in full rebellion against the whole Establishment, are experimenting with or even thinking seriously about new designs for living.

It is assumed that the family of the future will be like the family of the past. However, family life is changing year by year, and the changes multiply as other innovations alter older patterns of American living. For example, extension of the years of education combined with early marriage and parenthood means that young couples may be parents long before they are financially independent. Yet we go on defining the family as a financially independent unit.

Awareness of the population explosion is leading some young couples to decide against having children. Yet we continue to treat marriage as the first step toward building a family rather than as an adult relationship cherished for its own sake. As such discrepancies accumulate we may come to value a shadow form of family life that no longer has substance.

There is also the great danger that blind attachment to a traditional kind of family as the only good way of living and bringing up children may in the end frustrate our most serious efforts to improve the quality of our personal and national life.

As long as architects, urban planners, economists and politicians assume that what is needed is simply more homes for individual families, the housing crisis can only grow more acute. As long as many women must carry the double burden of caring for a home and of making a career with whatever energy they can muster, women will be cut off from the full partnerships in the world's work that are rightfully theirs. As long as children grow up in homes in which love and intimacy are bound up with family isolation, and in which concern for the individual in the family is divorced from concern for the community, young people will both perpetuate and rebel against the conflicts set up within themselves.

By holding on to a style of family living that has become incongruous with our newer expectations, we shall have lost what we have most valued: a way of bringing up children that prepares them to live their own lives, to make the future their own—and different from the past.

Is there an alternative?

I think there is.

In the past Americans were willing to work very hard for a better life for their children. Significantly, the forms that the "better life" should take seldom were spelled out. Instead, people concentrated on creating the conditions in which a better life was possible and on rearing children who could make innovations in the style of living appropriate to their own generation. This still should be our goal.

Our more immediate aim, I believe, should be the development of a setting in which each family would retain its identity but in which each would be an integral part of a larger group, all of whose members would carry some responsibility for everyone within it, adult or child, man or woman. Because such a group would be complexly organized, it also would be complexly related to the larger community.

In fact, such groups already exist in embryonic form here and there around the country. So far as I know, they have no formal organization or even a descriptive name. I have thought of them—and so I shall call them—as "cluster groups." What I shall describe here is nowhere the reality. It is an ideal picture based on fragments that are as yet only possibilities.

In a cluster community, couples with children would live very close to many people. There would be in each cluster some families, some childless married couples, older and younger, some individuals not yet married, some previously married, some working or studying and some retired, some with strength for energetic play and talk with children and some very fragile persons whom even children could help care for.

In such communities children would come to know adults who differed in their personalities and interests. The only child would have the warm companionship of other children, and no child would be dependent on parents alone as adult models or on one parent to carry all adult responsibilities. The experience of "mine" and "thine" would be modified by both the difficulties and the rewards of interdependence. Some things would be owned personally; other necessary resources would be owned and used within the larger group.

Clusters of this kind should not have a common occupational or economic base. A nationally guaranteed annual income would enable very young people—students and others —along with the elderly and with mothers who choose homemaking and child care as preferred activities, to join clusters of their own choice. But differentiations would continue to be made between working relationships established in the larger community and relationships of love and friendship within the cluster. By having a working life outside, each adult would become a link between "home" and the larger world.

Nor should families and individuals necessarily make long-term commitments to membership. It is necessary, I think, for people to keep the sense that they are free to change and move. Only so can they feel that the choices they make carry with them personal responsibility. Americans are easily put off by things they "have to do"; the feeling that one has elected a course of action can carry one through many difficulties.

Young people who advocate the building of communes will ask at this point: Why not make such associations into real communes and bring up the children communally?

It may be that the commune idea will continue to spread.

But I believe that there are very real objections to the economically self-sufficient, ideologically barricaded commune. It is probable that children who grow up without intense relationships with particular adults are spared some of the emotional conflicts experienced by family-reared children. But children who grow up in communes such as the *kibbutzim* of Israel or the religious communities of the Hutterites in Canada and the United States, become extremely dependent on their age mates and on the continuance of the commune way of life.

Communes are a solution for those with a special inspiration. It is a solution that emphasizes sharing, but one that can be shared only on a small scale. The commune should certainly be a permitted form. But we should recognize the fact that it is as special in its appeal as is the celibate monastic community.

Americans have overvalued personal autonomy and independence. Bringing up children within the isolated nuclear family, we can do little else. Growing up instead within cluster groups, children would experience new forms of interdependence and responsiveness so much needed in the modern world. But they would still wean themselves from their particular families and, leaving childhood attachments behind, would make their own way and form new deep and personal attachments.

How can we make a beginning?

On the whole, I think experimentation with new styles of living should be voluntary and carried out by groups whose members care about the development of new social forms. There is no use waiting for special facilities to be built. Those who want to try out some form of cluster living will have to make do with what they can find. Large old houses, converted apartment buildings, summer cottages—all these have possibilities.

But this would not be enough. Very small communities might be too ephemeral and some cluster groups might develop the cultlike characteristics of a group made up of over-committed enthusiasts.

We also need experimentation that will draw on the talents of architects, social planners and other experts from the beginning. There is one setting very appropriate for the development of cluster groups. This is the academic community. In every part of the country new educational facilities are springing up, and old ones are being transformed. Within short periods the numbers of students leap from hundreds to thousands. Almost everywhere there is a drastic shortage of housing.

Moreover, we are rapidly approaching the situation in which people from adolescence to retirement will be intermittently involved in some form of education or special training. A man or a woman may come to a university for a summer refresher course or settle down for a stay of five or even ten years. But after a certain period all students expect to move on. Many would be willing, even eager, to try out an unfamiliar style of living.

After World War II it was student fathers living in cramped quarters with their young families who revolutionized the relationship between fathers and their infant children. In the 1970s it could well be students who carried the idea of cluster living to every part of the country.

In an academic community the members of a cluster might include boys and girls away from home for the first time, married students with and without babies, grandmothers who enjoy young people, young instructors and scholars from distant lands. One cluster might be made up entirely of academics. Another might bring together town and gown. A third might be made up of people from different institutions—space scientists, musicians from a symphony orchestra and zoologists from a field laboratory. No two would be alike. Bridging time and space and areas of knowledge, children and adults living together in such a cluster might learn to see past and future through one another's eyes as they shared the present.

No one can predict the outcome of experiments with new designs for living. Children who had grown up in cluster groups would have a very different view of what they might become from the view we are able to have today, thinking about their possibilities within the framework of our experience of living each in our own separate family home. Clusters would be built on trust in our children's ability to make their own choices for the future.

In the long run what happens to the style of family living in the United States will be affected, as such things are, by a combination of consensus and happenstance—by decisions taken in Congress and in state legislatures, by the influence of experts and discussions in meetings of professional societies, by the presentation of news in the mass media. But in the end what counts are the acts of each person that implement old choices or initiate new ones.

Singles in Our Midst

NOVEMBER 1973

Are there any singles in your lives?

The majority of young couples—unless they are married students—would have to answer no to this question: "No, not really." But perhaps you have friends whose marriage has broken up; most people do today. Then a likely answer is: "Yes—and that's a problem!"

But nowadays isn't it equally pertinent—perhaps more pertinent—to turn such questions around and ask: If you are single, how much time do you spend with married friends? When your friends marry, do you keep up your friendships with them? When you break out of a marriage that hasn't worked, do you still include married friends as an integral part of your life?

The answers are likely to vary a lot in tone. But regretful, matter-of-fact or edged with defiance, the reply the unmarried and the no-longer-married make is, in effect, about the same: "Married couples go their way and I go mine."

It is all so new, we hardly realize yet what this means. But the truth is, our social life is splitting apart. We are well on the way to developing two kinds of social life, each of which excludes a large part of the generation now coming into its own.

Most young married couples with children still are following, however uneasily and restlessly, the style of living set by their parents, the style that took over the country in the 1950s, when Americans were conspicuously the most married—and remarried—people in the world. The ideal of family living still is a home designed exclusively for parents and their growing children, usually in the suburbs. Vacations still are pictured as family affairs or, alternatively, as brief holidays during which young couples meet other young couples just like themselves. And many party styles still require an even number of men and women with no extras—no unattached girls or roving males—to complicate the situation.

It is true that many young families are struggling to achieve some new kind of identity—for the family, for husbands and wives in their relationship to each other and for both of them in their different relations to a wider world. But basically, for married couples the old style of living persists as if there were no other possibility.

Yet an extraordinary change has been taking place of which we have become conscious only recently. In the 1950s the country really was like a Noah's Ark in which virtually everything was arranged for those who went two by two. But since the early 1960s the number of singles has been growing at an accelerating pace. Between 1960 and 1970 the population as a whole increased by 16 per cent, but the population of the unmarried increased by 38 per cent and that of the divorced and widowed by 34 per cent. Even more significant is the fact that in 1970 almost half of those who were single—unmarried by their own choice or as a result of misfortune in marriage—were under 35 years of age.

When you think about it, these figures are quite astonishing. Over 20 million Americans fall outside our conventional expectations for people of their age group. All over the country young people are saying they don't want to marry now or soon or perhaps ever. They want to be free to explore the world. And many more people who have been married and have children are not eager to marry again. They want to make a go of it on their own.

They are the new singles—the new outsiders. But they are, many of them, outsiders who are busily working out styles of living of their own. Commercial interests have not been slow in discovering them as a group. Singles bars and other forms of entertainment, sports groups and clubs, vacation tours for people of specified ages, computer matchmaking and living facilities for singles only are burgeoning. The singles way of life is currently given a lot of attention in the communications media, and the image presented is one that contrasts conspicuously with married domesticity in its emphasis on detached independence, defiance and experimenting.

Actually there is no one life-style for singles. As you who are trying it know, many adaptations are being tried by young people who do not want to marry or have children, by those who are trying out an "arrangement" instead of marriage, by loners and by some experimenting with communal living.

There are also the adaptations made by single parents. Some are women who believe that if they stayed home until their children were grown, they would never have a chance to find themselves as persons. Some are fathers stranded with children to bring up and educate. Some are delighted by new prospects opening out before them; others are harassed by new problems of living without partners.

Taken all together, the new singles are a very heterogeneous group indeed. What they have in common is their search for new ways of living outside the still-accepted pattern of married adult life.

But is this what we really want? Do we want to develop a kind of social life for adult Americans that is split in two: one way of living for those who are currently married and bringing up children together and other, unrelated ways of living for everyone else?

It seems to me a dismal prospect. For the number of singles, however defined, will keep on growing as men and women, especially young people, insist on greater diversity in their human relations. It will certainly not end in our abandoning family life, as some extremists predict—as, of course, extremists have always predicted the breaking up of the family during times of transition. But I do think that family living will become increasingly narrow, cramped and frustrating unless married couples open the doors of their homes and bring some singles into their lives. And I also think that singles cut off from friends with families will seldom gain a sense of wholeness in their lives.

The time to mend the growing rift is now, while so much is in flux; and the initiative, I am sure, has to come from those who are enjoying their marriage and their family, who have something to give and something to gain from a wider range of friendships.

Essentially, all we have to break through is the outworn belief that every single person is looking for a spouse and the unmarried are at best unfortunate and at worst somehow abnormal, untrustworthy and too far outside the main stream of life for anyone to want them as neighbors or friends. That this is a myth is self-evident today.

Once we accept the reality around us, a host of possibilities opens up, possibilities of friendships with individuals in their own right.

An old college roommate, as a welcome visitor, not only provides a link to the past but also fresh views of what is happening now. Younger brothers and sisters, instead of presenting terrible problems of providing them with dates, can widen the age range of those who come and go as they themselves are enjoying the company of slightly older people. A fellow musician can turn a husband's monologue about his most passionate interest into a lively conversation into which even an unmusical wife can enter. Where the point is friendship, couples can be free to choose individuals for who they are. And three—or four or five or seven—can join together and explore interests new to all of them, basing friendship on the mutual enjoyment of the discoveries they make together.

Children benefit by an assortment of adults who will take them swimming or read them a story, take Johnny to a chemistry lab and answer the questions that he alone in the family knows how to ask or enjoy going on nature walks with Mary to listen for birds. There are the children, too, of single parents, who need a little extra mothering—or fathering—and the warm experience of a family, a whole family, with expandable limits. In my childhood fictive aunts and uncles, the individual friends of my mother and father, were important and delightful guests to whose visits we always looked forward with excitement. Now we need, in addition, fictive aunts and uncles who will welcome another child into their homes as a delightful young friend.

A happily married couple who are willing to share their home and their children part of the time with their chosen, unmarried friends of different ages, both sexes and varied interests can open a wider and very fascinating world to their children. Their children growing up—their own and those who come as visitors—will discover that there are many possible kinds of life ahead of them and they in turn will be freer to choose, regardless of sex or marital status, what kind of persons they want to become and how they want to live.

It is also true that a great many single people, having chosen a different mode of living, miss some of the activities of a family home. Given occasional but lively access to children, they can happily maintain the single state that they have found fits them best. Besides this, they may enjoy providing able hands to help in the garden, to build that new brick walk or to redesign the family recreation room. The domestic-minded can contribute their specialties—and bachelors are often proud of their cooking—on holiday and party occasions in an ample setting. And a friend who takes pleasure in quiet may welcome a house-sitting weekend away from city noise.

Just as important are the things today's singles have to offer. Opening doors of friendship to them not only would bring a family blessed relief from the daily repetition of the same themes and the same controversies through the welcome diversity of other views and other interests. It also would give married couples a chance to enjoy the diversity of experience others have found. For it is a fact that our determinedly unmarried friends may have much more time to devote to finding out about the life around them and more opportunity to experiment and explore.

The inclusion of single friends in a family's life would not mean that a single person would become wholly dependent upon a particular family or that attachments to married friends would become the only recourse of the unmarried. They have already found ways of forming groups among themselves, trios and quartets and larger groups, sometimes of one sex only and sometimes of both, in their search for new kinds of warmth and companionship.

A new kind of mutuality between the married and the unmarried would make it possible for each to draw on many kinds of households and friendship groups for intimate and meaningful companionship. The family, I believe, will remain at the core of relationships between adults and children. But important adult relationships would have a broader and more diversified foundation in social life.

This is what can happen but it is not necessarily what will happen. So much depends on the way young married people respond to the new styles of life developing around them. And only if the married and unmarried alike see these new styles as very tentative and creative solutions to problems they, as members of a generation, all are facing will they find common ground. Then perhaps they will be able to entrust themselves to one another in the belief that friendship as well as married love can be a rich and valued adult relationship.

It is not certain, but it is a possibility. The 1950s were a grim Noah's Ark, with everyone outside looking wistfully in. The late 1960s were a time of tremendous confusion as the signals changed—as the pressures for everyone to have children relaxed and as women and men alike began to demand freedom from too-rigid and highly typed sex roles. We are still in a state of transition, but I believe we can, if we will, enlarge our sense of humanity—choose others for themselves, diversify our most meaningful relationships and let others know us too as individual persons.

Parents in Prospect

JUNE 1973

Young couples today are faced with a new challenge. Should they have children? Marriage has committed them to a partnership in life, a partnership based on their loving choice of each other. But they have another choice to make as well. Should they become partners in parenthood? Should they commit themselves to the task of bringing up children together?

The possibility of choice is entirely real and is rapidly gaining strong social backing. But it seems to me that this choice becomes meaningful only as those who are making it have gained some sense of what the prospects are for themselves, for each other and for the children to whom, as parents, they would commit themselves.

And yet how can they know? How can any two people know what kind of parents they might become? Are there ways of trying out parenthood without becoming parents? This is the real challenge.

Six years ago I proposed that we move toward two kinds of marriage—an individual form of marriage for those who did not intend to have children then—or perhaps ever—and a second form, more binding and much more cautiously approached, for couples who were preparing to become parents. I thought of this proposal as one way of illuminating the choices that were opening up before us. But there are other ways too. One of these might be called trial parenthood. Young couples who hope someday to have children can try out how good they are at the kind of marriage into which children can be safely welcomed.

120

As there are many kinds of parenthood, adoptive as well as biological, and also foster and godparental relationships, a couple can explore thoroughly their aptitudes and mutual capacities *before* they elect to have children. Although they cannot be trial parents in fact, they can be parents in prospect and discover what having children would mean to their lives.

Even in the very recent past such an idea would not have made much sense. In a social setting in which almost everyone was expected to marry, it was assumed that all those who married wanted to have a family. In recent years we have argued furiously over a woman's right to delay having a child and her right to accept or reject a particular pregnancy. But we have continued to take it for granted that every couple sooner or later wanted a family and that only those who suffered from some tragic defect or disability would remain childless. So it was those who deliberately chose not to have children who had to justify their decision. Parents and parents-in-law—candidates for grandparenthood—speculated about, admonished and scolded the childless, and many of those who remained childless eventually considered adoption.

Now all this is changing. Although marriage still provides a way for young people to get away from parental homes into a home of their own, there is no longer extreme social pressure to make every marriageable person marry. And in the light of our better understanding of the population explosion and what it implies for children now being born, social rewards are beginning to go to those who have few children or none at all. No longer pressured into marriage and parenthood, and consequently freer to make a choice, young couples can ask: Would we make good parents?

At the same time, of course, our ideas about parenthood and bringing up children are changing quite radically. Living as a family no longer means a simple division of labor in which Father is a good provider and Mother cares for the home and children. Being good parents now means something that could hardly have been imagined a hundred years ago, when the continuity of the family was always threatened by the catastrophe of early death, though divorce was virtually unknown. Considering marriage, our grandparents in dark hours asked themselves: Is he strong? Might he die before our children grow up? Is she sturdy enough to bear and rear children?

Today the basis of good parenthood is the capacity of a man and a woman to live together in amity—to have the mutuality of feeling and the will necessary to stay married to each other at least until the children are grown—until the youngest child has left home. And the questions young couples ask are very different ones: Will he stay? Will she stay? Can we keep in communication with each other? Can we carry the responsibilities of parenthood together?

So the first step for parents in prospect is to try out the expectation of a long-term commitment and their mutual willingness to make the necessary adjustments and sacrifices to get—and keep—the commitment going. Such sacrifices may take many forms. A wife as well as a husband may be engaged in a long period of study and preparation for a career; this may mean a new style of living—and many minor crises—for both of them. Preference for a specific kind of work may necessitate living in a particular place, perhaps thousands of miles from home and familiar friends and diversions.

Daily living together—especially where both partners join in caring for the home—means an inner acceptance of each other's idiosyncrasies—her never being on time, his continual mislaying of his small possessions, her briskness in the morning and his wakeful discussions at night—as well as the inevitable bickering over where to stop for gas or lunch on an auto trip or whether to watch a sports program on television or go to a movie. These are not the kinds of things that can be settled in the glow of courtship or the first experience of living together. It takes time, too, to find out how much boredom each partner can stand, and in every relationship one has to come to terms with some boredom as one or the other tells the same story or makes the expected observation not twice but a hundred times.

Can the marriage endure through sickness and health, in good fortune and bad, on vacations as well as during the working months, on blue Monday as well as on Sunday? Until this seems to be a realistic expectation, parenthood may be tried out in imagination—fantasied children can be born, named, played with, sent to school and projected into a world of the future. But real children need not be conceived until the prospective parents feel reasonably certain that they will have a continuing home together.

And what about the children around whom young people build fantasies? How does a couple's picture of childhood match the actuality of children growing up today? The question is not only whether prospective parents can more or less agree with each other in their expectations about bringing up a child. Even more crucial, perhaps, is the problem of how well their most cherished fantasies of childhood accord with changed realities. For even parents who do not recall their own childhood with nostalgia—who want something very different for their own children—tend to relate what will be "different" to the remembered past rather than to the living present.

So I think it is important for young couples, as part of the process of making up their minds, to spend a good deal of time with children in their daily activities as one way of exploring their own reactions to contemporary childhood. Serious volunteers are in great demand, and nowadays men as well as women can be drawn into contact with even the smallest children in community centers, in play groups, in day-care centers, in day camps and summer camps and many other settings. Finding time for this will take planning and certainly will mean giving up desirable alternatives—but far less than living with one's own children.

If possible, I think, a couple should work together at such activities, and so enrich each other's perceptions of how they feel and react in a children's world. Some will discover unexpected talents for teaching and play and care. Others may conclude that they would certainly want to swim against the current in bringing up their own children—but at least they would have some idea of how strong the current is. Still others may realize, however reluctantly, that they fit best in a wholly adult world.

At the same time a couple can find out how strong an interest in—and a toleration of—children at different stages of growing each of them has. Both parents don't have to be easy with children of all ages, but one or the other of them has to be able to cope at each stage. And if by chance the husband is better than the wife at soothing a restless baby, this had better be known and faced in advance.

Many parental situations can be tried out for a few hours, a day, a weekend, a month. A couple can spend Saturday afternoon with a sister's new baby while she gets her hair done. They can have a child at home overnight or for a week while a friend takes his wife with him on a business trip. They can spend a vacation in a house full of youngsters. Prospective parents can discover how they respond to an evening dominated by a crying child, perhaps, or the calls of an insistent three-year-old; to the impossibility of discussing an urgent problem because the whole house, turned into a playpen, provides no place where parents can have a quiet talk; or to the miseries of a long cross-country trip with two restless children and a dog.

They then can get some sense of the balance—for them—between inevitable adult frustrations and the delights of discovering the often-unexpected directness and humor of children and their uninhibited imagination in response to the everyday world.

Young people may feel that these "tests" still are not like the actual situations of parenthood, and in a sense they are right. Standing them well is no guarantee that one can stand the long, unremitting years of parenthood. But if a couple—or one of them—cannot stand such "as-if" experiences knowing that the duration is limited, it is time to stop and think again. Living through difficult periods with their own children, parents cannot depart. They can only help a child reach another stage of growth, and sometimes this takes a very long time.

Realistically, there is another possibility that cannot be left out of account. Suppose that, after all, the marriage—undertaken with the best intentions and the deepest commitment—does not endure? What would each be like as a separated parent, singly responsible over long stretches of time for the care of the children? How willing would each one be to share the love and trust of children who no longer were part of a united home? How willing would either one be to join some form of community living with neighbors and friends to share the burdens of single parenthood?

There is no way, I think, of trying out a failed relationship—nor would anyone want to do so. But it is a possibility, however remote, that should matter to parents in prospect. All they can go on, perhaps, is their own and each other's responses to other couples who are in trouble.

All these are considerations for the future for those who do not yet have children. Young couples have a choice to make, and since they cannot turn to the past for precedents, they must find ways of using the present to set a new style of living as husband and wife alone or as partners in marriage who also consciously choose parenthood and the life of a family.

But how about the millions of men and women who did not so much choose parenthood as simply accept it as an inevitable part of marriage? Do they have to mull over what they might think or say or do if they were getting married today instead of ten years ago?

Of course not. Nothing is so fruitless as trying to relive one's life on the basis of what one might have done at some other time and in a different world. Ten years ago the dangers of the population explosion had not been generally recognized, there was no effective women's liberation movement to raise consciousness levels and young men and women alike accepted marriage with parenthood as a matter of course. And where simply getting married meant accepting the children that came, parents and children together shared in the fate of a kind of family over which individuals had little control.

But this need not cut children off from the future. I do believe that each generation *can* choose—if not for themselves, then for the benefit of their children. Those who married in the older style can bring up their children to believe that parenthood is a vocation for which not all individuals have an aptitude and which may be as responsibly rejected as it should be accepted. They can encourage their daughters and sons, as they grow up and prepare to marry, to think of elective parenthood as a choice they have the freedom and the responsibility to explore.

And finally, bridging past and present in their experience and that of their young children, those who already know a great deal about the hazards and rewards of parenthood can— if they are deeply honest—become a principal resource for parents in prospect. They too have an important part to play in developing a style of living in which the children who are born are positively wanted and welcomed by both parents, who have put parenthood on trial and have decided for it.

Marriage Insurance:
A Stronger Base of Security

MARCH 1974

Today we have come to expect that a great many marriages —especially first marriages—will end in divorce. We even have come to admit that many marriages *should* end in divorce —marriages that were entered into too hastily or built on too flimsy a foundation or based on very divergent expectations. But as yet we have not revised our ethics to fit our behavior. We have not thought through the difficulties of ending a marriage that is entered into—in theory, at least—with a lifetime commitment.

Marriage has become a hazardous venture in which the fear of divorce shadows the hopes and promises of every loving bride and bridegroom. And we still treat a broken marriage as a failure. We have no way of saying: That was a good marriage. They brought up three delightful children who see a lot of both parents, and they are on good terms with each other. Or: They have given a great deal to each other, and now they can go their separate ways, yet follow each other's different paths with understanding.

The fact is that a fully responsible divorce is still unusual and an amicable divorce is a rarity. Instead, the man and woman who came so close together in the beginning of their marriage now, when divorce is contemplated, regard each other as adversaries—even as enemies—who must be got out of the way before a new future can open up. Relatives and friends are expected to choose her side or his, very seldom both equally or in accordance with their personal inclinations. The responsibilities that the new husband and wife accepted so gladly or so lightheartedly and unthinkingly have become

127

a burden to be cast off as quickly and completely as possible.

The children, who love both parents and are loved by them, are torn this way and that, and all too often are treated as pawns in working out conflicts or as unhappy reminders of a denigrated and discarded past. Statistics can tell only a small part of the story, but the very fact that within one year of divorce a very large proportion of fathers—over 40 per cent —have fallen down on child-support payments is significant.

Can't we do better than this?

I think we can. In spite of the complexities of marriage and divorce today, we can take an important step toward a more constructive attitude by realizing clearly that our conceptions of marriage and divorce involve a conflict of strongly held beliefs.

Most Americans still accept as the ideal a marriage in which two adults freely choose to bind themselves together in a unique relationship for as long as both shall live. This ideal symbolizes at the same time a recognition of each individual as a person, free to choose and be chosen, and our belief that given this freedom of choice, a woman and a man willingly will take upon themselves the responsibilities of caring for each other and of fulfilling their roles as parents and members of a family in a community of families.

Almost everywhere in the Western world people have idealized romantic marriage, the kind of marriage that is founded on passionate love. It carries with it the optimistic faith that over a lifetime, lovers can work out the problems of a monogamous relationship. The Judaic tradition, in contrast to the Christian tradition, always has recognized divorce as a possibility. But in a sense the Jewish community, by admiring the man or woman who has endured successfully the hardships of a difficult marriage, has given even greater support to the realities of a lifelong marital and parental relationship.

Actually, everyone recognized the fact that even a very

promising marriage might break down. But as long as every kind of social backing was given to an enduring marriage, a great many people were willing to work at keeping alive a relationship that was far from ideal. In such circumstances, when a marriage broke down it was indeed a failure.

But Americans also believe in an open future. It is our firm conviction that no one should be bound forever by the consequences of a mistake. And today, at the base of our growing toleration of divorce, our easier divorce laws and our lack of any punitive sanctions against divorced men and women lies our belief that everyone should have a second chance—a chance to make new choices, to correct old errors, to fashion a new dream and live it in reality.

Divorce is a solution that is wholly congruent with our belief that people can cut their losses and go on to a better future. But it clashes with our still-accepted belief that marriage should be a lifetime choice. It is this conflict that all but forces a husband and wife who are at the point of getting a divorce to see each other as adversaries who must carry the blame for the "failure" of the marriage—a failure for which no provision was made. And so with divorce we also get broken families and a breakdown of the responsibilities built into our kind of marriage.

It is in this context that we have to see the "arrangement" —living together without marriage—as an attempt on the part of many educated young people to avoid the disasters brought about by unwise choices. Their preference for such an arrangement, openly entered into and openly acknowledged, is not essentially an avoidance of marriage but an awareness of the instability of so many marriages. Rather than hurrying into marriage, one had better take a long time and perhaps make a lot of trials to be sure before one actually gets married. This arrangement takes into account the modern realization that sexual compatibility is not a gift from heaven. Those who enter into an arrangement also may have some awareness that compatibility of life-styles—ways of making a home, ways of handling money, expectations about the future, attitudes toward responsibility—affects the creation of an enduring relationship between a man and a woman.

Many people speak of the arrangement as if it were an experiment with a new form of terminable marriage. But an arrangement gets its validity, its ethical support, from the fact that the two people entering into it are saying, "This isn't a real marriage. As a couple we are not ready for a permanent commitment." So every arrangement, undertaken with full awareness, still supports the traditional ideal, a way of living in which each partner takes full responsibility for the other and for their children.

There is an alternative to both lifetime marriage, with its possibility of divorce, and the very impermanent, fragile arrangement. This is the idea of the contract marriage, with which Americans first experimented after World War I and which is being revived at present as a possibility, and to a very minor extent as a practice. Contract marriage treats two people, however much in love they may be, as partners—business partners or partners in a game, essentially—who pledge cooperation for a limited period only. The marriage contract is renewable at the will of both, but it is also automatically terminable at the end of the stipulated period.

Contract marriage has the advantage of encouraging the partners to talk out their preferences and prejudices, which otherwise seldom surface during courtship. But its great advantages are that there need be no divorce, and theoretically that neither partner need feel neglected or abandoned when the contract terminates because no long-term promise was made. But it makes marriage a wholly secular institution like any other contractual one; and on the whole, Americans feel that contract marriage, by eliminating what is unique in our form of marriage, eliminates what is most essential—the hope that two people can remain together for life.

Despite the conflict that is set up by the opposition between our ideal of marriage and our conviction that individuals should be free to make new choices, we are not willing to opt for a terminable form of marriage. The best we can do is to be clear about the conflict.

This at least will enable us to introduce some safeguards that will make marriage less hazardous, and divorce less shattering when it occurs. And today, particularly for young wives and mothers, it is the fear of what divorce implies for their own security and their children's that drives them toward divorce while they have a chance to make a life of their own, instead of waiting to be abandoned.

One proposal gaining currency today may do a great deal to allay such fears. As it has been discussed it has been called "divorce insurance." But I think we would understand its purposes much better if we were to call it "marriage insurance."

Insurance, especially life insurance, is a peculiarly American institution. It fits both our ideas of responsibility and our basic optimism. You take out as much insurance on your life as you can afford so that if you do not live, your death will not spell utter disaster for the people you love.

Similarly, marriage insurance could remove some of the anxiety, the fear, that haunts every mother of young children, and increasingly every responsible father, that a breakdown of the family will prevent parents from doing what they have every good intention of doing: caring for each other and for their children. Like life insurance, for which almost all families carefully budget their resources, marriage insurance would give a stronger base of security to the whole family, whatever the future held for its members. In this sense it would also protect an ongoing, good marriage.

Marriage insurance could be developed as one aspect of life insurance that would come into play only if a marriage broke down. Otherwise, in an enduring marriage, it later could be turned to all the different uses to which nowadays we have put life insurance, once the children are grown and the investment in insurance is transformed into benefits for those who have fulfilled their earlier responsibilities.

I know that many people will object that "merely" providing financial support for one's children after divorce cannot replace the steady affection and the give-and-take that is so essential a part of life in a functioning family. But knowing that the children are certainly and safely provided for can help avert the sense of overwhelming disaster, and so alleviate the fears and hostilities that too often mark divorce. By keeping the future safer for the children, both parents have a much better chance to keep alive their parental relationship and to protect the trust their children have in them.

Marriage insurance is not the only possibility, but it indicates the direction in which we should be moving in our search for ways to give marriage greater stability and make divorce, which we accept, a responsible relationship that we can honor—not simply the severance of a relationship.

If we are to have divorce, and we certainly shall continue to do so, we must aim at having good and responsible divorces and viable relationships between all those who once formed a family. A marriage may no longer be viable, but a good divorce carries into the future the responsibilities we once accepted—and a continuing concern for the person we once chose as a lifetime partner.

If we make this our aim, we shall not only protect those we care for most in our lives, but we shall also open the way for our children and the children of others to make happier and more enduring, fulfilling choices in their own lives.

Every Home Needs Two Adults

MAY 1976

Home is the place where we create the future—the place where children are prepared to grow toward independence and a way of living in the wider world. As parents we hope that our children will keep happy memories of home and a clear sense of trust and love, given and received, to sustain them throughout their lives. But we do not believe that children should be tied to their past. Home, for most Americans, is a kind of launching platform, and families set the launching process in motion.

But families in America—like families almost everywhere today—are in trouble. Living in a time of transition, some parents are clinging obsessively to old ways, including family ways, while others are trying to break very abruptly with the past. Neither way is a solution. For both children and adults, we need to consider much more carefully what must be changed and what was—and still is—most valuable, and also find new ways of providing for needs that have not changed.

The continually rising rates of separation, divorce and remarriage obviously reflect the current uncertainties of our beliefs about how adults can best live together and the tentativeness of our commitments to our most important adult relationships. One outcome of this is that more and more children are expected to adapt themselves not once and for all to one set of parents, brothers and sisters, but twice or even several times to new family constellations. In fact, it has been predicted that soon more than half our children will be living in households that do not contain both biological parents but

133

instead, perhaps, one stepparent who may—or may not— assume a parental role of love and responsibility.

Even more symptomatic of our difficult situation is the rapidly growing number of families headed by only one parent, in nine cases out of ten by the mother. The number of single-parent-and-children households has more than doubled in the last 15 years. In 1975, 7.2 million households were headed by women alone, and they formed 13 percent of all households. We do know that there is a very direct relationship between this large proportion of single-parent families and poverty, particularly in our inner cities. But going it alone with young children is also a choice made deliberately nowadays by women—and a few men—who are well able to support a family and who feel that by taking the whole responsibility, they are demonstrating their independence.

Of course, there have always been widows and widowers left with children to rear. And especially in troubled times there have been deserted wives with children, and girls left to care for their illegitimate infants. But in other parts of the world and until relatively recently in our own country, it has been common for husbandless mothers and wifeless fathers to be incorporated into larger family and household groupings so that the children were not left with just one harassed adult to depend on.

Single parenthood by *choice* is, in our society, definitely an innovation. Is it a good one? Can it work? What does it mean for children?

We can begin to answer these questions only when we know what it means to have *two* adults in a home. So it is worthwhile, I think, to go beyond the problems of broken family ties and scattered children who suffer because their parents have separated and to reconsider the needs that are met in a traditional two-parent household—needs to which we have given little thought because we have taken them for granted and have met them almost intuitively. We cannot, of course, go backward in time, but we can work out how these needs can be met today to give our children a good start.

For the sake of this discussion I shall assume that the parents are loving and caring people and that they can give a child at least modest economic security. The dangers to both children and adults caused by lack of love or lack of money for the necessities of life are those we are already aware of. What I want to discuss here are the positive factors that we may not always recognize in the traditional household.

In our society, a family with two parents provides the growing child with a sense of choices and of an open world. This is basic. Having two parents, the child discovers that individuals can be different, very different, and yet equally loving and lovable. And having parents who are different from each other, the child senses that she too can be an individual, different from both parents.

It is not merely that one parent is a woman and the other a man. As individuals, their build and coloring and features are different, their family background and history are different, their tastes and capabilities overlap but are by no means identical. What makes one parent laugh delightedly, groan with boredom, fret impatiently or glow with enthusiasm may be a constant source of surprise to the other. Even their most serious expectations for their children may have some very individual elements. They disagree, but in the end they work things out—not once, but time and again.

What a child learns from all this is that she or he can love and be loved by more than one kind of person, and that congeniality does not depend on two people's being alike in any simple sense but on their mutual enjoyment of each other's capabilities and their awareness of the concerns they share.

Parents and children seldom are conscious of what is learned, or how. It happens because this is the way members of families relate to one another. Parents provide an infant with two kinds of laughter and two kinds of comforting. From the first days of her life the baby hears two voices, different in pitch and cadence, and learns to expect two kinds of fun—being hugged in arms that are soft and smooth or tossed by hands that are strong and firm. And when one parent is silent or tired, the other may come in the door at any minute or at least may arrive very soon. Even to a baby, these things give intimations of an open world.

In contrast, the child who lives with one parent alone becomes ingrown and dependent on unvaried expectations. The amiable little girl, enjoying her mother, learns to respond to her slightest cue. But it may be a very long time and a difficult struggle before she learns that there are alternatives.

The child growing up in a two-parent home takes in the idea that there are at least two sides (and maybe more) to every question. Father likes to drive with the car windows open; Mother hates drafts. Mother is active politically; Father sticks to sports. Father always is sleepy in the morning, when Mother is most wide-awake. Father likes reading aloud; Mother likes to sit quietly with the children, listening to music. The two adults in the home assure their daughters and sons in a thousand different ways that the world is open and that each person can safely and happily make many choices.

And there is something else. Living with both parents, children hear them talking at an adult level about adult concerns. New words open the way to new ideas, and conversations about what has been going on give children glimpses of many kinds of adult experience. They discover that their parents can be irritable, frustrated and angry—but also forgiving and willing to be forgiven. There is flow and continuity as children's consciousness of the adult world expands.

An adult alone with a child tends instead to keep on the child's level. The mother knows the words her little daughter has learned and uses those words. She tries to explain the world in terms appropriate to a small child. This is necessary, of course, for all children; but it does not shed enough light on what, unconsciously, the child already needs to know about the adult world. And in the single-parent home a dreadful, engrossing monotony can develop, for there is no one with whom to alternate tasks—washing the dishes or taking the dog for an airing—and no one to help when one is worn out or depressed, no one to reflect affectionate pride in what the baby learned today or what the three-year-old taught her mother.

By concentrating so much on what a child needs (two parents as models) and, in other circumstances, what a spouse needs (a sex partner), we have somehow obscured the need of adults for the company of other adults, for people who are not little people two feet high but full-grown individuals who can share the tasks of providing for the children—who are adults in the making. In a household with two adults there is another adult to share the mother's—or the father's—joys and worries and annoyances, someone to talk things over with, someone who takes a different stance in looking at the children and has another set of insights to modify and expand what you yourself understand.

This is an adult need. But it is one that can make all the difference for the growing child. Through the care given by two articulate, devoted adults, the child learns not merely about these adults who are her parents but very substantially about adulthood.

What I have been talking about are ordinary attributes of the everyday, biological family of parents and children. No two are identical or are likely to find exactly the same solutions to the problems of living together; very few can succeed in meeting all the children's—and the adults'—complex needs. The sad thing today is that so many give up the attempt; so many fail altogether.

Yet when we really come to think about it, much of what children need does not depend on their biological but rather on their social relationship to their parents. Parenting is modeled on the interrelationships of two adults with their own young in a shared home in which both generations teach and learn, value privacy and intimacy, enjoy being together and the freedom to go out and come back. In our American version of the family, parenting is continually modified to match the growing skills and self-confidence of the child who is becoming an adult. The important thing to know is how the model works.

There is no intrinsic reason why parenting must be limited to one or both of the biological parents. In today's world it cannot be.

If every divorce is followed by an attempt by the mother or father to go it alone, if government agencies favor the woman who has no man friend and all aid is cut off as soon as a mother remarries, then opening the future for our children becomes very difficult.

What we need to do is to devise other kinds of homes in which two adults—at least two adults—can have a continuing, loving and responsible relationship with each other and with the children living there. In fact, we have a double task. Parents need to prepare their children both to appreciate the strengths of a two-adult household and to accept the many ways in which such a household can be well constructed.

And for ourselves we need flexibility. The binding tie between the two adults in the home may be, but need not be, a sexual one. Affection, regard and responsibility can be built on friendship and kinship as well. Although the two-adult household in which one is a stepparent is at present likely to be the commonest form, it need not be the only one. In fact, it is the alternatives, I believe, that a separating or divorcing couple need to consider rather than deciding that one of the parents must live alone with the children.

For example, two-adult households can be formed by adults of the same sex—two sisters or two friends and their children or the children of one of them. Or it may include adults of two generations—a mother's mother or father or one or both of the father's parents. Sometimes the adults may be more remotely related and sometimes there may be more than two. A brother who does not live in the household but who spends a lot of time there and takes a responsible, continuing fatherly role with his nephews and nieces can give a new kind of life to a one-parent home.

I believe that children today need to be prepared for such flexibility in family life. One way to prepare one's own children is to talk with them about the variety of families they themselves encounter. How they respond will depend in part on our own criticism, approval or compassion. If there is a single-parent family nearby, the children of that family can be brought in a lot "to help their mother because she is alone and has so much to do." When friends come from families with stepparents, the fact of stepparents and adoptive parents and foster parents all can be faced openly.

Everyone knows that it is not easy, particularly for women, to form an unusual kind of household with their children. It will be easier to do so when all of us who are concerned for today's children and tomorrow's adults succeed in creating a climate of opinion—a firm belief that at least two adults are needed in a home with growing children.

On Being a Grandmother

JULY 1970

On October 9, 1969, I became a grandmother.

Curious! Through no immediate act of my own, my status was altered irreversibly and for all time. It is always so, of course. The birth of a child, an extraordinarily small and fragile creature, changes one's own place in the world and that of every member of a family in ways that cannot be completely foreseen.

Someday parents- and grandparents-to-be will know whether the child they are awaiting is a boy or a girl. Perhaps, having made the choice, parents will feel the unborn baby already has an identity. But the waiting still will be mysterious and the birth a surprise. For even when the child's heritage over many generations is known, the child itself is a new person and unique.

Years ago, long before my own child was born, I steeled myself against some of the traits I loved least in my relatives, characteristics a child of mine might inherit. Like every family, mine had its anomalies—unexplained great-aunts who had been a little peculiar, a few individuals with extraordinarily trivial minds, a whole line of men whose charm was too great for their own good. My English husband did not have many living relatives and I had met only a few of them. Although I had heard scraps of his family history—stories about one person's oddities and another's distinctions—the things I knew were hardly enough for fear or imagination to feed upon.

I was fortunate in not caring whether the child I was waiting for was a girl or a boy. For if one finds oneself (this is how I feel it is) having a very strong preference for one sex or the other, this makes it much harder to wait for the stranger who will change one's life forever. I thought about the future during those waiting months. In the background was the implicit decision that if the baby was a boy, we would probably live in England, but that if it was a girl, we would live in the United States because a girl would have more freedom in this country. I feel sure that this guided my thoughts just below the surface. But I sternly refused to daydream about the kind of child this baby, yet unborn, might be. I have always been very conscious of how my personal daydreams might affect the life of a child or a student, someone helpless before them.

What has this to do with being a grandmother?

It seems to me that one begins to think about grandchildren from the time one's son or daughter marries. One's daughter-in-law or son-in-law will bring new elements into the line of descent. And then when the first grandchild is expected—especially when the child is a daughter's child, as in my case—one lives again, one step removed, the hopes and fears that accompanied the birth of one's own child, who will now be a parent.

Again I resolved not to daydream. But I had the kind of assurance that makes one an optimist. I had inherited a most fortunate combination of my parents' traits—my father's mind and my mother's feeling for people. And I learned quite early that traits—intelligence, for instance—are not determined by sex; even as a child I realized that my father had his mother's kind of mind. My daughter too had received an especially felicitous inheritance, so conspicuously combined that in a long sequence of photographs of her as a child one saw her father whenever she became quiet and pensive and her likeness to me whenever she moved and spoke.

My daughter's husband, who is Armenian, had come to this country as a student from Aleppo, halfway around the world. The possibility of any intermarriage between their ancestors was a thousand years in the past—and then only if one of my daughter's ancestors had been a Crusader, an event too remote to have been recorded. When we met, the closest tie on which we could build our first acquaintance was the fact that his mother had studied at a college in Turkey that had been established by one of my mother's classmates from Wellesley. The discovery of a shared belief in the importance of education a generation ago can give one a warm glow. But it gives no clues about what one's grandchild might be like.

In fact, I told myself that I might never see even one grandchild. When my daughter was born I was 38. Some of my classmates were already grandmothers, and living to the age of a great-grandmother is not yet something anyone can take for granted. So after my daughter's marriage, while she and her husband were studying and designing a life together, I simply took delight in the present and its promise for the future. I thought of their life as one a child might happily choose to enter.

This sense that a child has somehow chosen its parents is a very deep and old human feeling. It is, I am sure, a feeling we should not lose. It gives a child—one's own child and a child adopted with love—a status as an individual in his own right. And this, I believe, is one of the best gifts we can give children—from the first, the freedom to choose their own path.

My granddaughter is named Sevanne Margaret Kassarjian. Sevanne is the feminine form of an old name famous in Armenian literature; it is also the name of a lake in Soviet Armenia. Her parents chose for their first-born a name (Sevan for a boy, Sevanne for a girl) through which the baby's sex would be fully and happily acknowledged. They call her Vanni, in this way preserving the assonance of the sounds of her three names.

It was several days before I first saw Vanni. Nowadays

many hospitals have yielded in the matter of natural child-birth, and fathers are treated not as irrelevant but as partners in the enterprise of having a baby. But with characteristic tyranny such hospitals now keep grandparents and other relatives out. So I knew there was no use my waiting nearby for the baby's arrival. With a second baby a grandmother can be useful at home, taking care of the first child. But only the father has an immediate role to play in the hospital room with the mother and the new baby.

When I saw Vanni at home after her birth—and even months later—I had the same strange feeling of improbability that I had experienced with my own child. The resemblance of other babies to their kin is something I take for granted. But somehow, perhaps just because I know so much about the particular past—the journeys that might not have been made, the meetings that so easily might not have taken place—I feel there is a kind of miraculous improbability about *this* child, my biological descendant. And I think I am not alone in this. It is the kind of feeling that makes one tiptoe into a baby's room with irrational frequency, just to listen to her quiet breathing as she sleeps.

Now, fully inducted into the status of "Grandma," the name I called my grandmother and my daughter called my mother, I think back to myself as a child with my own grandmother.

The grandmother who lived with us was my father's mother. Looking back, I realize that she gave me an extra century of life through the tales she told me about the little town of Winchester, Ohio, where she had grown up. Although it was 60 years before I myself saw Winchester, Grandma made every person, every house, every nook and cranny and the whole style of living familiar to me.

She read me books she had read as a child and books my father had read. She told me, in a voice that I had learned I could fully trust, how times had changed. She explained to me about the telegraph, the first automobile and the men who were then just beginning to link far places in a new way, by flying.

All her life my grandmother had been a teacher, experimental, curious and exploratory, avid for new ideas on how to open the minds of small children. She taught me algebra before arithmetic, and wherever we went for our summer holidays she had me make a herbarium, using new methods to preserve the colors and outlines of plants.

She talked and I listened, and I talked and she listened. Later she used to tell me that after I had chattered to her all day, when evening came and the day's work was done, I would say to her in an expectant voice, "Now let's sit down and talk."

It is hard to know which is more important for a grandparent to do—talk or listen. But adults must keep time—the years before the child was born—firmly in mind. When Edward VII died, my grandmother sighed, "Poor boy, he had so little time to be king!" But she did not ask whether I remembered Queen Victoria. She knew exactly what I knew and what had to be explained to me. She kept the rhythm of my life in her head.

Now it is my turn to keep in mind the sounds to which Vanni dances. She is very sensitive to the qualities of different voices, and in the first weeks of her life her mother let her hear music on the radio, played softly, as a background for startling noises and the sound of unfamiliar voices. Long ago I rocked her mother to sleep to radio tunes, songs requested by men driving trucks on lonely roads at two o'clock in the morning. Related, but not the same.

Since her birth we have had an eclipse of the sun. Later I must not ask her if she remembers. She was still too young, younger than my brother was when he was wakened in the night to see Halley's comet—and the next day recalled nothing about it. But my grandmother knew that I did remember when she told me about other comets or when a meteor fell through the nighttime summer sky. She always remembered and differentiated among what had happened in my life and in my father's life and what she alone of all of us in the house had actually experienced.

I hope I shall remember in the same way just who Vanni is and what she can remember, so that I can make real for her my past and her mother's childhood, and in doing this give her the time depth she will need. Reciprocally, Vanni will keep me in the present that we both can share.

The mobiles over her crib are unlike any I ever saw before. She is surrounded by patterns new-made for the eyes of children growing up today. She will never know a world without television carried by satellites and bringing messages from the moon, as her mother never knew a world without radio or without warfare shadowed by the bomb and by man's new responsibility for the whole planet. But Vanni will also discover a world that is only now emerging, and I shall understand it partly through her responses to it.

In dedicating two of my books I have tried to express something of this link between generations. In 1942 I dedicated a book for Americans about American culture to "the memory of my grandmother and the future of my daughter." Last autumn Vanni was born on the very day my book on the generation gap was going to press; I dedicated it to "my father's mother and my daughter's daughter."

Grandparents need grandchildren to keep the changing world alive for them. And grandchildren need grandparents to help them know who they are and to give them a sense of human experience in a world they cannot know. In the past this was literally so. Now and in the future, when more adults will be concerned with the care of young children who are not their own descendants, this remains a model of mutual learning across generations.

I believe that Vanni and I will be able to talk across the chasm separating her childhood and mine because I know the gap exists and also because my grandmother, talking and listening to me, translated her world into mine and opened a past to me that did not bind my future. Remembering that past now, I know that Vanni will have a future I have no need to see.

IV
Children—Our Future

A New Understanding
of Childhood

JANUARY 1972

We Americans continually try to envision the future as one way of telling ourselves by comparison where we stand now. One question I am often asked is what our descendants, looking back at the 20th century, will think of as the greatest accomplishment of our time.

There are, of course, many possible answers. No one can really foretell what future generations will select out of the complex past as most relevant to what they have become. But as an anthropologist concerned primarily with our understanding of ourselves as human beings I believe that, looking back, our descendants will regard as one of the great accomplishments of our age the discovery of the nature of childhood and our attempt to put this new knowledge to work in the upbringing of our children.

In my lifetime there has been an extraordinary readiness to accept a kind of understanding about children that was only beginning to shape the thinking of a very few people in my own childhood. Yet we have growing up around us—here and in many parts of the world—a whole generation whose lives have been deeply affected by our initial efforts to put into practice (as well as, for far too many children, our failure to put into practice) this new knowledge. We cannot know how it will all turn out, for nothing on so large a scale and with so many variations has been tried before. But others in the future may see these first attempts as a turning point.

A great many people, I feel sure, will disagree. After all, they will say, children have existed always and everywhere— seen and heard or seen and not heard, they have been there

149

and have grown up to become adults. We all have been children, reared by parents and teachers and other adults who knew very well the difference between children and adults. Others, mostly young parents in mid-course of bringing up their children, will think about their hesitation and doubts— what choices to make, how to help their children make their way. Is this a change?

I think it is. What has changed is the old, absolute certainty people had that they knew about children and childhood—knew the one right way to proceed in rearing a child, a girl or a boy, from babyhood to become a functioning adult. But one thing we have discovered in this century, by looking at different cultures, is that there are—and were in the past —a great many "right" ways, each different from the others.

The theory that childhood should be regarded as a period of carefree play seemed entirely wrong to those who believed that childhood was a hard apprenticeship to adulthood. That children learned best by making their own mistakes seemed an incredible attitude to people who believe firmly that children must learn what to do and how to do it before they could safely be allowed to take the initiative. When I went to Samoa in the mid-1920s I could ask the question whether adolescence is, the world over, a period of storm and stress, as it undoubtedly was at that time in Western societies. Yet in Samoa it most certainly was not.

What we were learning then by careful observation was that each culture shapes the processes of growth, at whatever stages are recognized as significant, in its own image of a human life. But we were just beginning to ask questions about the processes of development—about what is involved in the conception of the child's "becoming" a person.

Every people has a quite definite image of what a child is at birth. Russians, for example, see the newborn as so strong that they swaddle it firmly to protect it from harming itself. The French, in contrast, see the baby as fragile and vulnerable to anything harmful in the environment—and they softly swaddle the infant to keep it quietly safe.

In Bali a baby is not given a human name at birth. Until it seems clear it will live, the Balinese refer to it as a caterpillar or a mouse. At three months, when it is given a name, it becomes a participating human being whose mother, speaking for it, says the words of polite social response. But if the baby dies before this, people reproach it, saying, "You didn't stay long enough. Next time stay and eat rice with us." For the Balinese believe in reincarnation. They believe the "soul," without any specific personality, is reborn every fourth generation within the same family.

Such beliefs as these—that the newborn child is intrinsically strong or delicate, assertive or compliant, naturally good or bad, a traveler from a different and better world, a soul given one chance for eternal salvation or a soul moving in an endless round of reincarnation—give people assurance that they know what to expect and how to rear a child. And long before the child learns what a child should be, it begins to know whether it fits or doesn't fit the expectations of its parents.

But it is not only conceptions of human nature that are expressed in such images. The basic relationship of parent and child and the procedures of education also are described by analogy. In many Western European cultures the child has been pictured as a plant and the parents as gardeners tending the plant. And there is, in fact, a kind of parallel between the way a people treats plants and children both as living things.

In the English image the gardener, it is believed, must provide the best environment for the plant's own natural growth. In the French image the child is often likened to a young tree that must be given space, with some idea of what it should become, and must be trained, shaped and pruned unremittingly for its best eventual flowering or fruiting by an experienced gardener who knows what the aims of cultivation are. But in the German image the child is more like a flowerpot in which seeds are sprouting, some of them flowers and others weeds, and it is the gardener's duty not only to tend the flowers but to uproot the weeds—weaknesses, errors and faults—so that in time he will produce a sturdy plant that can survive on its own.

In complex societies, of course, analogies like these provided only some of the simpler models for what children and childhood are. But as long as a people considered themselves as somehow representative of what is human and right, they could hold on to traditional beliefs or, from their ideas of what children should be, judge the children they saw around them.

In our time, however, two things in particular changed all this drastically and brought into focus many attempts to think about childhood in another way—not as a stage or state but as a process based in human biology and shaped by the child's relationships to the world of people and things.

One was our growing recognition that although there are extraordinarily different routes from childhood to adulthood, there are also regularities in children's growing—regularities of timing, for example, within wide individual limits, of when children begin to walk or begin to talk. In the face of this our older dependence on absolutes—our insistence on one right way—broke down as students asked how children's capabilities come into play in response to different forms of teaching and learning.

The other discovery grew out of the explorations carried out by the psychoanalyst Sigmund Freud with his patients in which they traced the paths of experience back to childhood —to long-"forgotten" memories, fantasies and conflicts. Freud's belief was that if troubled individuals could recover what was lost and understand what went amiss, they could free themselves to become happier and more productive. But what was also gained was a sense of the wholeness of a human life and of the continuing interplay of past and present in man's relationship to himself and the world around him.

The sequel has been a flowering of work with children themselves—children in many cultures. So for the first time we are beginning to see and understand the relationship between the child's developing capacities and what he experiences from day to day and from month to month, responding to and initiating responses from the people around him. We are discovering too that many of our most fixed beliefs were simply myths. There was the belief, for example, that for the baby the world at first is, in the phrase of William James, a "buzzing confusion." Far from this, we are finding out that the youngest infants have a working sense of space, that they respond with preference for certain kinds of visual patterns and, especially, are alert to movement and change in what they see and hear.

Equally important, we are finding out that little babies very soon begin to enjoy new variations, and by the time they are a year old are delighted with their own attempts to make quite complex variations on what they have come to know. These are things for which we have so far devised explorations in which babies themselves become partners in the enterprise.

Mothers—observant, loving mothers who enjoy their babies —may have an intuitive sense of what their own babies are reaching out for as they grow. But intuition does not fill the gaps. In our culture, in which babies often are left to lie alone in their own room staring at the blank ceiling, it is a matter of chance whether a mother notices how her baby responds to patterns of light and shadow accidentally cast on the ceiling and whether she finds a way of making these light-birds appear on another day. For her it is this baby—her baby—who responds with delight to the moving play of light and shadow. What we are finding out now is how babies' developing capabilities come into play at two weeks, four weeks, four months, a year, two years—and also what happens to the child from whom no one, except accidentally, elicits responses of interest and renewed recognition. We need to build this new knowledge into the kind of relationships of babies with those around them that almost any adult, given a lead, can establish—as traditionally mothers and grandmothers and fond aunts played nursery games just for the fun of it.

As our knowledge grows we can also look to the traditional ways of rearing children in different cultures as a way of understanding better the effects on children of special kinds of emphasis. For example, the Chinese give babies a great variety of experiences of looking without touching. The French emphasize sound and believe that to be alert a baby needs to be almost continuously in contact with human voices. In our own country we encourage babies to be physically active—to move and explore, wriggle and reach out, testing the world and their own ability to get what they want. As we examine these varying traditions in child rearing, what we learn from the world's children can be given back to them in new forms to enrich their lives and ours.

It is true that in our first attempts to bring up at least part of a generation in the light of new insights and a growing understanding of how a human being becomes a person, our efforts have suffered from all the difficulties of transition—inconsistencies, reversals, misunderstandings and the discouragement of hopes set too high. As the children have grown up they—and we—have suffered from shocked surprise at what the world looks like through their eyes.

We have not yet asked the kinds of questions about the developmental processes in later life that we have asked about childhood, questions that helped us alter and broaden our conceptions. Our attention so far has been narrowly fixed on this one early phase of life. But what will be the needs and capabilities of children reared to greater openness and self-discovery when they, in turn, become the elder generation?

We do not know. With our studies of childhood we have only made a beginning. But it is a beginning on which future generations may build.

Summer Camp Changes a Child

It is August, and the second month of summer is upon us. Parents who have sent a child to camp for the first time realize, perhaps with surprise, that this is the halfway mark, the turning point. After the first long days of wondering and waiting for news, the weeks began to slip away more quickly. By now some questions—the ones that loomed so large at the moment of parting, when the queue of small children moved toward the waiting bus two by two, stranger partnered with stranger, hand in hand—have been answered. The first few nights were lonely ones and the first meals were difficult to get down, but the newness of the round of camp activities also was absorbing.

Camp letters from a six-year-old, an eight-year-old, even a ten-year-old, are sketchy. They report, a little awkwardly, a succession of events: We went fishing yesterday. I caught a sunfish. We had a campfire. The moon came up. The water is warmer now. I learned to float. We play baseball every afternoon. Can I have a catcher's mitt? The black dog has new puppies. How is the cat?

Letters from counselors are a little more informative and even answer questions: Johnny is eating well now and has gained two pounds. Mary is making friends with the children in the cabin. Yesterday she helped two of them make their beds. Don't worry about Jimmy's glasses. He puts them on to read.

At first they were like messages from the moon or from a new-found land—all the names strange and no map to guide the reader from place to place. But gradually the names became attached to people, and glimpses of life in this distant

156

world began to appear in snapshots: This is me on my horse, Whitefoot. This is Peter. He takes us for hikes. This is Blueberry Hill, but the blueberries are still green. This is our picnic place on the beach.

But now it is August. Soon, very soon, the children will be coming home. While it is still quiet—often too quiet for a mother who is used to listening all day and every day—new questions begin to take shape. Was it worthwhile? Will all the happy promises of the summer be fulfilled? Will things ever be the same as before? Or changed? Changed how?

Such questions are being asked in every part of the country, for more children than ever before are going to camp. Parents who never had a vacation want their children to have some camping, even if it is only two weeks at a Scout camp not far away. Parents who spent short holidays at a nearby lake want their children to have a whole summer outdoors with time to make friends, time to learn how to swim, time to enjoy the whole changing scene of summer from daisies in the fields to the nights of the harvest moon and the first flare of red autumn leaves on a high hill. Parents who spent every summer in the easy familiarity of the same cottage community want their children to venture a little farther away and make discoveries on their own. Parents who recall their own camping summers, in the days when every hour was planned from the moment the bugle sound of reveille woke them to the moment when in the quiet darkness they heard the long, slow notes of taps— these parents want their children to enjoy the freedom of new kinds of camps.

Parents' daydreams are part of the picture of children going to camp, part of their expectations of what camping can do for their child now in camp for the first time.

But there are many other reasons for sending a small child to camp. Parents hope that living with other children will help the shy and clinging child to become more sociable and independent. They hope that learning new sports will train the hand and eye and foot of the active boy and teach him to use his superabundant energy. Mothers hope that the little ugly duckling will become less self-conscious during weeks away from her prettier sister, or that the left-hander, who irritates his right-handed father because he can't catch a ball, will surprise everyone with his swimming. Fathers hope their sons will come home bigger and sturdier, ready to do the things men and boys can do together.

Children are sent to camp so that they will grow up a little. So that they will learn to tie their own shoelaces without making a knot, wash their hands and face without being prompted, share activities with other children more amiably, get themselves up in the morning or go to sleep at night without diversionary activities.

They are sent off to give someone else in the family a vacation—perhaps only the mother, perhaps both parents. This is a reason seldom faced frankly. American parents are made to feel that they ought to enjoy their children all the time. To say it is magnificently peaceful without young George may feel like treachery. The child who goes off to camp may feel this too. Coming home, he will wonder and need to be reassured.

Parents are franker about the relief afforded other siblings. With two children actively competing day after day, it is easy to recognize the fact that it would be good for both of them to be apart for a while, especially for the older one who is smaller and less vigorous, for the little shadow of an assured older brother, for the girl who wants passionately to do everything her brother does. Mary Fisher Langmuir, who had four children, used to say to the mothers at the Vassar Summer Institute, which she headed: "Every child has the right to be the only child for a while!" The corollary to that was: "Only children have the right to share their lives with other children and find out what a large family is like."

Early in the summer parents worried about whether their

child—not very old, after all, and away from home for the first time—would really make it. Then expectations began to build up about all the good things that could come out of this camping experience. But now in August parents begin to wonder about what to expect *after* camp.

Whatever this first summer away was like, every child has gained something from the experience. The diffident boy may come home proud and possibly a little defiant about his new accomplishments. Or as sometimes happens, he may have un-learned something he did well before. Parents look forward hopefully to the effects of camping. But the outcome may be wholly unexpected. The returned camper, having learned something about independence, may be more of a problem than before he went away—less willing to pick up clothes, less responsive to family rules, more openly resistant to any voice of authority.

Parents have to be prepared for such unexpected and even unwelcome effects. Dealing with the aftermath of mosquito bites, poison ivy, sunburn, exposure to a very mixed vocab-ulary of four-letter words, overeating or undereating is not difficult. These are minor matters. But once in a while a child returns with new fears rather than with old fears conquered, or with a feeling of loneliness in a crowd added to the loneli-ness of being an only child. It will take time and patience to discover such new difficulties and help the child to overcome disappointments. It is a mistake to assume that because a child was sent (or asked to go) to camp for a particular purpose that that purpose was accomplished. Something quite differ-ent—very good or not so good—may have happened.

Looking ahead, parents can be very sure of only one thing: The returned camper (even the child away from home for no more than two weeks) will be different. A momentous event has taken place. The child has met a challenge and has found his or her own way of coping with the unknown and the strange, something no one could tell the child how to do. But few, if any, children can put into so many words how they managed or how they feel about it all. It will take a lot of listening to find out.

Moreover, the obvious things that happened to the child during the summer may turn out to be not the ones that mattered most. It is easy to praise a child for new accomplishments—for learning how to play on a team, for turning a lump of clay into a well-observed representation of a dog, for learning some of the skills camps are supposed to teach or for a new ability to listen to another child's account of his doings. But the high point of the summer may have been something quite different, something that went unnoticed by others or that had a special significance for him.

Daring to walk alone in the dark past shadowy trees may have meant conquering a very private set of fears. The discovery that every plant has a name and can be classified may have been extraordinarily exciting—the first step into a new world of how to think about things. Or it may have been the delight of having a friend to share secrets with—not just a playmate, but a friend.

Whatever it was, it may take a lot of listening for parents to learn what really made the summer special. The returned camper, not so very changed in appearance, in some ways will be a stranger, a child to become acquainted with again.

But there is something else to take into account. In the camper's absence the family has changed. Too often the person who is away thinks of home as static, waiting forever for him to return to his niche. But in a home full of living people nothing is static. Father may have got used to shaving without advice and help. Mother may even have had time to read the mail in bed. A brother may have spread his possessions out in a shared room. A sister may have abandoned her own toys for her brother's bicycle. The baby may have graduated to a youth bed. Home may still look the same, but the people will be different.

In the long summer weeks, parents will have found out things about the small, absent camper they hadn't known— just how much he was part of morning joy or morning grief, how they counted on his shout to greet the day or his tousled and resentful head, his sleepy voice, to set the tone at breakfast.

They will have found out things about themselves as well. A father may perhaps realize how often he compared his own son with other boys, not always to his boy's advantage, and now with nostalgia wonder whether he wouldn't prefer to have his son home again quite unchanged. A mother may become conscious for the first time of how much of what she sees and hears becomes associated in her mind with some thought about her daughter—how the child would enjoy the early raspberries, how she would laugh at a joke, how she would frown and tell her mother, "Your lipstick is on crooked again."

Returning to a new configuration, aware that his parents talk to him in a new way, the child will feel strange. He will have to find his place in a new pattern. This is harder, often, than learning how to adjust to a completely new situation, a new house or a new school. All the familiar things at home have changed a little; the noises in the morning sound different; conversations have a different tone; the balance of power has shifted. Johnny may not be quite sure he is as close to the center of things as he remembers. Mary may have moments of feeling left out.

The child who earlier felt unhappy at home may return much happier to be there. The child who was happy at home may have experienced such acute and unrecognized homesickness that later he can't understand why he felt the way he did in camp—or why home isn't quite what he dreamed it was. Both children feel a vague sense of estrangement, the more difficult to break through if no one realizes what is so puzzling and disturbing.

Not long ago a young friend who has been working with the high-school students who are brought to the United States for a year's stay by the American Field Service remarked with insight, "The kids know they have changed and that their parents expect them to come home changed, but the trouble is, neither of them will realize that the parents have changed too." That, I think, is the crux of the matter. Parents have to include themselves in what they expect of their children's first homecoming. It is a time of rediscovery for everyone and children need the comfort and reassurance that change makes no difference to love except to enrich it.

Coming home from camp is a rehearsal for something that will happen again and again and become more important through the years as the absences grow longer and visits home shorter. What parents and children succeed in making of this first venture out of the home circle will affect all the reunions in later years—the return from college, from summer jobs, from trips abroad, with a wife or a husband, with a first baby.

Why Can't Mary and Johnny Write—and Read and Compute?

AUGUST 1976

Mary can't write! Johnny can't write!

The plain fact is that today the majority of young Americans cannot write simple, grammatically correct and well-organized prose. They have not learned how to express themselves in English, their native language.

How has this happened? I believe it is because teachers and pupils alike have become dropouts from the learning situation.

The complaint began as a low rumble of dissatisfaction about a generation ago, when we were much more worried by the question of why so many of our children were failing to learn how to read—a question we have not yet succeeded in answering. Then it often was scornfully said that the complaints about writing were made by the purists, the traditionalists, who were against any kind of change in the usage of our written language. Wasn't it better for students' writing to echo contemporary speech?

Today the complaint about writing has become all but universal. High-school teachers of every subject spend time fruitlessly correcting spelling and grammar, time they would prefer to spend, and should be spending, teaching social studies or literature or chemistry. Many teachers have become so frustrated that they have given up written exercises.

Things are not much better at the most advanced graduate level. Even the students sometimes complain. Recently an able college senior explained to one of my colleagues why he could not take a final, year-end exam. "It's an *essay* exam," he said, "and I don't know how to write!"

163

But the problem cannot be tied down to writing or reading, as some people seem to think. Last spring, newspapers began to catch up with the very sorry statistics about the shabby state of education. Quite abruptly this year we have been brought face to face with difficulties that over the decades have plagued teachers in elementary and high schools, faculty members in colleges and professional schools, specialists in child development, school superintendents and local school boards. Theorists and practitioners who have argued endlessly about methods of teaching and the content of the curriculum, boards of regents and boards of trustees and recently even state legislators have become involved—indeed, almost everyone connected in any way with the formal education of our children and young people.

Even so, up to the present we have not come to grips with the fundamental problems. What the statistics show, and what we continue to argue about, are some of the more obvious consequences of educational failure. About these there can be no doubt. The College Entrance Examination Board and the American College Testing Program both report a steady decline over a decade and all across the country in the average scores of the college applicants they test. It is not only that too many Marys and Johnnys can't write—they cannot read with comprehension, add or subtract or divide with accuracy. And obviously this affects their ability to absorb information in any field they choose for study.

As a result, colleges and universities everywhere have been forced to devote an ever larger part of their precious resources —in some cases millions of dollars annually—to provide remedial courses in reading, writing and arithmetic so that the students they have already accepted can begin to benefit from college-level studies. Educators have exercised a good deal of ingenuity in naming these "compulsory workshops" and "laboratories" in order that the students who are gathered in by the thousands will not feel insulted and demeaned. But high-sounding names do not change what the courses are all about: the three R's in their simpler forms.

In turn, the need to provide state universities with special funds for classrooms, teachers and remedial teaching equipment has alerted state legislators to the problem. As might be expected, there has been a movement in many states to legislate educational rules. For example, Arizona now demands that in order to obtain a high-school diploma the student must be able to read, write and compute "at least at the ninth-grade level." Why not, after all, at the twelfth-grade level?

The education of our children has been one of our proudest boasts. From the very beginning, Americans have trusted, supported, fought and worried over whatever schools there were. The local school has been—and usually still is—at the heart of the community. It was in the schools that colonists learned to become Americans, creating a new kind of civilization. And in our schools the children of immigrants, generation after generation, have learned a new culture along with the three R's: what to eat and how to dress, to feel at home in a language their parents would never learn completely, to cope with authority and live with their peers, to tell the truth or face the consequences and—most important —to value achievement and work hard to get ahead.

Americans seldom have idealized scholarship as such or set scholars and scientists apart as an elite group. We do not admire dwellers in ivory towers. But successful men remember the teachers who set them on their way. Former President Harry Truman, recalling his schooling in the small town of Independence, Missouri, wrote: "I do not remember a bad teacher in all my experience. . . . They were the salt of the earth. They gave us our high ideals, and they hardly ever received more than forty dollars a month for it." What Americans have most valued about education is that it opens the way to free choice. Children are not compelled to become what their parents before them were. Education, by giving them a chance to make the most of opportunity, supports and enhances their personal independence. The child begins to find herself as a person; the young woman, like the young man, can make a place for herself in the world and fulfill herself.

Because these have been our beliefs, concerned and progressive people have continually wanted to expand our educational system and have fought for more education—especially more free education. They have fought for more years of schooling for more people, for a better chance to learn, a greater opportunity to become someone with a significant place in the world.

The big push to open high schools to every child got under way after World War I, and after World War II we began to open wide the doors of our colleges. And finally, in the 1960s, the supporters of Black and other ethnic groups—the students with the least chance to enter the main stream of our national life—fought for open admissions and for community colleges where women and men who had been left out earlier could have a second chance.

Looking back, it is astonishing how far we came in just one generation. In 1940, fewer than half the young Americans in the 20-24 year age group had completed high school and less than 10 per cent in the same age group were then enrolled in colleges. By 1972, well over 80 per cent in the 20-24 year age group were high-school graduates and some 24 per cent were enrolled in colleges. The figures are still more astonishing, even taking into account our population growth, when we compare over a century the number of those to whom colleges and universities have granted degrees of all kinds: 9,372 in 1870, when the first land-grant colleges were just getting established, compared with 1,313,000 in 1974! Surely this educational accomplishment should be a source of great pride. But how can we take pride when so much has gone wrong? Seeming to offer students more, we are actually giving them far less. While we have exposed our children to more and more years of schooling, we have been cheating more and more of them of the promise that education—true education—holds out for the future.

Part of the trouble has been the rapidity with which our educational system has grown, so that few adults fully grasp the reasons for the continually rising costs, particularly of the new kinds of education we want our children to have.

In the past, children could get a thorough grounding and learn how to learn even in a one-room schoolhouse and a small-town library. With good teachers and conscientious parents they could relate what they were taught to their own familiar world; books, which they could read and read again, were their windows on the past and on the wider world.

Today, children's experience is utterly different. The most distant places and peoples converge, through radio and television, on every home in every small town; unfamiliar sights and sounds are continually presented to children's consciousness, but ephemeral, sensational and highly simplified. Information comes in one ear and goes out the other, and the child seldom has a way of amplifying what she has heard to make it intelligible or of verifying what she thinks she may have heard or seen. Children need somehow to give shape and meaning to this flood of sights and sounds from far away.

And, of course, a teacher who is completely confident of her ability and her authority can easily handle a class of 50 pupils. But they must be children who have learned at home to sit still and listen and in school to recite when they are called upon; they must be pupils who have acquired from their parents the habit of obedience and a willingness, most of the time, to keep their thoughts and questions to themselves.

But this is not the kind of teacher and these are not the

kind of children we have in our classrooms. And an attempt to impose a form of authority, a hierarchical relationship, that neither the teacher nor the pupils believe in, can be dangerous. Not so much because it leads to violence, though it well may, but rather because it destroys the trust that is the necessary foundation of good teaching and successful learning.

Our changing attitudes toward one another have deeply affected our conceptions of the relations between children and adults. Today we have come to believe—and rightly—that children are persons. Many educators also believe that students, from the smallest kindergartner to the candidate for a higher degree, and at every stage in between, have the right to be active participants in the learning process. They must be engaged—"interested" is the word students use. The hindrances to spontaneous participation are considered to be "mindless" routine and "meaningless" subject matter.

This has meant one thing for many of our most privileged youngsters, who attend progressive schools where classes are small and hard-working teachers follow the development of each child. Here most rote and routine learning has been abolished. In some of these schools, there are no penmanship exercises, no alphabets, no spelling bees, no arithmetic tables or mental-arithmetic exercises, no bits of poetry committed to memory, no grammar rules, no dates of great events—no mindless memorizing at all to stifle the imagination, no routine to hinder questions and no immovable facts to get in the way of creativity.

At best, bright and interested children can learn a great deal by this system—as bright and interested children can manage to learn by almost any system—and they include some of our best and most engaging students. But too often what they know floats unanchored and awash; they cannot organize their thoughts.

Our emerging, still-muddled educational philosophy has been applied in quite another fashion to our least privileged children, crowded into poor, neglected and underfinanced schools and taught by teachers far too harassed to keep track of any one child's development. As those who entered school came more and more poorly prepared, the educational fare got weaker. In many public high schools the old curriculum became almost unrecognizable as Greek, Latin, French and German were dropped, mathematics and the sciences were taught sketchily, and history, even American history, was passed over quickly. Children who were not taught to read well were seldom asked to write, and for the same reason— no one had time to work with them to correct their individual errors and improve their individual understanding.

But the outcome has been very much the same. Two movements—one to make school easier for minority children for whom we have scant respect and the other to make school interesting and undemanding for privileged children—have had the effect of turning many teachers as well as children into dropouts; teachers who are as unable to teach as children are unable to learn.

There still are, of course, teachers who are gifted and conscientious enough to be able to "turn children on" to the attractions of learning in almost any situation and children who are receptive to education under almost any circumstances. But in a world in which so much depends on accuracy and on each person's ability to pay attention, to organize and to communicate facts and ideas, we are turning too many of our children into barbarians without access to the knowledge to which they, together with all the world's children, are the rightful heirs.

The fact that Mary can't write is more than a symptom of failure on our part. It is a protest on her part. And it is our responsibility to participate in a quite different way in Mary's education so that she can begin learning again.

Children Can *Learn*

NOVEMBER 1976

Children *can* be taught to read and write, and to do both with some measure of ease and competence. In spite of all the evidence today to the contrary, that is one thing we must keep in mind. Now more than ever before, the ability to understand what others have written and to express oneself clearly are necessary adult skills. They are skills no one is born with and that everyone who is to become literate must learn.

Given a chance, children *can* learn to use words exactly and vividly to write about the world they are so busy discovering, as well as to express their thoughts and feelings. They can learn how to tell a story, how to describe accurately an event they have watched or taken part in, how to give directions to another person who wants to go somewhere or make something, how to organize an argument and how to share with others their moods of pleased excitement, anger, fright and happiness. This much is within the reach not of just a few especially talented or privileged children but of every child—or it should be. Given a proper chance to learn how to write, children can even learn to enjoy the process of discovering how to communicate more and more meaningfully.

An English philosopher, R. G. Collingwood, once said that you cannot fully know what the poem you are writing is about until you have finished writing it. It is equally true, I think, that you cannot fully know your own thought until you have succeeded in expressing it clearly, either orally or by writing it down. Learning to use words is not only a way of reaching

170

out to others; it is also a way of finding yourself.

But the evidence cannot be dodged. Our children are not becoming competently literate. Great numbers of elementary-school children fail to grasp the basic elements of reading and writing and each year fall further behind. The majority of adolescents are incapable of expressing themselves in good, clear English. And the average adult has little confidence in her own ability to read rapidly and with understanding, to conceptualize what she wants to say and to say readily what she has in mind.

The facts are well-known. The question is what we are to do.

First of all, I believe, we must scrap most of the current theories as to why our children are not learning. They are simply poor excuses for our own failures. It is said, for example, that television is so attractive to children that it is keeping them from reading. But watching television—for reasonable periods of time and with some attention paid by parents to the quality of the programs—is at least as useful in learning to read as the same number of hours spent roller skating or playing ball. It is certainly true that many children would benefit by more active play out of doors—but this would not turn them into readers. Just because children learned to read in the past does not mean that they spent all their free time reading or keeping diaries or writing stories. For one child who was a delighted bookworm or a precocious author, there were thousands who read no further than their school lessons required. But it is also true that children today who do learn to read and write do not treat television as their *only* resource.

We must also realize the pernicious effect on almost everyone of our continually rising anxiety about our children's education. Two generations ago the young adult who for some reason had not learned to read and write English could still get a job. Today this is not so; the illiterate person is a social cripple. And as we have raised our standards our ability to teach the necessary skills has diminished.

This is not the paradox it seems. For high standards can be used, not only to increase care and to provide timely warnings about things that may be going wrong, but also to frighten people with the specter of failure. And anxiety of this kind is paralyzing both to parents, who fear for their children's future, and to teachers in school systems where no one suggests workable remedies. In the end, of course, this adult anxiety paralyzes the children most of all, and they cannot learn.

Concern is legitimate in some cases. Parents and teachers must be alert to the needs of handicapped children and the special kinds of help they must have. But what I am speaking of here is the vague, unplaced worry that is extended to all children and that serves only to aggravate the difficulties along the way without providing remedies. In many schools, teachers, uncertain about the effectiveness of their methods, discourage any efforts made by parents—even though we know that the best way for a child to learn basic literacy is in the natural, everyday give-and-take with literate parents who are close to each child's interests and learning habits. Deprived of help, healthy children become handicapped, deprived of the ability to learn through no lack or failure of their own.

The children of illiterate parents need more help, and in the past we used to give it to many of them. And elsewhere in the world today, in new countries and postrevolutionary countries, whole adult populations have become literate almost overnight—because educational planners and teachers and students alike believed in the importance of reading and writing and had no doubt that these skills could be put within everyone's reach.

In our own country, in fact, during World War II, we had a splendid literacy program in the armed forces that was designed, not by educators who had given up on half the children it was their responsibility to teach, but by highly sophisticated people who respected their students as adults interested in adult things, who happened not to have learned to read and write but were perfectly capable of doing so. And they learned. Somehow we have forgotten what we have done and have not observed what others are doing.

Our most immediate task, then, is to change the level of our expectations. Instead of indulging in worry that carries with it the expectation of failure—and our contempt for those who fail—we must be convinced that what other children have done and are doing, all our children can do. We must establish a nationwide expectation that *all* children can and will be taught to be literate. And we must not be deterred by educators' quarrels over the methods of teaching or by shibboleths about such things as the McGuffey Readers or the dangers of permissiveness. Children have learned to read by being beaten—and also by learning their letters from cookies coated with honey. As long as the society—and so the teachers and parents—expect children to be able to learn, they will learn.

It is when that expectation falters, when a society believes that any group of children is incapable of learning—whether they are physically handicapped or the children of mountain people, whether they come from rural or urban slums or are Black or foreign-speaking, whether they are barefooted, or girls, or twitchy and unused to sitting still—then such children will become "social dyslectics," children who suffer from an impairment in the ability to learn to read that is social in origin.

Expectations have to change equally in the minds of educated, anxious parents who have accepted uncritically their children's failure to learn for complex psychiatric reasons. As I began by saying, we must keep firmly in mind that children *can* learn to read and write.

Our second task is to recognize the fact that education is

costly as we now define it in a very complex world. And it is costly as it applies not only to beginners but also to all those in search of higher education—indeed, to everyone who wants to learn. There are those who say we should not raise our level of expectations until we are ready to pay for what we will need. Certainly the two go together. But on the whole, Americans are willing to commit themselves only to working hard for and spending money (especially tax money) on activities they accept as necessary and good and likely to succeed.

And in making plans for education and budgets to implement those plans, we must provide not only for children, adolescents and college students, but also for adults who want to advance and for the dropouts—the neglected, the deprived and the damaged—who want to enter the main stream of living. As Americans we have never believed in penalizing people for their past, and any plan we make and advocate broadly must take into account those who have suffered. Today we have a vast number of parents who have been marred by the experience of their schooling. If we do not realistically give them a chance, we shall endanger the chances of their children, and so the well-being of still another generation.

But what about time? What about *my* children—now? Isn't there something we can begin to do now, immediately, for the children who are already in school and the still smaller ones who will come streaming into schools next spring and next fall? This is a legitimate demand. For every child, childhood happens only once and is always now.

There is, of course, a great deal we can do—parents and teachers and everyone involved in the teaching side of the educational process. We can begin by drawing on what we know worked in the past and adapt it intelligently to the kind of children we hope, at best, to bring up for tomorrow's world.

And we are not without help in the matter. Here and there

in the country some children—a few—*are* learning to use their language very well. They are learning to write correctly and much more individually than the best-taught children did in the past. And there are teachers—not only very young teachers, and many more than we know about—who are struggling successfully with the problems of how to teach children the kind of literacy they will need and can take pride in as they are acquiring it. I have talked with some of these teachers and I have read some of the lively and interesting work that their pupils are producing.

One thing we have to realize is that the ability to read and to comprehend the meaning of written material does not give a child proficiency in writing. It is true that reading and writing are linked tightly together, so that unless a child understands that someone has written the words she is asked to read, and learns to write those words herself, reading remains a kind of mumbo jumbo. The child needs to see the teacher (or the parent as teacher) write the words that the child then reads. And then the child herself must write what she has read.

And she needs to practice writing all the time in order to begin to do it well—and better still as she goes along. We don't object to tennis players' or skaters' or jazz musicians' or ballet dancers' practicing incessantly, or to their knowing the technical names of the tools they use and how exactly to produce their formal, highly stylized actions. Why, then, should we let our old rebellions against admittedly outmoded disciplinary forms dominate us so that we call all practice and memorizing and technical study "dull drill"—and throw it out? Surely children have as much right to gain proficiency in a most basic skill as they do in learning a sport. And certainly they have as great a need to know how the language works and to have an accurate, specific way of talking about what they and others have tried to do in their writing.

In fact, children need to understand the whole wonderful

literary process, from the first struggle with an idea, a fantasy or a muddled bunch of "facts" to printing and publication and reading and criticizing and weaving new patterns of ideas out of ones that have become familiar. And it can be done.

What is different now, I believe, and what differentiates the best of modern teaching and learning from the best of the past is that we recognize the fact that learning is a social process in which every participant plays a crucial role. The teacher respects the child, knows where the class is headed and how her students will proceed. But at the same time the teacher, like every child in the class, is a participant in the learning that is taking place for each child and for all the children together.

This is the true beginning, I believe, and it depends on a mutuality of trust and respect between teacher and pupil and among all the pupils. It depends on a belief shared within and outside the school that what the student learns is valuable to herself and her whole society. Learning to write takes time and much effort, but it can be done. And the joy of writing well is that this skill, learned early, stays with you and continues to grow through the whole of your life.

Our Youngest Commuters: Children on School Buses

JANUARY 1977

Have you ever tried to add up all the hours in a week or a month or a school year that your own child—or a child in your neighborhood—has to spend traveling to school and home again in a school bus? Sit down with your daughter or son some evening and do the arithmetic.

Thirty minutes, 40 minutes, even an hour, for a single trip does not seem a great hardship for a sturdy girl or boy. But add in the time spent getting to the bus stop and waiting for the bus to arrive and, for quite a lot of children, the time involved in changing to a second bus. Then multiply that total by ten trips a week—forty trips a month—and a picture begins to emerge that no one really wants to see—a picture of far too many wasted hours, empty hours, in our children's lives.

Suburban fathers often complain about the boredom and fatigue of commuting. But how many parents are ready to admit that their six-year-old daughters and sons are commuters too?

Our sympathy goes out to children who are being bused to a distant school as a way of achieving a better racial balance. If the school bus is carrying a Black or an ethnically disadvantaged child out of a poor neighborhood to a better school, parents—and most other people—stifle their doubts; it may well be worth the price. But in all honesty, most of us also sympathize with the children who are being bused away from a safe and pleasant neighborhood where everything is familiar to a faraway school where they are strangers. Should

177

children be punished because adults will not solve their social problems?

Actually, busing to bring about desegregation involves only a relatively small proportion of the children who ride in school buses. Recently it was estimated that busing for this reason involves no more than 3.6 per cent of the national public-school population. It also has been estimated that well over 50 per cent of all public-school children travel daily by bus. Of course, a national estimate of this kind is deceptive. There are places where only a few children are bused to school. But there are also a great many places where as many as 80 to 90 per cent of the pupils depend on busing and where school buses in a district may aggregate half a million—or more— miles in a school year.

Over the last 30 years a growing emphasis on busing has brought about a radical transformation of school life. What is astonishing is that most parents treat the situation as if it were a natural phenomenon, like the weather or the tides or the seasons—something you always have to take into account but can't do anything to change. And curiously, the passionate arguments about busing to alter the racial balance in schools have done very little to raise our consciousness of what busing means to a great many children, particularly the younger ones. If anything, concentration on the goal has almost totally obscured our ability to realize the dull tedium or the teasing and hazing to which the means—busing—subjects an annually increasing number of children.

All over the country during the last generation, neighborhood schools—even schools for little children—have been disappearing. They have disappeared from the countryside as farmers have been driven off the land by agribusiness, from cities because of the deterioration of inner-city neighborhoods and from suburbs as walking has become dangerous on roads without sidewalks and as communities have voted down school budgets. Neighborhood schools disappeared in the years when so many Americans, believing that bigger was better and signified progress, enthusiastically supported the consolidation of school districts and the elimination of small schools. They also believed—mistakenly, as it turned out—that consolidated schools would mean lower school taxes.

From time to time parents—and even the whole country—may be roused to indignation over busing. When there is a disaster, an accident in which schoolchildren are frightened and injured or even killed, the whole country becomes aware and alarmed—for a few days. Here and there across the country, parents and school boards raise questions about school-bus safety. But who asks about the ordinary, everyday ride? We hear a great deal about the empty time children spend in front of television sets looking at stupid and inappropriate programs. But what about the precious hours children waste sitting doing nothing on buses?

In many districts the characteristic school-bus load is made up of children of mixed ages who are picked up and dropped off in different places. The bus driver—the only adult present —has more than enough to do to drive safely and is lucky if he or she has the kind of personality to enforce the dullest kind of quiet. The bus travels the same route every day, and after a while most children stop looking out the window. Anyhow, as the landscape speeds past there is no time to notice a bird or a new cat or even a house that has been painted— or anything else. The lucky child sits next to a school friend, but the friend may get on and off the bus miles away from where she herself lives, so they seldom can play together and become real friends. Less lucky, a child may be crowded in with strangers, often big, noisy strangers who step on her toes and shout over her head, careless of the feelings of anyone so much smaller.

One reason, perhaps the main reason, we have become so inattentive to what busing is doing to children is that we don't see any way out. While parents concentrate on getting a better education in better schools for their daughters and sons, they have accepted busing as the price that must be paid. They accept the sacrifice without realizing that it is the children themselves who are sacrificed.

Isn't there anything we can do? Of course there is.

The long-term solution is clear enough. We must concentrate on building good communities where children of many different backgrounds can walk to school and come to know one another well as pupils with very different talents and interests and as friends they will keep. It is possible that the grandchildren of today's young mothers and fathers will be educated in such schools. But for the time being we have to accept the fact that school busing is unavoidable for a great many children.

Nevertheless, this need not mean that we have to put up with things as they are. Certainly parents and teachers and school boards will have to overcome their apathy, the peculiar apathy that comes from a continual, resolute, dodging of an uncomfortable issue. If people can take that step, then with common sense, a little imagination and some technical know-how they can accomplish quite a lot.

Once in a while the children themselves, backed by an interested—and probably amused—school-bus driver, have come up with some astonishing ideas of their own. In one community I was told about a busload of children of mixed ages who got the idea of forming themselves into a kind of orchestra and practiced on their daily travels. At the end of the school year they gave a concert at which the bus driver was their honored guest. As I have traveled around the country it is stories of this kind, told me by parents or children and once or twice by school-bus drivers, that started me thinking. Unfortunately, a highly original effort seldom can be duplicated, and in any event, very few drivers would willingly follow the children's initiative. The rules say explicitly that the children must sit still, and with all those lively children just behind their backs, who can blame drivers for trying to enforce the rules?

But the rules can be changed in ways that are safe and in keeping with activities from which every child can gain. It is impossible for children to read or write comfortably on a bus, but as they ride they can learn with their ears, a way of group learning that has been terribly devalued in our schools for more than a generation. Children can learn by singing together, by memorizing together and by forming themselves into groups in which older children take responsibility for younger ones and the ears of all of them respond to sounds, sounds made doubly desirable because they are both produced and heard in a group.

In my grandmother's childhood a good part of necessary learning—of the alphabet and numbers incorporated in songs, of the multiplication tables, of spelling those intractable words that sound alike and are spelled differently, of the names of the states and all our Presidents, and best of all, of poems— all this kind of learning was accomplished by ear and repetition in a group. We have grossly neglected children's capacity to memorize and store knowledge that will stand by them all their lives. We will have to decide anew what it will be useful —and delightful too—for today's children to learn by heart in groups. But it can be done.

In the "outback" of a country like Australia and in the village schools in Papua New Guinea, where I have spent much time, today's children learn about the world they live in and the world far beyond their reach by radio and by listening in a class to teaching tapes; and adults who may never learn to read and write are learning about their country by listening to the programs on their little transistor radios. Is there any reason our own children, living in the most technically sophisticated society in the world, should not have a chance to learn by hearing? Is there any reason our children should not discover how to learn by listening and, reciprocally, by using their own voices?

There are problems, yes. But mostly these are technical problems that always attract and challenge people with lively, innovative minds. Obviously the first need is for buses in which children can use their ears and listen to one another's voices, as well as to voices telling them things they want to know, to music they enjoy hearing and to rhythms to which they can respond—in all those ways restoring some of the sensitivity to sound that is being destroyed by all the prevalent noise.

It will take planning, too, by many kinds of individuals who are concerned with children—beginning with parents, who must take the initiative, and including the children themselves, who, after all, are the most concerned.

Parents can begin by demanding buses that are adapted to learning by hearing. For the present, this certainly means adapting the buses that are already in use, rearranging the seating and most likely giving the driver the necessary privacy for safe driving. This in turn would necessitate having another responsible person on the bus—a teacher, a student teacher, one of a group of parent or other community volunteers or even one of a group of older, trained students—someone committed to the program, traveling with the children.

Radios are certainly the most immediately useful resource for this way of teaching, and I believe that public broadcasting could be drawn into developing—together with schools and children—programs carried in the morning and afternoon busing hours, with ties perhaps both to television and to programs in the schools. Citizen's-band radio offers another local choice. And tape recording, with the use of cassettes that can easily be duplicated, is a resource that would allow schools in a district—or children traveling on a particular bus—to develop individualized programs under the supervision of technicians and especially with the guidance of teachers who understand about children's doing things together. Once such programs got under way, I have no doubt, the educational media would pick them up as a new fashion in teaching, and the most exciting ideas would spread across the country quickly.

But whatever we choose to do, the main consideration is that we begin to think about that everyday trip our youngest commuters have to take five days a week for so many months of the year. We have made busing an essential part of a way of life for millions of children. But it need not be something to which they are condemned. We can do better than that. And perhaps we might even do some fresh thinking about the millions of adults who also are daily commuters.

V
Celebrations

At Christmas I Remember . . .

DECEMBER 1969

On the afternoon of Christmas Eve the tall tree stands in its accustomed place by the window, green and bare, its boughs bent upward like folded wings, its outdoor fragrance still muted. By the door there is a pile of holly. Crimson ribbons, cards and rolls of crisp paper have spilled onto the floor; they are for presents not yet wrapped.

We lift down the big boxes of tree ornaments from the highest shelf in the storage closet. Where are the scissors to cut the cords? As so often before, lost and found and lost again. Now the ornaments lie in bright disarray on the sofa, the table, the chairs. Lambs for the crèche, gilt stars, a carved wooden Santa Claus, a raffia cornucopia, crystal icicles.

The marmalade cat pokes stealthily at a tinkling bell. We look at the tree speculatively, wondering about the design that will emerge—always new, for no two trees have the same asymmetry, yet evoking all the Christmas trees of a lifetime. I pick up a small angel framed in tarnished tinsel. This comes out of my childhood, 60 years ago. Someone asks me: "Do you remember . . . ?" And, of course, I do.

The golden balls, the silver bells, the bright chains of fragile blown glass, the woolly Norwegian skiers, the Viennese horses with their satin saddles, the angel riding a shooting star —each of these comes from a different Christmas. When we were children my mother's friends brought us ornaments from abroad as presents—those exquisite miniature musical instruments, that tiny Mexican basket.

And there are the special ornaments, also from faraway places, that mark the years of my daughter's childhood—the

187

little Greek dolls made of yarn, the painted star from Mexico, the Japanese ship and the slant-eyed Japanese children, the birds with iridescent plumage. Each represents a different year in our lives, and now all are becoming part of this Christmas, the pattern of which is slowly emerging out of this particular afternoon's cheerful confusion.

Holidays, especially Christmas, bring together all the scents and savors, the sights and sounds, the colors and the music of voices that are part not only of this home but also of the homes one lived in long ago, the island visited only once, tears and discomfiture as well as delight.

For people with my kind of precise memory, it matters a great deal that the day should be right, that nothing happen to mar the tone. For it is feeling that binds together all these disparate memories: candle flames and burning logs, poinsettias framing the door of a tropical house, cedar trees in the snow, the fragrance of cake baking, the slightly acid smell of chewed betel nut, the sound of a wooden spoon beating the hard sauce for the plum pudding, a carol carried on the wind through palm trees, the lost scissors, the treacherous feel of artificial snow spilled on the floor and the pale reflections of early sunset on the snow out of doors.

When the plans that were so long in the making go wrong, a holiday is not a passing disappointment but a permanent loss. Each year the memory of it will return, a pricking pain —the time the presents didn't arrive, the time there was a blizzard and none of the guests could stay to enjoy the goose, the time all the children were sick in bed.

Sorrows and the anticipation of sorrow can be woven in. Knowing that this may be the last year we will have Mother with us, listening for laughter newly silenced, realizing that this is the last celebration in the home where we began our life together—heartbreak and the anticipation of heartbreak are as much a part of a lifetime as a baby's first Christmas, the first celebration in a new home or the welcoming of a bride or a bridegroom into the family Christmas circle. But the surprise that was no surprise, the perfect gift that was a fiasco—these petty miseries can forever tarnish the brightness of a remembered day. And always, as on this afternoon of Christmas Eve, I wonder a little anxiously whether this will be one of the good years. Perhaps it is because I was the oldest child, the mediator between my parents' hopes and the younger children's dreams.

Looking back, the Christmases of my childhood blend and merge, each echoing the others and resonating from other moments of excitement, pain and joy. Only small incidents come back as memories of different years. There was the Christmas when I was nine; that year I trimmed the tree all alone because my mother was having a new baby. There was the year I played a naïve Lady Bountiful and carried six little trees with handmade ornaments to six poor families, only to find that they had big trees with store-bought trimming. And the year we carried ten hand-painted lampshades on the crowded train because the paint had not yet dried.

The individual Christmas celebrations I remember best are those when I was far away in the field. They have a life of their own. I remember the people I shared them with, but for everyone here at home they are only names, faces seen in photographs, children in books, not the elderly people I know they must be now.

The most uncomfortable Christmas of all I spent in Samoa in 1925. My college friends, who shared the excitement of my first field trip, sent boxes of fragile ornaments, months ahead, on one of the slow ships that were the only links then between home and the Pacific islands. As I lifted each one gently out of its cocoon of wrappings and held it in the brilliant sunlight, it seemed to glow with a strange intensity.

Happily I set up a small, green-leaved bush as a Christmas tree and hung from its branches the new frail, exotic fruit. I don't know what I expected—perhaps a gasp of surprised pleasure. Instead the children—my preadolescents for whom I had made this glittering gift—rushed the little bush, tore off the ornaments and broke the balls into fragments, which they pressed on to their skin.

I think that now I would see it differently, but at that moment, caught between my world and theirs, it seemed a hostile act. The next day more than 100 people came, bringing me strings of shells as presents. Of course, I had no individual gifts with which to repay them, and they made long speeches about the generosity of the Samoans and the stingy meanness of the *Papalangi*—the skybursters—the white people. They, and I too, felt aggrieved.

Christmas in Manus, New Guinea, in 1928 was filled with laughter. This time my friends sent me a collection of plastic rattles for the babies. But it was the small boys in our household staff who shook them delightedly. The presents had come wrapped in red cellophane straw, the first I had ever seen. I draped long strands of it on the children's crinkly hair; everyone laughed with them.

Later, in their young adulthood, these same boys became revolutionaries who brought their people into the modern world. But then they knew nothing about Christmas. In Pidgin English "Christmas" was simply a word meaning "year," only vaguely conceived. The Manus had no calendar; their feasts were related to particular occasions, when someone reached puberty, married or died. They had no conception of the world from which I came, nor any idea whether rattles and cellophane were everyday objects or as exotic to me as they were to them. They were neither gratified nor aggrieved, only amused. Lacking a real meeting point between our two worlds, we could not even misunderstand each other.

Christmas in our mountain village in Bali, in 1936, was a great contrast. The Balinese have a crowded ceremonial calendar and fully understand both Western Christmas and the Chinese New Year. These are times they can give gifts that will be reciprocated at the Feast of Faluengen, which comes every 210 days.

In our courtyard with its many pavilions, our household staff decorated every post and window with greens. Poinsettias that grew ten feet high were carried in from neighboring villages. As a climax to the feast our staff had hired a troupe of traveling players to present us with a kind of review of reviews. The main point was the skill with which the actors mimicked other actors in a different play, actors who themselves had been taking off the actors in still another play. Though we couldn't understand all the jokes, we sat attentively through the long hours in proper appreciation. And all day we noted carefully which of the many gifts of fruit and cake were *langseran*, offerings to the gods that were taken back and so were unfit to be offered the gods again. These we could eat or pass on with a word of caution. The others, not yet offered, we could give as gifts, more appreciated by our neighbors.

In 1965 I made a fourth trip to Manus especially to celebrate Christmas with the people of my village, Peré. It was a political as well as a religious occasion, for some 2,000 visitors had been invited to admire the new village—the second one built at Peré since the Manus had remade their way of life—and to celebrate the far-flung unity of the revolutionary movement through which this transformation had taken place. In these brief years the Manus had moved thousands of years in time, and our world was now one.

When I arrived I found that for two months getting ready for this Christmas had been the main preoccupation of everyone down to the smallest children, who were practicing carols. People went to bed at sundown, the better to rise energetically at dawn. Mountainous piles of food had been accumulated, and the whole village husbanded the precious supplies of kerosene for the lamps and cooking.

And with each passing day excitement and tension mounted.

What if there was a bad storm? What if the school children could not make the crossing from their mainland boarding schools? Like everyone else, I gazed anxiously out across the reef at the distant horizon. Then, just before Christmas, the schoolboys arrived, wearing their modern school clothes and laden with their books, their guitars, their transistor radios. And in their wake came the canoes crowded with guests. In the end only one canoe had to turn back, and no one was drowned.

The Christmas services lasted until dawn, in mixed remembrance of midnight Mass in the years when the Manus were devout Catholics and the all-night sessions in the brief period when they had sat waiting for their ancestral ghosts to bring them miraculous cargoes of white men's goods. Now, having made a different future, they sang the familiar hymns, waiting for morning and the great feast, while I listened, dozed and dreamed, remembering the little boys dancing with red cellophane in their hair, remembering my own childhood, remembering starry nights in New York City when we walked down the cold streets of Greenwich Village to St. Luke's Chapel to welcome Christmas with the same melodies.

I remember one Christmas Eve at home that brought together the faraway and the familiar. While upstairs we trimmed the tree, downstairs my daughter and her husband prepared an Armenian feast. The main dish was to be a whole lamb, stuffed with rice and herbs and roasted on a spit in the garden. An ingenious machine made from an old phonograph turntable was to turn the spit, but in the end it had to be turned by hand in the darkness under falling snow—a strange sight in a New York City garden. The guests drifted downstairs to watch and back to the warm living room, wanderers between two worlds who were told first, "It will be hours yet . . ." and then suddenly, "Come at once—the lamb is ready!"

As on many other Christmas Eves when we gathered to

celebrate—family, friends and children together—folklorist Alan Lomax sang for us the "Cherry Tree Carol" and the melancholy and passionate Christmas songs Black singers had taught him in the South. A little Pakistani boy, here for his first American Christmas, sat wide-eyed. On this evening there was a meeting of traditions, partly familiar and partly strange to each of us—and Christmas came, known, yet as always a mystery.

This year at Christmas, my granddaughter will be just old enough to enjoy the glitter of the lights on the tree, not knowing yet that it is more than a new pattern of light and color.

Woodstock in Retrospect

JANUARY 1970

Friday, August 15, 1969, was a hot, clear summer day. Even before the sun rose, long lines of cars—new cars and old cars painted with slogans, sports cars, Volkswagens, pickup trucks, jeeps, trailers, almost anything on wheels—converged on Route 17B, the road leading to Bethel, New York, where, on Max Yasgur's dairy farm, the stage was set for "three days of peace and music." Some 70,000 young people from all over the United States had paid $18 in advance to hear rock music at the Woodstock Music and Art Festival. Perhaps twice that number were expected in the course of the weekend.

The earliest arrivals on Friday discovered that they were not the firstcomers. Far and wide, fields and pastures already were dotted with tents and improvised arrangements for living in that green and smiling countryside. By seven o'clock in the morning every approach was clogged. The cars slowed, stopped, started and ground to a final halt. Now the only way into the festival was on foot. Four miles . . . eight miles . . . ten miles. Toting sleeping bags, knapsacks, shopping bags, hibachis, soft drinks, a bag of doughnuts, a can of beans, a couple of apples, the endless stream of boys and girls poured into the festival area and, always moving closer together, settled on the ground in the amphitheater.

The crew of technicians still was struggling with the massive sound system on the improvised stage. The gates intended to control admittance never were put up and the attempt to collect or sell tickets broke down almost at once. By noon the young producers accepted reality. The festival, they an-

194

nounced, was free and open to everyone there. The crowd cheered.

The first scheduled performers, caught in the jam, had to be airlifted in. (It was the helicopters that ensured mobility. Three had been planned for; eventually 12 were pressed into service.) And still the crowd poured in. No one knows what the total festival population was. The best-informed guess was about 400,000. And no one has even tried to guess how many thousands more were turned back on the crowded roads, far beyond walking distance.

Overnight, the young people told one another, a whole city, the third largest in New York State, had come into being—a fantastic city in which everything was improvised, drugs were omnipresent and anyone over 30 was out of place ("an up-tight guy, you know, who wanted a drink"). Overnight, they said, almost as many came together there voluntarily as there were men involuntarily fighting the war in Vietnam. And while they sat through that first night, listening to the performers, rain poured down and the countryside was churned into a sea of red mud.

The first news of the festival that reached Europe called it a catastrophe. I was in England, where the BBC was broad-casting harrowing accounts of the rioting going on in Northern Ireland between Catholics and Protestants. In almost the same tone of voice in which newscasters described that futile battle, in which some were killed and many were wounded, they told the listening world that a state of emergency had been de-clared in Bethel, where 300,000 (later half a million) young enthusiasts were in dire straits as a result of rain, lack of food, shelter and sanitation, rising disorder and the uncontrolled use of dangerous drugs.

It sounded extremely frightening. But the few pictures in the newspapers made me wonder. One, I remember, was of a young boy lying on the hood of a car—"out, asleep, drugged" —or perhaps just exhausted? Another photograph showed a young couple pushing a baby carriage across a field. Certainly the disaster—if it was a disaster—was happening in a universe very different from the one in which men could still murderously attack each other in the name of religion.

When I returned to New York three days later, the Woodstock story was being told and retold as young people, dazed and tired, drifted home. What might have been a disaster had turned instead into a kind of miracle. Listening to those who had been there, you heard wonder in their voices, saw it in their eyes, as they said, "We were all there together. It was beautiful."

No one denied the struggle merely to survive. That almost everyone did survive was part of the delight. Those who had been at Bethel talked freely about the lack of food and water. The mud. The breakdown of sanitation. The smell of garbage. The cuts and lacerations as thousands walked barefoot on the littered ground. The bad trips. And again the mud. ("Can you imagine my *parents* sitting on a wet sleeping bag for two nights and two days?") The crowds. ("They kept saying, 'Remember, the guy next to you is your brother,' and we did!") And when I asked what it meant to them, the answer was almost always: "We were there."

Like most other adults—the local people who sent in truckloads of food, the doctors who came in to look after the injured and the sick, the police who concentrated on keeping the roads open, the photographers who brought back their way-out pictures and those who only listened afterward—I was convinced. Something very good happened at Woodstock. In spite of everything, the young people achieved what they had gone there for—three days of peace and music. Even those who never heard the music.

When my contemporaries tried to say what it was all about, they were puzzled. Most people, of course, marveled at the absence of fighting, the almost total absence of any kind of violence in a situation in which, it would seem, the smallest incident might have touched off a riot. But putting it like this, negatively, somehow misses the point.

This is a generation that can be fierce and angry on behalf of others. They have marched in sympathy with the children in the ghettos, in protest against the war and the killing in Vietnam, to rouse others to the plight of children in Biafra. And when they are led to expect violence, they react violently. Excluded from planning that involves their lives, feared, scorned and provoked, the young strike back and shout words that in turn provoke and horrify.

On this occasion the extraordinary thing was their spontaneous gentleness. They had come of their own free will, because everyone who cared would be there and it was a way of showing one belonged. Strangers for the most part, they spoke the language of people who trust one another.

The sheer size of the crowd astonished everyone. But after all, such huge gatherings are not unknown. The best parallels are the great religious pilgrimages—the medieval Christian pilgrims who traveled from all parts of Europe to Santiago de Compostela, in northwestern Spain; or, today, the Moslems who, in enormous crowds, make the journey to Mecca; or the orthodox Hindus who go to bathe ceremonially in the Ganges River.

There is one very striking difference, however. In the case of religious pilgrimages, tradition sets the style of behavior in every detail. Hostels exist to receive the pilgrims and strict rules are enforced to protect their safety.

In contrast, at the Woodstock festival everyone was on his own and each crisis called for some new improvisation. Looked at superficially, the whole thing had the appearance of something created overnight. The emphasis on spontaneity, the lack of overt forms of organization and the unexpectedness of what happened blind us to the fact that there was a kind of structure, an image of what it was to be together. Because of it, people survived and the occasion had deep meaning for them.

True, the facilities originally provided turned out to be totally inadequate, but crises were met. Extra helicopters were found. Doctors and medical supplies were flown in. The roads were kept open; no one felt trapped. Members of the Hog Farm commune and others like them, only a little older and more experienced than most members of the audience, fed the hungry, counseled the distressed, helped care for the sick and those whose experiments with drugs miscarried.

Above all there were the voices, sometimes identified and sometimes anonymous, that rang out between performances, telling the lost where to find their friends and keeping everyone in communication.

This, it seems to me, provides a key to understanding why it was that the young who lived through it all could say, "It was beautiful." The planning, the improvisation, the stream of communication about what was happening, were part of the event itself. Those who carried the main responsibilities were also very young, and from this emerged the sense that everyone spoke the same intelligible language.

This was the true happening at Woodstock—the realization by these "Aquarians," who think of themselves as the first generation in a new age of peace, that they have a voice, a viable style, a community of trust.

What does this mean for the future?

It must be admitted that Woodstock might have been a disaster but for two things, one an accident and the other owing to the exercise of intelligence, that can be elaborated on. The accident was the rain. The young, in addition to being numerous and gentle, in search of music and peace, were drenched. Chilled, exhausted but still enthusiastic, they moved the hearts of everyone. Moreover, the rain kept away many of the television cameras (and so, also, hordes of merely curious sightseers) until it was all over. It was the kind of accident one cannot count on happening twice.

The second circumstance was that the responsibility for the festival was in the hands of young people who could think, respond and plan in the style of the audience. The very acuteness of the crisis also meant that they remained in responsible control. Their choice of a location, away from a large, settled community, turned out to be the only feasible one. Their choice of musicians drew the crowd. The choice of the Hog Farmers and others like them to act as intermediaries made sense to everyone. Their protective use of human resources probably saved the situation.

This is something others can build on, not only for other festivals but also for any event in which masses of young people are involved. With the responsibility in their own hands, they worked things out. It all made sense.

But it must also be admitted that there was tremendous inadvertent destruction of property. Farmers' fields were trampled, their fences burned for fuel, their crops looted and destroyed—all things that farmers do not take to kindly. The astonishing thing is that these very real losses caused so little rancor and led to almost no immediate reprisals. Instead, a very large number of people responded to trust on a massive scale with trust and friendliness. "They were such nice kids!"

In these circumstances most accidental destruction can be avoided. We have the technology to set up, if we will, the necessary facilities for caring for the needs of an enormous temporary "city." We have the human resources to protect the citizens of such a city and those among whom they come. If great gatherings of this kind are part of the style of living of present-day young people, we can ensure their safety.

But I believe we must differentiate between facilitation and exploitation. The crowds that gathered at this festival, part of an affluent generation that has seldom been cold or hungry except by choice, found the hardships exhilarating. The message they got was that this was a spontaneous, uncommercialized event. We must help them keep it so; to do otherwise would be to destroy what is at the heart of the event.

For older people the lesson of Woodstock is that such gatherings do have structure, however invisible it is to the eyes of members of another generation. But no outsider—who does not speak the language, who cannot set the pace, who does not move with the rhythm of those involved—can foresee what will be needed long ahead or from hour to hour. The responsibility must be in the hands of those who, as members of the whole generation group, are creating the new style as they all move together. This is the reality of a new kind of world that only a new generation can bring into being.

I do not think the Woodstock festival was a "miracle"—something that can happen only once. Nor do I think that those who took part in it established a tradition overnight—a way of doing things that sets the pattern of future events. It was confirmation that this generation has, and realizes that it has, its own identity.

No one can say what the outcome will be; it is too new. Responding to their gentleness, I think of the words "Consider the lilies of the field . . ." and hope that we—and they themselves—can continue to trust the community of feeling that made so many say of those three days, "It was beautiful."

Halloween: Where Has All the Mischief Gone?

OCTOBER 1975

Halloween poses a dilemma for parents: Can children celebrate in ways that are safe and still have fun?

In the huge city apartment building in which I live we have made a choice. As far as I know there never has been any discussion, but quite clearly we have opted for safety and treats. Halloween in our house begins at dusk and continues into the early evening, for as long as parents think neighbors will tolerate their small, bell-ringing children. The essential intimacy of the event is accentuated by the fact that on this one occasion in the year children scamper up and down the service stairs that connect kitchen with kitchen. So the children move, in some sense, from the inner life of one family to that of another—in safety.

Last year the first to come to our back door was a pair of small, masked witches carrying hearth brooms and wearing black, conical hats. They danced a jig as they shouted, "Trick or treat!" Like most families, we had assembled on the kitchen table a bowl of polished apples, some candy and raisins and nuts, bagged and tied so they could be carried home without spilling—and without being eaten—and a stack of shiny dimes. Unexpectedly, the little witches thanked me most politely.

The next to appear was a very skinny skeleton in jeans. He rattled a box instead of his bones. He was collecting for UNICEF, the United Nations Children's Fund, but he didn't object to a treat as well. After that came a very small monster with a fierce crayon face drawn on a brown paper bag. She couldn't see very well through the slits for her eyes and she

201

wasn't quite sure why she had come to our door, but when her adult guardian coached her in the magic words, she held out a huge shopping bag.

We took turns answering the door, so I did not see every ghost or witch, devil or monster who came up the stairs. But the last, I remember, was a tall, casual, adolescent trio, two slim girls and a boy, who wore no disguise and made no pretense of collecting for a good cause. I must have shown my astonishment, because one of the girls hurriedly explained, "It's Halloween, you know, and—well—we just thought we'd make a little mischief ringing bells."

A little mischief! That was the ingredient that was missing! In this building, which is friendly to young families, parents need not telephone first to ask whether Mary or Johnny or a whole party of youngsters carrying jack-o'-lanterns (lighted with safe flashlights instead of candles) will be welcome at your back door. And no one, I am quite sure, ever complains about these Halloween visitors. The children are quite safe and most adults enjoy them. But it is all treats and no tricks. There is no mischief at all.

Parents, and especially grandparents, can remember with nostalgia when Halloween was fun—mischievous fun. It was the one night in the year when the child's world and the adult's world confronted each other and children were granted license to take mild revenge on adults. Long ago in medieval Europe, there was a folk belief that Halloween was the one occasion when people could safely invoke the help of the devil in some enterprise. We no longer believe this, but somehow the notion of deviltry still is associated with what is permissible on Halloween—or was permissible in a safer past.

All older adults have stored away memories of some outrageous form of mischief perpetrated by the older girls and boys on Halloween. They can chuckle at the annoyance they once caused and the edge of fear they felt as well.

I remember very well how some boys would stamp up onto

a porch and bang a heavy sack of broken glass against the wall and then run. Did the old maid indoors behind the drawn shades really believe that the boys had shattered a window? Or they would remove a gate and hide it in the bushes. I wonder—did the owner ever really believe the gate had been stolen or destroyed? Using soap, boys would scrawl words on a glass door or window that they never would say in the presence of a woman. But there was nothing permanent about soap-writing. Or with their slingshots they would aim staples or pebbles at upstairs windows. Did anyone believe a thief was about to break in?

Who were the foolish people who left full ash cans standing by the side of a house? Were they just very careless or were they collaborating in the adolescents' mild destructiveness? And once in a while there were the children who went "too far." There were, for example, the boys who stretched an imaginary rope across the road and as a car approached in the darkness mimicked pulling the rope taut. Naturally the startled driver stood on the brake, and there was a real danger that someone could be hurt—and occasionally someone was. "Would you do something like that?" we asked one another. No one was quite sure. But by asking such questions we policed ourselves.

Looking back, one thing is clear. All this was small-town mischief, country mischief, neighborhood mischief, contained within the bounds of familiarity. The children knew quite well which neighbors it was safe to plague and which ones to avoid —and the neighbors knew them. The younger children, not yet old enough to go out after dark on Halloween night, sat in the dark by the windows, watching and listening. They had been in on some of the planning and they could guess who was sticking pins in the doorbells so that, ghostlike, the bells would ring—and ring—without anyone in sight.

The mischief-makers also knew in which houses they had friends and where they were expected to come at the end of the evening for a treat after all the tricks had been played. And then when they laughed over their exploits they felt quite secure. After all, who would give away the Jones boy or the Smith boy, when everyone knew they had been up to the very same tricks as their older brothers before them?

But that was a far safer world, a world in which adults still believed in adolescent mischief and adolescents believed that mischief had its limits. Mild destructiveness disguised as mischief was displaced quite long ago by angry destructiveness disguised as Halloween activities and carried out by alienated youngsters against anonymous adults—strangers and the unidentified people who run things. In the vast stretches of suburbs tricks became expensive and dangerous. Some parents even took out insurance against the physical damage their own children might do. In the cities some adults—as well as hostile adolescents—came to treat Halloween as the occasion for unlicensed destructiveness. Every year parents have to caution their trick-or-treating children against biting into an apple that may contain a razor blade and against eating a piece of candy that may make them very sick.

In response, communities have long since tried to take steps to protect homes and shops and public places and, equally, the more innocent and less destructive among our adolescents and children. From time to time shop owners have given prizes for the best drawings put up in their windows. Community organizations have sponsored Halloween parades or free movies or hot dogs and soft drinks as treats for all comers. Some towns have even arranged trips for teen-agers to historic sites —paid for by anxious citizens—as one more device to keep them safely occupied and out of the way.

And most commonly children of every age have been drawn into good works. Instead of ringing doorbells to ask for treats for themselves—treats that may or may not be safe—they have learned to ask for trick-or-treat money for a good cause.

Who can chase away a child who is out not for mischief but to do a good deed?

So actually, almost all that is left of Halloween nowadays focuses on smaller children, and they are the ones for whom parents have to plan. Traditionally this was the night when graves yawned, ghosts and skeletons walked abroad and witches and hobgoblins were free to play tricks on mortals. In my childhood, youngsters in their permitted mischief played out the roles of these characters. Today small children wear the scary costumes, but the characters themselves have been rendered harmless, unfrightening or comic in modern children's literature and television fantasies. It is now the mothers of very small children who get a kick out of Halloween, buying or making the costumes for them and leading them on trick-or-treat expeditions close to home while the small performers, trying to overcome shyness, hardly grasp what it is to be a witch or a ghost.

But this is not enough for children who are a little older. The eight-to-ten-year-olds are eager for something more, some bit of license, something a little scary. Halloween is still associated with tricks, even though for so many children "trick or treat" has become an empty formula without any hidden threat for those who refuse to treat. On this night, fun and mischief and something scary still go together—and parents have a problem.

The task for parents is how to contrive a framework for an evening that is safe and scary and fun. One of the best solutions I know is an early-evening party in a succession of three or four homes, in each of which some games and a different kind of slightly scary experience await the children. This arrangement spreads the responsibility and the work among several households. It also takes the children out at intervals into the dark night, which itself is a little mysterious.

Bobbing for apples in a bowl of water or trying to take a

bite out of an apple suspended from a string or playing blind-man's buff may be a tame entertainment if that is all there is. But combined with a few puzzles and tricks—and in the end some treats—the old games evoke a great deal of happy laughter. Listening to a ghost story by firelight, especially accompanied by a few appropriate thumps and whistles, can set the scene. Going into a darkened room and shaking hands unexpectedly with a wet rubber glove filled with sand can be startling. And making one's way alone through a dark tunnel (constructed of sheets for the occasion) and hearing queer sounds (recorded and played back on a tape recorder) can be quite scary enough.

Of course, this means a lot of planning by adults and careful supervision to be sure that the tricks are really not dangerous and only a little scary. However, the fun and the scary part are much greater if the children themselves are involved in the planning and the execution of the tricks. The mild mischief children work out for themselves is the best of all. But parents are needed to help implement some of the ideas ten-year-olds think up and to make sure that they can carry out the tricks they plan for one another.

It is true that this kind of Halloween party is a break with the past. Instead of a confrontation between the children's and the adults' worlds, the children are confronted with the problem of how to handle, among themselves, a game of frightening and being frightened by one another—knowing it is a kind of game. Each of the children will be involved in planning some of the tricks and will be supervised by others. Discussing with them beforehand what is possible and what may go too far not only involves them fully in this Halloween game but also can give each of them some sense of the protectiveness that is part of true play, even scary and mischievous play. And afterward, learning the mechanics of the trick that was a surprise can make what seems scary more manageable next time.

But what about the older forms of mischief?

I do not think we can safely allow children to roam by themselves on Halloween in a big community, even in a community or neighborhood where many of them are known. At present there is no way of telling whether the children who come are one's own or unknown invaders or whether the people inside the homes will take for granted that the mischief is all in fun or will be angry and hostile to all comers. Taking adults along is no help. By doing so we only end up pitting adults against adults with children as the instruments—a very different thing from perpetrating childish mischief.

The collapse of traditional forms of Halloween fun has not alerted us to the very pressing need for a new ethic of protectiveness in our communities. Perhaps in the course of helping our smaller children to make a safe Halloween for themselves we shall begin to do some fresh thinking about what makes a community safe for everyone who lives there.

Pictures from the Past
for Our Children

Our country's 200th birthday, which we are now celebrating, belongs to all of us—to you and to me and to all our children.

Whoever our actual forebears in this country were—the original Americans who met the first European settlers or the newest arrivals—this celebration is for them as well as for us. And whatever their origin—whether they came from the British Isles, the steppes of Russia, the great plains of China, or the plains of North America, from the cathedral cities or the little villages of Europe, the rain forests of Africa or the sunny Mediterranean coast, from farms or fishing hamlets or the back streets of ancient cities—they have made our history rich and variegated. Through their lives, the life of our country as a free and independent nation has become our common heritage, and the bicentennial celebration is a way of binding together the past, the present and the future for every one of us.

So that we may better understand what we are celebrating, members of local bicentennial groups have been ferreting out the lost moments in the history of every region, tracing the trails and roads made by pioneers traveling into the wilderness, excavating the sites of blockhouses and gristmills, stripping away ugly false façades from beautiful old houses, searching for treasures in family attics and the lumber rooms and forgotten files of town halls to bring back into lively remembrance those 200 years of our past.

As they have brushed away the dust and cobwebs, reproduced the fading photographs and deciphered the barely legible signatures on old declarations and charters, they also have been looking to the future. For by conserving all these things that might otherwise be lost forever, they are restoring the past to become part of the ongoing lives of all American children.

But we as parents have an important part to play too in linking together past and present for children. The bicentennial commissions and committees, working in their particular ways, are providing the framework and the background of events and people and places. But for all this to become more than a splendid pageant, our children will want to know more intimately about the lives of people who are real and very close to them—how they lived and what they looked like and what they made of the world around them. These, I think, are pictures of the past only we can assemble for our own children.

How can we do this?

One of the best ways, it seems to me, is by making "grandmother and grandfather books"—scrapbooks or albums that will reflect a family's own history as far back as the oldest member can recall. The whole family can join in gathering the material, and the books as they take form will be full of surprises and discoveries for everyone.

Young parents and students often tell me how essential it is for children to have grandparents who are close to them. Yet in most American homes there are two tones of voice for visits to and from grandparents. The children's voices are expected to ring with joy and expectancy and the parents speak of such visits with anxiety or resignation. The differences between generations have been so great in this country of immigrants, continual mobility and rapid change that many parents and their grown-up children are desperately uneasy with each other.

In spite of this, young people in colleges and young parents at home all agree—it's good to have grandparents. Children ought to have a chance to enjoy their grandparents. "My grandmother," a student told me, "planted my roots in the earth."

Making grandparent books, then, is a way of giving our children their grandparents. It is a way for grandparents to pass on to their grandchildren their most cherished possessions—their memories of their own childhood and youth. And as parents move back and forth between the two generations, helping to put all the bits together, it is a way of rediscovering how they themselves came to be who they are and how all the different strands of family experience are becoming interwoven in their children's lives.

There isn't any fixed form for a grandparent book. A bride's book or a baby book can provide a kind of model, but your family will have to invent a form to fit all the kinds of things you decide are part of the family story. A big looseleaf binder and a large supply of strong paper might be good to start with, for memories, once stirred, tend to rustle on and on; and desk drawers, attic trunks and boxes in the cellar, once opened, spew forth old daguerreotypes, snapshots, wedding pictures and photographs of Grandfather as a little boy riding a studio bucking bronco or of Great-grandmother as a little girl in long skirts and button boots.

The first sessions had better take place around the biggest table in the house, where everyone can see the evidence assembled—the family Bible with its record of births and deaths, the old marriage lines, the faded passports that meant freedom and a new life for one set of great-grandparents, the old address books that tell where everyone lived a generation ago, the tags still attached to old luggage, the letters from relatives who moved away across the continent.

Grandparents can be asked to think back, to hunt out and to recall everything they know about *their* grandparents, so that their grandchildren can hear what they heard. Once when we were studying children's ideas about time, a little boy said that for him "long ago" was before his grandfather's grandfather's time. His own grandfather, he explained, told him the stories that *his* grandfather had told *him* about his boyhood. So real and lively were these tales that the boy today felt that he could reach out with his own hand and touch that distant time four generations ago.

If your family has a small tape recorder, or can borrow one, you can make a record of just how one story led to another. One of the children, minding it, can see to it that the tape doesn't run out in the middle of the most exciting account of how Great-grandfather saved his children from a prairie fire. And grandparents will remember, perhaps, how it made them laugh, as children, to hear how frightened people were when they saw the first automobiles, how exciting it was to see streets lighted with electric lights, where grandparents saw their first airplane and how marvelous the great airships looked, drifting slowly across a summer sky.

There will be many different kinds of things to put into the books. Old dance programs with tiny pencils attached by silk cords to write in the names of partners, a blue ribbon won as a prize at a county fair and souvenir post cards brought home from world's fairs, the lace collar that adorned Grandmother's first dancing dress, a bit of tattered shawl carefully laid away by a great-aunt, Father's first report cards, which Grandpa secretly kept, and Grandma's precious recipe for plum pudding, written out in her mother's spidery handwriting, lacy valentines, the front page from the "extra" hawked by newsboys on Armistice Day, 1918, a pressed white rose from a wedding bouquet—all these have their stories to tell.

Some books will need a lot of pages for the already well remembered past, in case some grandmother or great-grandfather kept the family tree well in mind and made records or kept a diary about events in the lives of relatives. In some few families there may be a straight line of eight, or even nine, generations back to the Revolutionary War, in which one ancestor may have fought bravely and another been jailed for being a Tory. All the known names and dates and places can be written in, with pictures—if any survive—to make them real and to give the children a way to trace back the heritage of curly hair or flashing eyes.

For other families, life in America began only yesterday. Grandmother came here as a young girl to find work or to visit relatives, and stayed to marry. "She and Grandfather came over on the same boat, but they only met ten years later." For these families there are the ties to European, Middle Eastern or Far Eastern towns—old letters in strange languages, foreign photographs of great-aunts and uncles and cousins who stayed in the Old Country. And there are the post cards of ancestral towns sent back by the GIs who went to them searching for their own past after World War II. And if there are no photographs of your own great-grandparents, the children can look for post cards and pictures to cut out of tourist guides showing the towns they came from. These can be pasted in the book to illustrate the warm golden light or the bleak gray landscape where one set of ancestors lived.

There will be gaps, of course, and many families today know little that is personal about their particular ancestors. But grandparents will be able to name the little town in the Carpathians or the tiny island off the coast of Scotland from which, it is said, their parents or grandparents came.

And never mind if the legends about them are romanticized, so that ancestors from Wales had a castle in the family and remote Irish ancestors were kings and queens and a slave ancestor was known to all his descendants as a proud rebel who won his own freedom. Possibly it isn't quite true that blue eyes in the family came from the one blue-eyed baby who was rescued when the wagon train was attacked by Indians on the Oregon Trail. Somebody's great-great-great-grandfather was saved. He might well have been yours. Family legends are as much a part of our history as the true events out of which they grew and the real people around whom we have built our romances about the past.

For we live in a country in which dreams and hopes have always blended with reality and our lingering knowledge about our own family also blends indistinguishably with the adventurous stories heard about other families that could have been our own. And because our ancestors are so much more a matter of memory than of carefully plotted lines of blood relatives, it is quite easy for us to share grandparents with our friends' children, easy for adopted children to enjoy the past of their adopted parents and equally easy for the children of second marriages to acquire whole new sets of ancestors. My mother's youngest sister, all of whose grandparents were dead, happily adopted my paternal grandmother as a grandparent too.

So there should be room in our grandfather and grandmother books for adopted children, foster parents, stepparents, godparents and all the kinds of extra relatives and ancestors, real and assimilated, who turn up as Grandma and Grandpa talk about the people who were important in their lives.

If there are family movies—and many families have some stowed away—still photographs can be made from these that show wedding scenes and family reunions and picnics and children, who are now staid, middle-aged adults, turning somersaults on the lawn. And after the family has relived what once was a minor tragedy and now seems so comic—the scene in which the two-year-old starring in the home movie broke the Chinese porcelain lamp—her picture can be set beside the others of Mother when she was growing up.

Grumpy uncles and critical aunts will seem more human when Grandma tells stories about their childhood, when they stole corn or watermelons or threw the winter wood down the well or ran away and thumbed a ride home in an empty hearse. Children will be comforted to know that their fathers and mothers sometimes made poor grades in school or played hooky or cut their own hair with the nail scissors. No one whose mischief and sad experiences and triumphs can be shared by the children can remain just a name or a stranger—no matter how long ago—because children too have been mischievous and sad and triumphant from time to time.

And history itself will come alive. You can make up a chart of memorable historical dates and in between these set down the dates when grandparents—and you, the parents of your children—were born, met and married. History won't seem so distant and unreal for the child who can say that Grandma was ten years old when in 1927 Lindbergh flew the Atlantic, that Grandpa was just 15 that day in March, 1934, when all the banks were closed, and that a great-aunt, just out of college, was sitting in a dentist's chair when she saw what looked like snowflakes—in full summer—drifting past the window. Of course, they were really the bits of paper people were tearing up and throwing from windows to welcome V-J Day in 1945.

So history will reach from a grandfather to his grandfather, from a grandmother to her grandmother, and from grandparents to their grandchildren, who can close the grandparent book by pasting in pictures of themselves celebrating, with their family, the 200th birthday of their country.

Beyond the Horizon

JULY 1976

What has happened to our belief in the future?

"Horizon," one of the three official themes of the United States Bicentennial, was intended to be both a climax to our 200th-birthday celebration and a look ahead to our Tricentennial, 100 years from now. It was designed to allow us, the whole American people, to give form to our dreams and hopes for our children's children, the first generation of the 21st century.

On this Bicentennial Fourth of July we shall certainly celebrate the past and make ritual speeches about the future. But the plans for "Horizon"—the third and final phase in our Bicentennial celebration—have, in any important sense, come to nothing. In the course of this year there will be a few symposia in which scholars will gather to discuss things to come, and here and there a few imaginative and optimistic people will make local efforts to look ahead. But nationally nothing is being done in a serious way to point out new directions or open our eyes to new vistas.

What has happened? Why have the American people, who have delved so busily and productively into past centuries, been so unwilling to reach out to touch the future?

I believe it is because we are at present throwing our future away—neglecting, denying and destroying almost everything on which we know the future should be built. In one sense, of course, the future is already here. The babies born during this Bicentennial year will be 24 years old at the turn of the century—young adults who will be blessed by our gifts but also burdened by the losses and unsolved problems we be-

215

queath them. What kind of women and men are we preparing them to be? And what kind of world are we preparing for them? Many of our predictions are necessarily grim. But as yet we are unwilling to admit that everywhere in the country we are letting disaster overtake us.

The issues are many. Here I shall speak only of two that directly or indirectly affect every living American—survival and impoverishment.

Survival must come first, for if the people of this planet, ourselves among them, do not survive, then of course all other discussion is idle. But knowing the danger, we continue to build nuclear weapons and plan to build advanced nuclear reactors as a principal solution to our energy problems. Our latest agreement with the Russians in effect permits both sides to stockpile more dangerous weapons than ever before.

In addition, our country is selling all over the world huge quantities of arms, no less lethal because we consider some of them out of date for ourselves. In doing so we encourage the spread of civil conflicts that can easily prepare the way for massive warfare. And by capturing fissionable material manufactured by a breeder reactor, any bold outlaw group in the world can make and threaten to detonate a nuclear-powered bomb. Defense and deterrence and, in prospect, the private production of energy from nuclear sources support tremendous, highly profitable industries. But I think we must ask much more bluntly than we ever have in the past: What kind of security is this that we are providing for our—and all —children? Could not these billions of dollars be better spent altering the conditions of people's lives at home and abroad?

Impoverishment is almost equally serious, for by impoverishing human life we narrow and destroy the future. Yet this is what we, a people who believe in progress, seem to be doing.

Day by day and year by year in our cities, older housing falls into disrepair and ruin—neglected, battered or burned to the ground. Old office buildings stand half empty as mammoth new office buildings, already anachronistic in their excessive demands on energy for light, heat, cooling and ventilation, are built for investment purposes with money denied to ordinary housing. Crowding becomes worse and taxes and rents rise in the housing that remains.

The only escape for the more fortunate is to cut themselves off from their human fellows. Families looking for decent living for their children and businesses looking for tax benefits flee to suburbs that also are growing crowded. And in the cities, as taxes soar without meeting costs, every kind of service necessary for a civilized and humane way of living is sharply curtailed. Teachers, social-service workers, policemen, firemen, sanitation workers, doctors and hospital personnel, inspectors and guards of many kinds, the vast horde of technicians who keep city services functioning and many others lose their jobs as city income fails to match city needs. In the interest of economy, the economy of the cities is being eroded.

In this year of 1976, unemployment officially stands at about 7.5 per cent nationwide. That is high enough, in truth. And although we do not like to admit it, we know very well that this figure masks higher—in some cases much higher— levels of unemployment regionally and among particular groups: older women and men who have given up looking for jobs, Black Americans and members of certain ethnic groups, young Americans, girls and boys who have never yet had jobs. Economists and politicians tell us that the economy is improving but that unemployment will remain high for some time to come. In recession periods, whole categories of jobs may be abolished. For some people this means no job to look forward to; for others it means learning a new skill.

But the prospects are not very good. At every level we are curtailing educational opportunity, once the source of our greatest pride, so that all over the country we are doing a great deal to ensure that the next generation will be worse educated than this one. Almost everywhere we are cutting funds for nursery-school and kindergarten education, crowding more children into elementary-school classes, cutting out special teaching in the schools—including remedial reading and arithmetic, the most basic skills. We are cutting down on the provision of school meals (as if hungry children could learn better) and school health services (as if children in need of glasses or hearing aids made better pupils), cutting the hours of schooling and cutting funds for books and teaching materials.

We also are closing night schools, where those who lost out earlier could try to catch up. And instead of insisting that every school be an excellent school where all children can grow and learn in peace, we have turned hundreds—more likely thousands—of good and poor schools into battlegrounds where children have become the captive pawns of acrimonious groups in the community.

Only a few years ago we could take justifiable pride in that most American educational invention, the two- and four-year community college, an institution designed to be almost infinitely adaptable to the special needs of its students, whoever and wherever they are, and yet capable of setting good, even excellent, academic standards. In these colleges dropouts of every age—students who made a poor start and want to make up for it, men and women who have developed new ambitions, and students, a great many of them women, who want to pick up where they left off ten or 20 years ago—all these students have a second, a third or a fourth chance to make it in life.

This is what America has always stood for—a new start, a chance that never existed in the countries from which millions of poor immigrants came, in search not of streets of gold but of golden opportunities, especially for their children. But now the funds for community colleges are drying up. Since student activism has died away, it seems safe to cut down and to take back what once was given in response to the demands of activists of many kinds. The fact that in recent years thousands of the students who made a new start in community colleges have become useful, more productive adults seems to be irrelevant.

In our cities it is in public libraries and museums that intellectually curious children have found and opened the doors to educational opportunity, often finding their way from illiterate homes into the worlds of science and art and the professions. But we are closing these doors too. Many libraries have been shut down and we are starving others so that they no longer can buy books, particularly expensive books for children, and can remain open only a few hours a week. In the 1930s, during the Great Depression, the unemployed in great numbers went back to school and found their way into libraries to prepare for a future they still believed in. Today we seem to be saying to many people: There is no future— for you.

We are no better off when it comes to caring for the nation's health. We know how to give babies and little children a good start in life—and we also know that early malnutrition and physical neglect can be permanently damaging; yet funds for child care are cut, and cut again. We know a good deal about caring for the elderly, but we have allowed the funds made available for their care to be used in ruthless profiteering that has divested thousands of helpless individuals of their humanity.

And as never before we can cure the sick, protect the healthy and give a great many incapacitated women and men a better chance to live as autonomous adults. But the current cost is overwhelming and we have not begun to solve the problem of how to make these different kinds of care safely available to all who need them. And it is the poor who suffer most grievously.

Today it sometimes seems to me that rather than trying

to find ways through which people, using their own abilities, can overcome the handicaps of poverty so that fewer among us will be trapped by it in the next generation, we are attempting by abolishing the services to the poor, to abolish the poor. And in so doing we ensure that they will be more helpless in a hostile world.

But poverty in the United States is not like poverty in a country like Bangladesh, where there is neither enough land to grow food nor any resources to export and sell in exchange for food. We have land and food and resources adequate to the needs of our whole nation, not just some parts of it, and we certainly have the knowledge and skills to implement any realistic plan we can agree upon to increase the well-being of all Americans. For this very reason our present acceptance of widespread poverty, ignorance and misery is a blight that can destroy all of us.

How does it happen that we are willing to spend billions in support of a very dubious sense of security and at the same time are wasting our most precious, irreplaceable resource, our children? They are young only once; they can be permanently maimed by adverse experiences in their growing years. But we could give them a new vision of human community to think about and work for in their lifetime.

One way of beginning, I believe, is to recognize the fact that the image of the horizon gives us a false cue today. The horizon, after all, is part of where we are; it is simply the outer edge of the world as we see and know and judge it. Our ancestors had to be willing to trust themselves to the unknown beyond the horizon; that was their future and they accomplished much. But for us it is too limited. In our time we have seen the turning earth from the vantage point of the moon.

And in this our Bicentennial year, our vision needs to take in the whole of our planet if we are to give our children faith in the future. That faith depends on our willingness to plan for our survival and the survival of all our children on this earth—and to carry out what we plan so that the quality of the human community may become the best that it can be. As individuals we must begin at home, working for what are the true necessities—child care and education, health needs and decent housing, safe methods of developing energy. In this election year we must support at all levels—local, state and national—the candidates who share our concern.

We have been a people willing to work very hard to realize a vision. Why should we now turn our backs on this vision in a shortsighted refusal to see?

The Gift of Celebrating Christmas

DECEMBER 1974

As autumn deepens into winter and the wind-blown leaves drift into rattling heaps and the first snow flurries darken the sky, Americans begin to measure time till Christmas—three weeks, two weeks, the last few harried days . . .

For everyone, these weeks before Christmas are a period of quickening expectation. Children's expectations are touched with mystery and wonder. Even children who enter into all the family plans know there are secrets that will be revealed for their delight only when the day comes.

But for adults, expectation carries with it as well a weight of obligation and responsibility for all the things they ought to do and all the people they ought to look out for so that Christmas can truly be a happy day of fulfillment. And there are the lonely ones, the elderly and those who live alone, whose expectations are tinged with doubt—who feel that someone ought to be thinking about them, ought to include them in festive plans. For adults the "oughtness" of life has become firmly attached to Christmas.

Thinking about these weeks of expectation, I began to wonder how the shift comes about from the child's pure, egocentric delight in a feast that seems to be planned almost wholly for her enjoyment to the adult's sense that this is a time when all obligations somehow must be met—quite heavy obligations to provide for other people's pleasure or to guard other people from loneliness or disappointment—if they are to satisfy their own feelings of expectation at Christmas.

My own earliest memories of Christmas are full of sensory delight—as all children's memories are if Christmas is not

222

marred by death or disaster. During the weeks before Christmas there were the wonderful accumulating fragrances that gradually filled the house. There was the sugary smell of the special candies we made of white fondant that was such fun to shape—flattened to hold English walnuts or curved to fold over a date or to cover an almond. There was the strange, spicy smell of fruitcake and plum pudding that mingled with the woodland smell of the holly and laurel decorations. And at last there came, drifting from the kitchen, the delicious, tantalizing smell of the turkey roasting in the oven.

Best of all there was the tall tree, fresh and fragrant, with its glittering balls and draped tinsel, its strings of white popcorn and red cranberries and tiny, homemade paper lanterns. And there were the mysterious presents wrapped in tissue paper, neat packages and oddly shaped bundles that when opened revealed books and toys, toy animals and dolls, and one year a pair of beautiful red shoes that I wore in the snow —and the dye turned the snow red.

Always as Christmas approached there was the early darkness, when the last light shone in our west windows at four o'clock. This early darkness is one of the strongest memories I have kept of the weeks of waiting, the weeks when we counted the days.

Perhaps, after all, it is the distinctiveness of this period of preparation that remains most vivid in adults' memories of childhood. Or perhaps the memory is reinforced as adults get caught up in the other side of Christmas, preparing for the enjoyment of others—children, parents, neighbors, faraway relatives and the friends associated with other times and other places, the distant people we do try to write to at least once a year and almost always at Christmas.

For myself, I know that every year as the days shorten and the lights come on early and curtains are drawn long before suppertime, the old sense of excitement persists no matter what my own particular Christmas holds in store. It catches me as I go home from work in the dark and see people hurrying homeward under the street lights and it seems to me we all are moving in the same rhythm of expectation.

Would Christmas be Christmas without this sense of expectancy, this tension of wondering? If we did not carry in our memory the almost unbearable anticipation of small children, creeping down in the dark of the cold morning of Christmas Day to find their stockings, each hoping to be the first to shout, "Merry Christmas!" to the still-sleepy adults following them down the stairs?

But the idea of "oughtness"—of obligation and reward—comes early too. Children soon learn that they ought not ask questions—too many questions—that they ought not get up too early on Christmas Day because the grownups were up very late finishing last things. And they learn that the delightful presents are somehow related to being good. This is an idea that is fathoms-deep in our tradition. You have to be good to be given a happy Christmas, and reciprocally it is a matter of obligation to give others a happy Christmas.

Just how deep this goes may depend primarily on when in childhood the shift takes place from concentrating on the presents you are given to what you do for others. And perhaps we are influencing a child's whole conception of a future role within a household if little boys are given money to buy presents but little girls are encouraged to "make something for Daddy."

In my own family no distinctions were made between my brother and my sisters and myself. We were allowed to share in some attempted elegance in the family present for our grandmother—which she almost always found unsatisfactory. But presents for our parents had to be homemade. And Grandma presided over the presents that, from the age of two, we made. We cut penwipers out of printed challis and we cut shaving papers for cleaning our father's straight razor out of colored tissue paper topped by a colored cardboard oak leaf. Later we made calendars and stone paper-weights, our emerging skills displayed in the hand-painted designs.

Dadda did not like to be given bought presents by anyone. Of course, it was easy for Grandma to knit him a new scarf. But my poor mother, who had no cultivated hand skills, tried every year to make him a tie, a tie that never got finished until the last hours of Christmas Eve.

In this way we were indoctrinated very early with the idea that Christmas included responsibilities for giving as well as the pleasure of receiving. This meant that my anticipation of presents to come always was clouded over by my uncertainty about the success of the presents I had made to give others. But it was the Christmas when I was nine that permanently shifted me over from being a child who could anticipate with delight to becoming the person in the family, once and for all, who was responsible for the delight of others.

That year my mother was expecting a baby, a baby born just two weeks later. So all the tasks of trimming the tree and filling the stockings and laying out the presents for each member of the family were turned over to me. My grandmother supervised, and she was very successful in helping a child experience real responsibility. On Christmas Eve I filled the stockings—put a tangerine in the toe and added little packets of nuts and candies and hunted through the presents that had arrived to find things small enough to fit into stockings. I filled my own stocking too, and so the tension of surprise was lost.

Overnight on that Christmas, my role was completely reversed. And it never changed. From then on I always trimmed the tree and filled the stockings. I had become responsible for other people's Christmas. The child's sheer delight in receiving presents others had chosen out of love and foresight or sacrifice or exuberant enjoyment of the object itself was dissipated forever.

In much later years, in the years of my most complex Christmas celebrations, preparations were a scramble against time. We were living then in New York in the bounteous aura of our friend Larry Frank's household of six children. My daughter was little, my parents were living in Philadelphia and were lonely and there were close friends with whom we celebrated Christmas Eve.

All this meant a Christmas Eve dinner with our friends and their small children, a Christmas-morning breakfast with the Franks amidst the shouts of children, and dinner with my own family. It meant starting to roast the Christmas goose at two in the morning so that it would be ready in time for us to catch the ten-o'clock train to Philadelphia. And in the station I would meet my sister, who was likely to be carrying a set of unmanageable presents she had made for the family, perhaps hand-painted lamp shades on which the paint was not yet quite dry.

In those years the late-night and early-morning hours left no moment free. There were the meals to be cooked, the dishes to be washed, the Christmas wrappings to be picked up, the train to catch, the lists to be made so no thank-you notes would be forgotten. Often I did not get to my own presents before Christmas night. Until then I was too preoccupied with all the things that had to be planned, arranged and watched over for the sake of what seemed the multitude of people for whose happiness I felt responsible.

It isn't that I do not recall many of those Christmases with pleasure in the particular constellations of trees and candles, special food, children's voices and people enjoying the feast. It is instead, I think, that I learned too early to take on the parental role of filling the stockings and worrying about the plans and provisions for other people.

As a result, it seems to me that at Christmas I have been in many ways an unsatisfactory child and parent, lover and wife and friend. People regularly complain that they don't

know what to give me—others have given me an abundance
of monogrammed handkerchiefs, potted azaleas, filmy scarves
or bottles of perfume.

If they are very close to me, they have heard me wonder,
as I opened a carefully planned present from someone who
would never know, to whom I could give it on another occasion. Or they have watched me groaningly set a carved and
varnished wooden turtle on my bureau, where it would be in
full view, because it was brought with affection all the way
from a Caribbean island just for me. They keep on trying,
my family and friends, but I feel they do it without the pleasure
they ought to have, because I am such a distrait and inattentive receiver of gifts.

And so it seems to me that children at Christmas should
have opportunities to experience pure, unalloyed delight—delight without responsibility. I know that most children receive
too many presents to be able to distinguish among them. I
know that many of the presents we give children are too break-
able, too mechanical, too expensive. But if Christmas is a
season that someday will be shadowed by obligation and responsibility, I think children need to learn both sides of the
giving and receiving pattern with equal happiness. Then later
their obligations will be lightened by the memory of how much
they enjoyed being given presents—presents that were planned
and saved for, thought of and dreamed of, by those who gave
and those who received them for their own.

Then Christmas preparations will be less of a burden and
adults, having lived through the weeks of expectation, which
for them were filled and overfilled with things that had to get
done, can still experience some of the joy of the delighted child
at receiving a gift. And the capacity to take delight in a gift
is heart-warming to the giver.

Some presents do give me great pleasure. They are slight,
often ephemeral things—two peacock feathers; a bouquet of
wild flowers; a single, incredibly beautiful rose, too fragile even

to take on an airplane; or something I have to eat or drink at once, where I am—a delicious bunch of grapes or an open bottle of champagne.

And once while I was lecturing I saw a woman sitting in the front row with a brown paper bag held tightly on her lap. At the end she came up to me and said, "I am an Omaha Indian from Nebraska. I have brought you some rocks from the reservation." I had worked there long ago, in 1930, and had never returned. This was a present I had no sense I should share with anyone else. It was meant for me alone and I had a right to enjoy it.

VI
Transitions

Earth Day and
Our Plundered Planet

APRIL 1970

We have arrived at a strange moment in human history. Women, faced with the possibility that their lifetime commitment to homemaking is coming to an end, are looking with uncertainty toward an unknown future. And men as they take their first steps into space are discovering that our planet is in truth a little island, a bounded territory whose limited resources, once they have been fully exploited, mined, burned, destroyed or polluted, can never be restored. The causes of this awakening awareness among men and women are the same—the population explosion and our technological revolution. No one is without some sense of the dangers of our situation, but we are only at the beginning of thinking about what we can and must do.

In a movement organized by students to initiate action for the protection of our plundered planet, workshops and teach-ins will be held on 400 college and university campuses throughout the United States on April 22nd, the first Earth Day. On this day students, scientists and many kinds of specialists in conservation will sit down and reason together. They will try to find some answers to this question: What must people everywhere begin to do *now* in order that our planet can be preserved as a fit habitation for the next generation of humankind?

April has been designated by concerned young people as a month for everyone to think soberly and imaginatively about the dire state we are in. The meetings are intended to give focus to that thinking.

Students of all political persuasions, disregarding their differences, have called for these meetings. They are coming together, not in angry protest, but to learn and to plan how best to pool their energies in work. The teach-ins and workshops are one way of taking stock of the resources at our command. They are also a call to action. The students, whose productive life is in the future, realize fully that the time is short, very short, before conditions will become intolerable—unless we act now. Already we can hear, in our imagination, the cries of children born into a world civilization that is choking to death on its own waste products.

An easy way out would be to treat the situation as a crisis. We could, without insuperable difficulties, take emergency measures. We could set in motion what would be in effect a glorious house cleaning—banning DDT, banning diesel engines, controlling industrial waste, forbidding the dumping of radioactive waste in the sea. Such one-shot actions are dramatic and would give many people a sense of accomplishment.

But we are not dealing with a crisis that can be overcome and afterward forgotten. What we must work toward, instead, is a way of thinking that will encourage all of us to become the vigilant conservators of our inheritance of earth and air, the waters of ponds and rivers and seas, and all the life of the world.

We have the scientific knowledge and the technical competence to make the first necessary inventions. We have a communications system through which people everywhere in the world can learn whatever anyone anywhere can devise for human benefit. What we need, beyond anything else, is a frame of reference, a model of cherishing care for the earth and all human needs.

Our contemporary picture of masculine attitudes toward the natural world is predominantly one in which men in the exercise of power have been ruthlessly exploitive and prodigal, arrogant in their disregard for the balance of nature, ready to change whatever seemed inconvenient and committed to the shortest route to a desired goal regardless of what was lost or destroyed on the way.

But this is, in fact, a very partial picture. Looking back to our own European past we can still see the expression of very different attitudes toward the earth. Across much of Europe and England we can still trace in the contemporary landscape the lines of very ancient fields fanning out from villages where men had developed a system that bound together the people, the land and the animals on which they depended. This was how the peoples of northern Europe lived during more than a thousand years, how they expanded their holdings and slowly subdued the great forests and wild places.

As long as the peasant farmer remained close to his land, feeding and tending living things day by day, plowing and harvesting and husbanding, he played a nurturing role, just as his wife did at her indoor tasks of child rearing and house-keeping. For in spite of the fact that men won more and more from nature, their continuous care gave back what they had taken away—and much of this land is still fertile today.

The sudden availability of apparently limitless land in the new worlds of the Americas and Australia radically changed men's relationship to the natural world. Like men in a hurry they recklessly exhausted the land they opened to use, cut down the trees, mined the soil and moved on. Then to make the soil yield again they invented synthetic fertilizers, pesticides to protect the crops and the machines that turned farming into big business.

Man the cultivator is an ancient image of nurturing care. But there is no way, I think, in which we can return in our imagination to the old, lost peasant attitudes toward the natural world. We are urbanites for whom the outdoors has become a playground, and massive mechanized methods of food production are essential to the survival of our huge urban populations. At best, looking back, we can reassure ourselves that human beings do have the capacity to cherish the earth as well as to exploit it.

Have we, then, another model?

I believe we have. It is women's unremitting care for their families and homes.

Age after age, women have learned to conserve, to plan for the next day and the next season, to use carefully whatever they had and to keep a continual balance between giving and meeting the needs of everyone in the home. Women's conservative tendencies were born out of the limitations of the household, a small, closed universe. They have always had to think: So much food to lay away for the winter and the distant spring, so many mouths to feed each day.

Men, even the most careful conservators, have been taught to think about the obstacles to be overcome and how to overcome them and so live in a more open world. But women have almost always been familiar with closed systems and understand very well that survival within them depends on continuing care and the continuing performance of the same tasks over and over again.

Women's conserving habits—which they have sometimes shared with men and sometimes have carried on in spite of a completely contrasting world view among men—have everywhere gone almost unremarked. They have been conservators without conscious thought, and as in so many other things, usually without the supporting formal rules and ceremonies that characterize men's important activities. So it is not surprising that women seldom have raised their voices in protest against the plundering and devastation of our planet. They have taken for granted the rightness of men's activities and have said of themselves, as vast numbers of women today are saying with regret or in angry self-condemnation: "I am only a housewife."

But at this critical moment, while women still are pausing

on the threshold of their homes, homes in which there is no granary, no storeroom, no milk shed, no harvest of beans or peas to be shelled, no ham smoked for the winter, homes from which their two or three children eventually will depart, it may be well to ask: Can women make articulate their understanding of the tasks they have traditionally performed, the tasks they learned, however reluctantly and rebelliously, from their mothers?

Before we recklessly incorporate women, like cogs in a machine-dominated world, into some great system in which individual human values have little meaning, it may be well to consider what would be lost. It would seem that modern women, who are running their homes in great part with machinery, buying much of their food from day to day in processed form and almost all of it in supermarkets, dressing their families in clothes made in distant factories, learning new ways of doing things from impersonal experts, driving cars as skillfully as men—living, in fact, almost wholly within the world men have made—it would seem that these women have little in common with women who lived only 100 years ago.

But these modern women still are, as women always have been, caretakers of persons and, equally, caretakers of the things that are essential to those they love and for whose well-being they are responsible. And it is just this—responsible and devoted caretaking—that is the key to the future. It is this capacity to relate things to the needs of many individuals that makes possible vigilance over a lifetime and for generation after generation.

The most radical feminists want to be part of the larger world, free to express themselves and use their talents. They want also to be recognized for what they are, women. Many other women, who are not yet ready to give up their commitment to their homes and private lives, have only the most grudging sympathy for the rebel activists. But I believe that women who have taken the most opposing stands can find a common bond in a commitment to the conservation of our planet.

They have a difficult task ahead of them. They must make articulate to themselves and others what they know at deep levels about conservation. They must make a tremendous leap in scale from the closed system of a single home to the closed system of a whole world. They must make a translation in terms from housekeeping for a family, each member of which is known as an individual, to housekeeping for all people, most of whom are strangers to one another. Above all, they must somehow convey the belief they sometimes accept and sometimes doubt—that responsible caretaking is a central value of life.

This does not mean that women should take over the running of the world's affairs as for thousands of years they have managed their homes. It does mean that women, within and outside their homes, will begin to develop new kinds of partnerships with men in which each can inform the understanding of the other.

Such a changeover from a focus on their own homes and their own small communities to concern for the whole world, in which their homes and families are included, involves long-range thinking and planning on the part of women together with men. It involves a process of self-education in knowledge we already have and the incorporation into this knowledge of attitudes toward protective care that women have not yet extended to the larger world. This is the first step toward partnership in decision-making that must be shared more equally by men and women for the safekeeping of the future.

Shared responsibility for the protection of our planet is the goal that concerned students, young men and young women, can set for themselves and that we can best support with our belief that the world is a home for humankind.

Thinking Clearly
about Clear Water

MAY 1974

How much can we really do about the pollution of water and earth and air? Are the damages reversible? Can modern technology invent safer ways of dealing with pollutants? And if we have the knowledge, are we willing to pay the price, especially if this means radical changes in our style of living?

These are questions about which many people are arguing very heatedly. But it seems to me there is a different, equally important question: How much do our own attitudes contribute to the difficulties of our endangered situation?

For I believe that we must go to the very center of our attitudes as Americans, as urban people and as members of the great industrialized world to get at the essential problems.

If we consider water pollution, for instance, this much is indisputable:

• The basic scientific knowledge for the recovery of good water exists.

• Many sound techniques have been worked out and put into practice on a small scale.

• Large-scale solutions depend on what we are willing to do—and the price we are willing to pay.

It is our *thinking* that we must modify if we are to make and implement the decisions necessary to protect the world we live in.

Americans know that science and technology are very rapidly changing the face of the earth. But a great many people still find it difficult to grasp the idea that the natural resources of our planet on which all life depends—water and earth, air and fire, in the old, prescientific vocabulary—are both

limited and very vulnerable to the unexpected and increasingly damaging effects of our extraordinarily successful in-
ventiveness.

In particular, we have great difficulty believing that waste
and decay, which are part of the natural cycle of life and
death and change, are getting out of our control. We deplore
the mountains of waste our huge population creates every
day. But we have little idea how much our accepted, everyday
practices have to do with the damaging effects of waste ac-
cumulation and the pollution we have brought about in our
world.

Consider what we are doing to the earth's resources of
water through our handling of domestic waste.

Today about 90 per cent of Americans live in homes and
work in offices and factories that are linked to public water
supplies and public sewage systems designed to dispose of
waste—waste that is flushed away by water. This is the sanitary system that developed out of the 19th-century realization
that people in towns and cities must have uncontaminated
water to drink if they were to be spared the horrors of recurrent epidemics. Clean water, drawn from streams, stored
in reservoirs and purified, was piped in for drinking and other
domestic purposes. And waste matter, instead of gathering in
cesspools or draining back into the earth, was flooded with
millions of gallons of clean water that carried it through the
sewers to be emptied elsewhere.

This system of waste disposal served us well enough as long
as urban populations were relatively small and the wastes
were of kinds that could be dealt with fairly adequately by
the natural processes of disintegration and change taking
place in the rivers, lakes and coastal waters into which sewers
were—and still are—emptied. But as populations have grown
enormously and as more and more people have become part
of the urban, industrialized world, we have been carelessly
and unthinkingly using up our resources of pure water to get

rid of waste. And the water one town discards, other people farther down the river have to recover and use for drinking purposes and in turn to carry away more waste products.

Now this water, always more contaminated with sewage, is choking our running streams, so that often nothing can live in them. It is saturating our lakes and bays and estuaries, the bottoms of which are terribly overloaded with stagnant filth. Beaches to which families come for recreation are strewn with refuse, and all too often signs are posted: Unsafe for swimming! And far beyond the shores of continents, wherever anthropologist Thor Heyerdahl sailed in the papyrus boats that succeeded *Kon Tiki*, he found garbage floating on the surface of the ocean water. The more sheltered seas—the Baltic and the Barents—have begun to die.

So we are faced by the paradox that cleanliness destroys what is clean.

Americans as a people have a more highly advertised dislike of visible dirt and malodorous filth than almost any other nation in the world. We have traps in our pipes so that the noisome smell of "the drains" that made Victorians, including the Queen of England, sick cannot come creeping back into our immaculate, tiled bathrooms. Advertisements describe and demonstrate the newest and most efficient methods of keeping our kitchens and bathrooms hygienically clean and sweet. Daily we are told how to keep the air as fresh as daisies inside our homes, where more and more windows are being sealed shut against the dust and dirt and pollution outdoors.

The smell of the mildest of human wastes—sweat—repels us, and everyone is exhorted to buy and use daily one or more of an enormous range of deodorants and antiperspirants, which ensure that whatever we eat and however heavily we exercise we will all have a similar, slightly cosmetic smell. Even the smallest baby is not exempt from the demand that everyone should smell pleasant.

Nor is it enough for our clothes to be clean. They must be

whiter than white, soft to the touch and smell not of the sun and wind (for how many of us can hang out laundry today?) but of one of the clean, fresh odors built into the modern laundry detergents, bleaches and softeners that contaminate our waters.

There is a striking contrast between modern urban homes and the farms on which so many of our grandparents grew up. There the horse and cow and chicken manure was returned to the farmland and gardens. Garbage, carefully sorted, was fed to the chickens and pigs. Coffee grounds and tea leaves were simply poured out on the grass to fade harmlessly into the soil. When I was a child we even carried out the greasy dishwater and poured it on the flower beds so that it would not be wasted. Almost without thinking, our grandparents adapted themselves to the rhythms of conservation in which most of what was used was safely restored to the earth to enter a new cycle of growth.

Today most rural and urban homes differ little in their practices. Human waste, garbage ground up in a disposal unit and hundreds of gallons of water electrically pumped up from deep wells for showers, dishwashers and clothes washers are flushed, with their added burden of detergents, into septic tanks from which sludge eventually must be removed. Fields are fertilized with chemicals that drain off into streams, dangerously overloading them with nutrients. And in rural as in urban America the tons of household waste—the paper and packaging, the newspapers and magazines that have used up numberless acres of trees, the tins and disposable bottles, the plastics that are not biodegradable, the old tires and all the castoff rubbish of modern living—are carted to dumps to be burned and buried, to pollute the air and the earth and the streams in ever-mounting, unmanageable quantities.

The paradox of modern living is this: As we have raised our standards of what is safe, sanitary, attractively clean and desirable for our homes and our own persons, we have progressively made the world away from our homes dirtier, more contaminated, more polluted and foul-smelling. But always at a distance—out of our sight and out of our minds.

For most of us there is a daily reminder of the true situation—our drinking water. Almost everywhere now this must be radically treated, and it comes back to us with the masking smell of chlorine, which simply substitutes one bad smell for another and protects us only from the grosser water-borne diseases. But only occasionally do people complain and even more seldom do they ask, Is there no other way? Instead we turn to bottled drinks—soda and pop and expensive water from "pure" springs—in this way increasing the numbers of bottles that come into our homes and go out again to add to the mountains of "disposable" rubbish.

The present-day system is first in the name of cleanliness to contaminate; then to use chemicals to purify; and always to use water, millions of gallons of water, to carry away wastes to contaminate the water needed by others and to contaminate as well the rivers and lakes and bays into which the polluted waters flow.

It is a system long outdated. Yet our efforts to achieve true cleanliness—cleanliness in the world we live in as well as in our homes and persons—are very hesitant, slow and at best local and piecemeal.

Why is this? Don't we care?

Certainly there is no single or simple answer.

It is argued that domestic waste is a secondary source of water pollution. Manufacturing and power plants, the runoff from very large-scale commercial farming and feed lots, acid mine drainage and urban runoff—these are major sources too, and these can be regulated, essentially, only by national and statewide legislation and control.

That is quite true. But it is also true that the managers of the corporations and the members of local governments who lobby against controls and protest the installation of newer techniques of protection and the legislators who must set up the controls and provide part of the funds are Americans like the rest of us. Their reactions reflect attitudes common to most of us, attitudes that will change only as all of us work toward a different climate of opinion. It is not, basically, how we treat this or that aspect of the problem of water pollution that matters. It is our over-all attitude.

It is also argued, as it has been argued for over a century, that flushing away wastes in water is essential to human health. Isn't it well-known that it is exceedingly dangerous to return human and animal wastes to the soil? Isn't it the unstinting use of water—washing, flushing and flooding wastes with water—that protects us from sickness and deadly epidemics?

The answer today is, No. On the one hand we now know that our handling of waste water permits the spread of virus diseases, such as infectious hepatitis. On the other hand there are now superior and economically practical methods of treating sewage so that it can be returned safely to the soil as fertilizer; and the water can be recycled to a state of purity instead of flowing, laden with waste, into rivers, lakes and the sea.

There are other arguments as well. But I believe it is our own attitudes that bind us, that prevent us from connecting our practices with the end results.

There is first our belief that we are consumers of water. The clean water that is piped into our homes and on which we pay taxes belongs to us and we consume it. But in fact we do not consume it. We are only users—and very temporary users—of water. We share its use with others in our communities and with strangers in communities we shall never know. It flows through our homes; we do not use it up. It remains a resource which we can gradually destroy or of which we can make ourselves the custodians for everyone's benefit, now and in the future.

But if we are to grasp the idea that water is a resource that is continually recycled, a resource that we use and use again, we shall have to recognize very clearly the fact that we cannot rid ourselves of waste and dirt (and every other thing we abhor) by washing it out of sight. We cannot rid ourselves of everything we regard as unsavory by increasing the distance between ourselves and pollution. The ecological behavior that is strangling our towns and polluting our water sources echoes and reflects our attitudes toward all that repels us.

If we are able really to *think* about the way we handle waste, we will be better able to face our problems squarely and take the necessary steps to change our practices. We need to make sure that our community is not polluting our own water or that used by other communities; we need to know how our local system of waste disposal functions; and we need to work through our town or city government to improve that system if it functions badly. We need to support legislation on the national level that safeguards our rivers, lakes, bays, estuaries and seashore against the dangers of domestic and industrial pollution.

If we stop pretending that flushing waste out of our houses will make it disappear forever, if we can face the fact that the waste returns, only a few miles away, to destroy rivers and beaches and seashore, perhaps we can face other problems too. For all the ways in which a people handle their problems are related. Honest respect for one set of facts encourages honesty in facing others. And we can no more get rid of our distasteful problems than we can wash away our wastes into waters that run endlessly into inexhaustible seas. What we wash away in water returns—and soon.

Our Lives May Be at Stake

NOVEMBER 1974

How many Americans are aware of what an all-out commitment to a nuclear program to generate power will mean to our own safety, and to the well-being of our children and future generations as far ahead as people can imagine?

At the height of the fuel shortages in 1973, Richard M. Nixon as President told us that the United States could become independent of other nations in the production of energy by the mid-1980s and that the Government was taking the necessary steps to see that this highly desirable goal would be accomplished. The nuclear energy program, on which the Atomic Energy Commission had been working for 25 years, would, he said, turn this bright promise into a reality. And because the AEC is a Government agency that Americans deeply trust, most people have felt less anxious about the future.

So for the time being we have lost the sense that we are in the midst of an energy crisis. We have come through a summer during which most people have had enough gas to go where they wanted to go, and there is no great worry about heating fuel for the winter. It's very expensive, yes, but it's there. And a great many people are saying, "That's what the crisis was really about—the price we have to pay!"

For the present, it is easy to be complacent and not ask questions about crucial decisions being made without our knowledge or participation. But I believe no alert and concerned Americans would be willing to pay the tremendous price of complacency if they realized that commitment to the proposed nuclear program carries with it a unique threat to human health and survival.

The nuclear program is still in the development stage. We still can consider what other options we have and make other, far safer, choices. If we take action now, we can protect the future.

On the face of it, the liquid-metal fast-breeder reactor (LMFBR) program, of which the Atomic Energy Commission has been the chief advocate and promoter for several years, has an almost magical sound. Indeed, from the point of view of those who think only of generating energy—vast quantities of energy—this advanced reactor looks ideal. For the LMFBR produces more fissionable fuel than it consumes and so, it is said, will conserve our supplies of uranium for centuries. The more nuclear material we put into the reactor, the more fissionable material it will produce; and the more reactors we build, the more bountiful the production of fuel will be. This in turn seems to mean that we can count on an adequate supply of electricity—the only major industrial application of nuclear energy—no matter how heavy our demands for energy may become over the next 20, 40 or 100 years.

As we listen to the forecasts of the Atomic Energy Commission about the possibilities of the nuclear energy program, it is almost as if—in terms of energy—we had at last realized the dreams of medieval alchemists of turning base metals into pure gold.

What we do not hear about from the Atomic Energy Commission or from the industries that are rapidly becoming involved in the advanced LMFBR program are the known risks. Yet these are risks so extraordinary that every citizen in the nation should have a voice in deciding whether this is the road to energy independence we—or anyone—should take.

Informed scientists have discussed these risks for years and as experience with the light-water reactor, the one now in commercial use, has grown, more of them have spoken out in warning. Most scientific discussions about the production of nuclear energy are very hard for even informed lay persons to understand; however, there are certain facts that any thinking person can take into account.

Atomic reactors produce plutonium 239, an artificial, man-made element that is perhaps the deadliest substance in the world. It is known, for example, that a microscopic amount of plutonium, if inhaled, would be enough to produce a lung cancer, and it is believed that the dispersal of a few grams of plutonium through the air-conditioning system of a large modern office building would be enough to kill all its occupants. But what is most astonishing about plutonium 239 is that it will remain deadly dangerous for 250,000 (some scientists believe 500,000) years. To almost anyone's way of thinking, that means forever. And scientists have no idea whether the toxicity of plutonium can ever be reduced.

At different stages of the fuel cycle of the LMFBR it will be necessary to transport nuclear materials containing plutonium to reprocessing plants and later back again to the fuel-fabrication plants. And plutonium will be one element in the nuclear waste materials for which safe storage will have to be found. What we have in prospect, then, if the proposed program ever reaches the commercial stage, is transport over public highways and eventual permanent storage not of pounds but of tons of lethal plutonium that must be guarded every instant—for thousands of centuries to come. And as yet, no one knows how to provide "safe" storage. None of the experiments we have made so far have proved to be safe even for short periods.

Inevitably, by committing ourselves to a nuclear program for the production of energy, we also are accepting incredible risks:

• There is the risk that during transportation reprocessed plutonium may be seized by conscienceless hijackers—or even by high-minded fanatics—and used by them as a terrible threat.

• There is the risk that plutonium, which is one of the fissionable materials out of which bombs can be made, may be stolen or acquired through some black market for the purpose of making an atomic weapon. The process of making a bomb is no longer a secret. Scientists say that anyone having the knowledge—and the plutonium—could make a crude but effective bomb in a basement workshop.

• There is the risk that a nuclear reactor could be an enemy target or that an accident to a nuclear reactor could release into the atmosphere enormous quantities of radioactive substances that would be far more lethal than anything we experienced during bomb tests. As we now know, many hundreds of what an Atomic Energy Commission task force report called "abnormal occurrences" have taken place in the few light-water reactors now in operation. According to this report, made public last January, about 40 per cent of the occurrences were related to deficiencies of design or fabrication. The rest "were caused by operator error, improper management, inadequate erection control, administrative deficiencies, random failures and combinations thereof." Luckily none resulted in massively dangerous accidents. But what guarantee is there that we would do as well if the much more complex LMFBR program came into commercial operation?

I think any automobile owner who has been obliged to return his late-model car to the factory for correction of some dangerous fault or any housewife who has had to deal with the vagaries of "experts" in the repair of simple household appliances will be doubtful.

• And there are the risks of permanent storage. To whom will we give the sterile task of guarding these potential pollutants that are capable of endangering every living thing for generations out of mind?

Dr. Hannes Alfven, Nobel Laureate in Physics, writing in

the May, 1972, issue of the *Bulletin of the Atomic Scientists,* summed up the viewpoint of many scientists:

"Fission energy is safe only if a number of critical devices work as they should, if a number of people in key positions follow all their instructions, if there is no sabotage, no hijacking of the transports, if no reactor-fuel processing plant or reprocessing plant or repository anywhere in the world is situated in a region of riots or guerrilla activity, and no revolution or war—even a 'conventional one'—takes place in these regions. The enormous quantity of extremely dangerous material must not get into the hands of ignorant people or desperadoes. No acts of God can be permitted."

But if all this is really so, you may well ask, how has it come about? Why don't more informed people protest? Why won't Congress take restraining action? Why are we putting so much money into the nuclear reactor program?

The basic difficulty of bringing the whole problem into the open, I believe, is the tremendous prestige we have accorded the Atomic Energy Commission.

The Commission was established after World War II to save us from the terrifying dangers of our own invention, the atomic bomb. At that time we felt it was a triumph—and it was—that we removed control of nuclear devices from the military and assured ourselves of civilian control.

A group of wise and devoted senators and congressmen gave the Commission great powers in order to protect us—and all-unknowing, gave over too much power. For the Commission was given the power to make all the rules, to establish standards of safety and to judge whether those standards were being met. It was given the power to decide what uses were to be made of nuclear energy, by whom, on what scale and for what purposes.

In a word, the AEC was made the initiator, the judge and the jury in everything to do with nuclear energy—all this to regulate its use.

But over the years, as possibilities for peaceful uses of nuclear energy emerged, the Commission became not so much the regulator as the promoter of new programs. And even today, when we know so much more about the risks involved, only the most outspoken critics have dared to challenge the recommendations of the Atomic Energy Commission.

The new Environmental Protection Law requires every Government agency to present an impact statement that describes the effect a proposed program will have on the environment and discusses alternatives. Yet the Atomic Energy Commission refused to prepare an impact statement on the huge and possibly disastrous nuclear reactor program until a court, responding to a people's suit, forced it to do so. Even then, after giving the task of preparing a draft to the very part of the Commission responsible for the program, the Commission apparently ignored the reports of its own convened committees. In particular, the draft impact statement virtually ignored, by playing down, the alternatives we have to the use of nuclear energy for the production of power.

These alternatives—solar energy, geothermal energy, wind energy, energy derived from ocean thermal gradients and possibly controlled nuclear fusion—developed and used, if necessary, in conjunction with one another, could provide us with safe, clean and reliable sources of energy to replace the dwindling supplies of fossil fuels.

But the fact is that the Atomic Energy Commission has no mandate to recommend the development of other forms of energy. It is concerned only with nuclear power, regardless of the country's real needs or environmental safety or the well-being of living people and future generations, or the dangers of setting up social controls powerful enough to prevent the misuse of nuclear materials.

In spite of this, most Americans still picture the Commission as the good watchdog who guards us from the demonic capacities of nuclear fission. We cannot realize that the watchdog in whom we placed our trust has become a killer dog with tremendous power for harm.

And if we do recognize this, what can we do? What can ordinary citizens do that scientists with their specialized knowledge and high prestige have been unable to accomplish effectively? The Atomic Energy Commission still rides high.

We have arrived at the crossroads of decision. We still have the choice of which road we shall travel. No commercially feasible advanced LMFBR has been built. Other options, long delayed, are still open.

We can insist that the whole problem be opened for discussion in terms everyone can understand. We can insist that *every* option for the development of power resources be explored with adequate funding. We can insist that the search for safe power be diversified so that we can make choices that will keep our children's future open. We can insist that no one agency, devoted to one form of energy production, will be allowed to usurp the power of decision.

Most immediately, we can insist that Congress refuse to pass the next multimillion-dollar appropriations bill presented by the supporters of the nuclear reactor program. We have succeeded on other occasions. We can succeed in this.

After all, we are not sheep to be herded by a watchdog we can no longer trust. As aroused citizens alerted to danger, we can be actively vigilant in our own behalf.

EDITOR'S NOTE: *President Ford abolished the Atomic Energy Commission in January, 1975. Two new agencies were created in its place, divorcing regulatory from developmental functions, as Margaret Mead and many others had urged. The Nuclear Regulatory Commission was charged with the licensing and regulation of nuclear power plants; the Energy Research and Development Administration combined nuclear research and develop-*

ment with responsibility for research and development in all energy fields. In 1977, the newly established Department of Energy took over the activities of ERDA along with those of the Federal Energy Administration and the Federal Power Commission.

The Air We Breathe
Means Life—or Death

APRIL 1976

There are only two ways of coping with the problems of air pollution that face us and—directly or indirectly—everyone in the world today. One way is to deal with each kind of pollution as a separate issue, a particular disturbance of our otherwise normal, everyday way of living.

The better way, I believe, is to recognize the central issue —the fact that in our extraordinarily complex civilization the air has made neighbors of every one of us, wherever we live in the world. Air knows no boundaries, and because the atmosphere is boundless—in reality as also in our imagination —we share a neighborly responsibility for the world's children and all living things. Realization that this is so provides us with a framework for thinking about what we must do to have good air. It does not simplify the problems, but it sharpens our judgment in dealing with the dangers and our appreciation of successful steps along the way.

When I was a child some people used to say, "Everybody's business is nobody's business!" That was a way of telling a child that responsibility was specific, particular—and limited. It was a way of teaching a child that she was living in a world with many boundaries—boundaries surrounding her home, her community, her state, her country. Within each of these boundaries she belonged and outside them she had few rights and (I could hear it in people's voices) probably no responsibilities. It never was a view that appealed to me.

Air travel has modified but has not fully set us free from our parochial and earthbound beliefs about boundaries. These beliefs are sustained by the efforts made by governments to extend to the air the kind of thinking appropriate only to the land. The Soviet Union, for example, has declared that its national air space goes up (or out) to infinity, and many nations treat their national air space as a private preserve.

What we completely fail to grasp when we treat the air as a mere extension of the earth is that it is not, like a pond, enclosed and static; like the sea, air is constantly in motion. The radioactive dust stirred by a nuclear explosion flows great distances away on air currents. And it is this continuous flow of air that links all communities, no matter how remote, into a world community. In the past the atmosphere was relatively untouched by human activities. But in our present technological society our very existence affects the atmosphere. Through the air, the business of each person and each community and each nation has truly become everybody's business.

How far we have come is illustrated by our perception of the weather. When I was growing up in Pennsylvania, weather was something our eyes could see and our bodies feel as thunderclouds blotted out the sun and the wind rose or, in winter, as a snowstorm blew across our valley, bending the trees and roaring down chimneys. Weather was "local."

Nowadays the daily weather maps and satellite photographs shown on television have expanded our perception. We "see" cold air masses coming down from Canada and storms sweeping up from the Caribbean. Because we are a large country, we get to see a large slice of the world's weather on any one day. And most of us, through television, now have seen the earth from the vantage point of the moon—an event that advanced our consciousness of the lonely vulnerability of our planet. We saw the patches of pollution drifting out from cities. But we still have to be convinced that there are no purely local problems when it comes to the air and the atmosphere that protects life on earth. We still have to learn how to think constructively about the air that shelters all of us.

During the last decade or so we did learn to ask some questions and take some action against the commoner air pollutants—the exhaust fumes of automobiles, for instance, and the heavy smoke that poured from the chimneys of some industrial plants. And we discovered the dangers of new chemical substances—sprays like DDT, in particular—that had promised so many benefits but produced so much destruction of life. But somehow we were not convinced that all of us as citizens and some of us as scientists must insist on a continuing careful monitoring of all—and particularly of all new—substances that are released into the air until we are well informed about their real effects, direct and indirect, on the living world.

One question we must always ask is whether it is the product or the process that pollutes. A product we can ban; a process we must control.

Some of the hazards of manufacturing in the modern asbestos industry, for example, have been well-known for a long time, and strenuous efforts have been made to protect workers from the cancer-causing dangers of free-floating asbestos dust. But not until recently was it realized that characteristic forms of cancer were also claiming victims among adults and children living near manufacturing plants and shipyards where wide use was made of asbestos products, and among workers who breathed in the snowfall of asbestos fibers sprayed as fireproofing on the girders of skyscrapers under construction. In 1973 the U.S. Environmental Protection Agency banned the use of asbestos sprays, and since then has much more carefully regulated the conditions of manufacture, storage and dumping—a course that has raised the cost of production enormously.

Recently we also have discovered wholly unexpected hazards to health in the process of making polyvinyl chloride (PVC) from vinyl chloride gas. PVC, a truly modern substance, can be molded into any shape and is used for innumerable products, from floor tiles and water pipes to upholstery and toys and clothing. In our country alone it is said to be a $12-billion-a-year industry today. The first reports of liver damage to workers in the manufacturing process came from Russia in 1949. By 1970, industry-supported research in Italy reported the occurrence of characteristic cancers among workers in PVC processing plants, apparently from gases released during manufacture. And now evidence is accumulating that people living in areas where PVC is manufactured also are endangered. Protective regulations are costly, and one manufacturer claims that the industry is "on a collision course with economic disaster."

Another question we must always ask is what happens when an industry is forced to take expensive protective measures. We already have considerable experience of what may happen when one state bans a dangerous, air-polluting practice: the manufacturer moves to a state where controls are less rigid.

And what about other countries? There is firm evidence that asbestos manufacturing is rapidly moving to countries where industrial regulation is minimal—Mexico, Venezuela, Brazil, Taiwan and possibly South Korea. Instead of exporting asbestos products, we are increasingly importing them. This may be happening with other "dangerous" polluting manufacturing processes also.

Can we condone this kind of escape from expensive responsibility? Every day on television, over radio and in newspaper advertisements, manufacturers and processors tell us how deeply concerned they are for the well-being of Americans. But what about the men and women in the countries to which these industries are moving? We cannot, it is true, force other countries to regulate air pollution. But we can work for international controls and meanwhile insist that the products we import be produced under safe conditions.

Much more spectacular are certain pollutants that quite certainly can—and most likely will—affect the quality of life for all living beings. Best known today are the fluorocarbon aerosol propellants, which as they rise from the earth's surface may be breaking down the ozone in the stratosphere. As a result, more harmful ultraviolet rays may reach the earth, endangering the health of people everywhere.

It is hard to believe that a convenient product as useful and apparently harmless as an antiperspirant or an oven cleaner or a furniture polish can possibly have so devastating an effect. We do not even need these propellants; other propellants that are not at all suspect are equally effective. The extraordinary discrepancy in the scale of cause and effect has caught our imagination, and most of us are familiar with this situation. Yet we still continue to argue instead of acting to avert danger! It is both amazing and ridiculous.

Indignation can be exhilarating and protest has its moments of drama. But after a time you are likely to lose your enthusiasm and get tired of listening and trying to understand the details of each case. Sooner or later you are likely to say to yourself, "Maybe it's not so bad. Maybe it doesn't matter so much."

But it does matter. Clean air—safe air—is necessary for every living being and all living things on our planet.

One problem, seldom mentioned, is common to all the efforts to protect human health and the human environment from the dangers of pollutants carried by the air. It is the problem of time: the time it takes to convince people that they must pay attention; the time it takes to make the highly necessary scientific tests, to publicize the findings of such tests, to set the legislative and judicial processes in motion and to insist that protective regulatory measures *must* be carried out. It takes a great deal of time for processes of correction to get under way. Often we cannot save those who in the meantime are harmed.

And for some things we do not have even a little time.

In particular we do not have time to think things over while government and industry plan and begin to develop a nationwide—a world-wide—system of nuclear-power plants as the main way of generating the energy we believe is urgently needed to keep our kind of civilization going. For once the plants have been built, the whole world must face the hazard of nuclear accidents that would release into the air radioactive substances far more lethal than anything experienced during bomb tests.

In addition, generations yet unborn will have to struggle with the unending difficulty of guarding tons of radioactive waste that will accumulate even within a few years—waste that no one yet knows how to store "safely," that will remain dangerous for 250,000 years.

We need to come of age now—at once. We can no longer daydream ourselves into the past, when seas and mountains and rivers and even man-made walls provided boundaries that could be defended. We must recognize the fact that because we share the air with all the world's people, we have become part of an interdependent world community. We must work not only in our communities for local controls of pollution but also through our national legislators for Federal controls. We must work through our Government for international controls and for the development of solar, geothermal and other safe energy sources.

The only way today that we can cherish and protect what is small and private and particular to us is by taking responsibility for protecting all that is cherished as small and private and particular to persons we shall never see.

The air moves, and somehow we must become a people who carry in our imagination an awareness of our interdependence with all living beings and with life on earth—through the air we breathe.

Welfare—Everyone's Responsibility

EDITOR'S NOTE: *The essay that follows describes President Carter's proposal for a new welfare plan, sent to Congress in 1977 as the "Better Jobs and Income Act." Although the program was discussed in committees but never reached the floor of Congress, Margaret Mead's essay on the reforms it embodied is included here as an insight into her social philosophy and an example of her staunch and spirited support of efforts to achieve rational solutions to the problems that plague us as a nation.*

MARCH 1978

How do you feel about the future?

There are people who believe that somehow the future will take care of itself. But most of us want to have some real part in shaping the kind of world in which we—and especially our children—will be living in the years ahead. And now we have an important opportunity to do just that.

For the first time in more than a generation—since the 1930s, in fact—we have the possibility of influencing the development and enactment of new plans that will affect the lives of millions of Americans directly and all of us indirectly. Instead of tinkering once again with systems we have outgrown, we have a chance to rethink what we want and how we can most effectively help all Americans to become and live as first-class citizens. In the 1930s the labor unions, feeling their newly growing power, made themselves heard. Today we know that as women we can make ourselves heard, for the first time, at every level of government as members of families, as working women and as active, concerned citizens.

258

President Carter is proposing a series of programs that, taken together, form a meaningful mosaic of social change. But perhaps the one that is most significant for us, because it redefines family relations, has to do with welfare reform, and it is incorporated in identical Administration bills before the House of Representatives and the Senate.

The proposed program is intended to provide welfare in a focused and rational way, and to make it basically uniform for the country at large. But it goes much further than this.

Whatever our particular, individual interests may be, I think we all must somehow come to grips with the problems of welfare. For the past nine months there has been a rising tide of discussion about restructuring the whole welfare system, but little has been decided—except that whatever plan is adopted, it will take time to implement. There will certainly be a new plan. But what it will be like may very well depend on what you and I, all of us thinking as Americans, are ready to back and support.

As a first step, it seems to me, we must clarify our thinking, and this brings us face to face with an extraordinary social contradiction. A great many Americans, if you ask them today, will tell you that they are "against welfare." But most of the very same people will insist emphatically that we must take care of the old and the disabled, the blind and the sick, women and children who are without resources and also single individuals who, for various reasons, have no jobs and are without any place in a community.

No one, I am sure, would have us go back to the dreadful situation in which we found ourselves in the early years of the Great Depression in the 1930s, when there was no national system at all to care for the jobless and the helpless. Then our poverty laws, such as they were, were long outdated and reflected a kind of morality in which being poor was equated with sin. Helping the completely destitute, people who had been struck down by catastrophe, was an act of private virtue for which the charitable would be rewarded in heaven; but helping the poor was believed by many to encourage dishonesty, idleness and debauchery.

Moreover, it was our fixed belief that able-bodied men should be able to support permanently their wives and unmarried daughters, widowed mothers and unmarried sisters, as well as, of course, their growing sons. The Depression demonstrated that vast millions could be unemployed and totally without resources or any form of property through no fault of their own, but we still clung to the belief that men should support their families.

The Social Security Act, passed in 1935, was a turning point. Then for the first time we recognized a national, though limited, responsibility for working Americans through the new Social Security program and for our fellow citizens who needed help through a program of welfare assistance. But back of the welfare system then and as it was developed bit by bit over many years there remained the fixed belief that assistance was designed for those who lacked a properly constituted family: women and children who had been deserted by the husband and father; the destitute old who had no adult sons to care for them, and, in addition, the blind and the wholly incapacitated or disabled who were dependent on others for survival.

By denying relief to intact families, welfare had the disastrous effect of destroying families. Unemployed men knew that their wives and children were better off without them, and so deserted their families or committed fraud by pretending to desert. Preference in public housing was given to single-parent families headed by women. And very little help was given to the working poor; men who worked without being able to support their families fully were still regarded as somehow blameworthy, and their families suffered as a result.

Over time a great many other unanticipated side-effects have contributed to everyone's dissatisfaction with welfare.

For example, benefit levels vary enormously from one state or city to another across the country, from a high (1977) of $6,132 in New York City for a family of four to a low of $2,556 for a similar family in Mississippi, and even lower for a comparable family in Puerto Rico. This has meant that welfare recipients have crowded into the cities where the provisions are most ample, thereby placing a burden on these cities that they do not have the means to carry from year to year. This burden is not only financial but also social in terms of the multiple problems of people who may be isolated and ill-adapted to coping with the difficulties of big-city life.

In the 1960s there appeared all over the country conspicuous groups of young people who began to live on the Government-sponsored Food Stamp Program intended for the needy—which many of these young people were not. But what is much more serious, we have begun to rear a third generation of welfare recipients—young people whose families have never known any other form of life and who are almost totally unprepared for responsible autonomy.

Then, of course, there have been cases of welfare fraud—and there have been many—and these have been publicized far more than the behavior of the much greater number of submissive, deserving welfare recipients. And the fact that some people have been getting something for nothing—on *our* money—haunts many taxpayers.

Welfare recipients themselves, faced with unintelligible and disheartening bureaucratic rules and with decisions made by biased or inexperienced case workers, have sometimes protested; but more often they have simply tried to find their way through the tortuous maze of programs, cheating a little where nothing else worked and accepting the fact that programs devised over the years to meet newly recognized problems were unintegrated and worked in different ways for different people.

So over the years criticism of welfare has mounted. Nowadays it comes from all sides—from those who still virtuously begrudge assigning tax money to care for the poor, from those who have felt themselves victimized by irrational bureaucratic practices and equally from those who are ablaze with indignation at the injustices of the system and the denigration of human individuality. By such different routes we have arrived at this paradoxical attitude of ours: rejection of the welfare system, coupled with a deeply felt sense of responsibility for human beings in need.

Is this discouraging? Not necessarily. Providing we realize that it signals a need—even a readiness—to change, it is a good thing. What we want to get rid of is not welfare but an underlying belief about the nature of welfare that we now, after 40 years of experience, no longer accept.

The Administration program as set forth in the bills before Congress reflects this need to change even in its name: "Better Jobs and Income Act." There is, it is true, an implied promise that those who are able to work will be required to work and that no one who can work will receive something for nothing. But there are also drastic changes. First, it is implied that the principal breadwinner in a family or of a childless couple may be, without prejudice, either the husband or the wife, depending on who has worked most over the past six months; and second, underlying the work requirement, there is the assumption that adults have the right to work, especially to work at a job in the open market, even though this entails partial public support to supplement low pay.

More important to those of us who are concerned with the setting in which children are growing up, the Administration plan is organized to strengthen the family by strengthening (rather than breaking) the ties binding a husband and a wife and a father and his children. Earning money will not, of itself, deprive the family of essential supplementary care until the earned family income, as now planned, reaches $8,400 for a family of four (possibly higher in states that supplement the Federal payment). This is a practical way of emphasizing the value of the whole family as a unit.

However, the welfare mother who is a single parent and whose youngest child is over seven years old must go to work part time; and she must work full time when her youngest child is 14. This decision appears at first sight to be punitive and cruel, when we consider the 9 million households without fathers, many of them made fatherless by the old welfare system. But clearly the intention is to promote stability of family life by recognizing not only that a poor mother whose children are small must care for them, but also that when they reach school age she is entitled to a job to help her keep her family intact. And this concern that people must work if jobs are available, which is strongly felt by the very Americans who are most critical of welfare, may serve to override our historic reluctance to help *men* support their families if they are working but earning too little and need supplemental assistance to help them provide.

We have gone a step further, however, in the new, modern assumption of the proposed Better Jobs and Income Act that the principal family breadwinner, who is entitled to a job, may be either a man or a woman. In the future people may look back and realize that the important principle here was the tacit acceptance of the equality of a man and a woman with respect to work.

There are several other very good aspects to the proposed plan. For example, the poor single mother who, with her baby, stays with her own mother or family is recognized for the first time as an adult in her own right—as head of her own family unit and as such qualified to receive aid for herself and her child. This is particularly important for the many very young mothers who need both the support of older adults and the recognition that they are not children any more. But the plan also recognizes that a relative other than a parent—a grandmother, for example, or an aunt—may make a home for a child and provide her or him with loving care. Under the Carter plan, such a relative would qualify for welfare aid in support of the child.

The proposal also provides better for those who have no family—the single men and women, the widows and widowers without kin—people who have been thrust out of the labor market, sometimes very early, and who now fall outside the system of care for the needy until they reach old age. With even a modicum of help—enough to pay for room and perhaps board for these helpless single people—charitable organizations and social agencies within a community would be much more likely to help them further, so that instead of being left to starve in solitude, they may have some small place and human contact in a community.

I have no doubt that there will be many criticisms of every feature of this bill and of its cost as it passes from committee to committee and from conference to compromise within Congress. So we must keep our eyes firmly fixed on the central purpose—to give every able-bodied adult a chance to work for a living; to protect and support the family, instead of destroying it; and, by what we do for adults and children in need, to give dignity to every person in these United States. A system in which we grudge help to those who need it demeans not only those who receive that grudging help but also each of us who is fortunate enough not to need it.

It is shameful that we need feel cheated because we believe that others are ripping us off. A simpler, comprehensive system of administration can prevent that. It is heartbreaking to have a system designed to protect the helpless end up multiplying the numbers of the deserted and the fatherless. The proposed new system can change this. It is archaic to let our punitive self-righteousness harm those who, through no fault of their own, are out of work or too poorly paid to survive. And it is stupid to put primarily on well-employed men the burden of supporting through taxes the five living generations in our

society. We merely increase the burdens of the few by excluding women and minority members, the young, the partially
handicapped and the elderly from a chance to work, to produce and in turn to bear their share of caring for those who
cannot work at all.

We can do better than this. But it will take time and effort
and a very stubborn belief that women, as mothers, as wage
earners and as citizens, have a part to play in shaping the
future for their children and their children's children.

VII
New Directions

Bisexuality: A New Awareness

JANUARY 1975

The time has come, I think, when we must recognize bisexuality as a normal form of human behavior.

The whole question of sexual preference has for so long been taboo in our and most other Western societies that the subject of bisexuality has seldom been raised or, until very recently, frankly and openly discussed. The idea that a woman —or a man—is capable of loving members of both sexes simply does not occur to most people.

In our culture it is well-known that very young girls may go through a period of falling in love with another girl or an older, admired woman. Usually we treat this as a more or less harmless phase of adolescence that will pass as soon as a girl enters into livelier relationships with boys and young men. Boys too may go through a period when they feel closest to someone of their own sex, but we treat such relationships, especially if they involve sexual experimentation, much more gingerly, for any shadow of doubt cast on a male's heterosexuality may adversely affect people's attitude toward him throughout his life.

Occasionally the transition fails—as we see it. But for the most part men and women, conforming quite easily to the customs within which they were reared, confine themselves to a heterosexual choice of lovers, companions and mates. So the question is never asked whether, as adults, they could fall in love with a member of their own sex, and the question of bisexuality in sexual choice and love is ignored.

But now the gay liberation movement, by its protests and demands, has brought into full light of day the problems of

269

men and women who, following deep personal preference, do choose members of their own sex as lovers and living companions. This, I think, should open our minds to a clearer understanding not only of homosexuality but also of our human capacity to love members of both sexes.

All the liberation movements of the last decade have given voice to groups in our society—Blacks, ethnics, young people, women—who have banded together to protest against gross discrimination and to demand equal access to good jobs and fair pay, equal housing and rights within the community and, above all, dignity as individuals. Members of the gay movement have fitted into this wider category of protest as men and women who have been discriminated against—even violently rejected—because their sexual behavior differs from all that their relatives, their neighbors and friends and the public in general were brought up to believe is normal. What the men and women in the gay movement are now demanding is that we break through our prejudices and recognize their adult right to their own chosen social identity.

But there is not, and it seems unlikely that there will be, a bisexual liberation movement. For the truth is, bisexual men and women do not form a distinct group, since in fact we do not really recognize bisexuality as a form of behavior, normal or abnormal, in our society.

Instead we tend to divide people into two groups, each the mirror image of the other. By far the larger group includes all heterosexually oriented men and women, most of whom cannot even imagine falling in love with a member of their own sex. A very small group (though we do not know, as yet, how large it may be), simply reversing what we regard as normal, confine themselves to members of their own sex in their choice of lovers and companions.

Vaguely, however, we do recognize the existence of men and women who unfortunately, as we see it, fall in love with a homosexual of the opposite sex. It is by putting the devoted companions of many homosexuals into this indistinct third category that we explain to ourselves that homosexuals often are married and the fathers—or mothers—of children. These we tend to believe are not "real" homosexuals. This is a belief that follows along naturally enough from our cultural belief that homosexuals are heterosexuals in reverse—people who, like ourselves, are committed to loving members of only one sex but differing from the majority in the fact that their commitment is to members of their own sex.

Changing traditional attitudes toward homosexuality is in itself a mind-expanding experience for most people. But we shall not really succeed in discarding the strait jacket of our cultural beliefs about sexual choice if we fail to come to terms with the well-documented, normal human capacity to love members of both sexes.

Even a superficial look at other societies and some groups in our own society should be enough to convince us that a very large number of human beings—probably a majority— are bisexual in their potential capacity for love. Whether they will become exclusively heterosexual or exclusively homosexual for all their lives and in all circumstances or whether they will be able to enter into sexual and love relationships with members of both sexes is, in fact, a consequence of the way they have been brought up, of the particular beliefs and prejudices of the society they live in and, to some extent, of their own life history.

Only when the whole subject of sexual selection has been far removed in time or space has it been possible, until recently, to think and talk candidly about homosexuality. But even then we usually have not put all the facts together realistically.

People with a classical education know that among the ancient Greeks young boys were loved by older men and that among the Spartans a young and a mature soldier were paired as companions and lovers as a device to provide an army whose members would fight side by side to the death. But even knowing this, it is usually left out of account that the older men also had wives and children. Students of the Far East know that in many countries there was a monosexual phase for boys; much less is known about girls, mainly because most studies have been made by male scholars. Later the boys married and had children, and then as older men had love relationships with young men. But differentiating phases of life has been only one way in which bisexuality has been built into a great many cultures.

Students of social conditions in our own society have been well aware that in any all-male group—in a boys' school, in a prison or on a ship on a long voyage—men have taken other men as sexual partners. Similarly in all-female groups—in a girls' school, a prison or a religious community—intense though not necessarily overt sexual relations develop between women. But it is also perfectly well known that the sailor on shore actively pursues girls and that women, as soon as they are allowed to enter the main stream of living, fall in love with and marry men.

The remedy in recent times has been to do away with one-sex institutions as far as this is feasible. But the long prejudice against homosexuality has blinded us to the full implications of the facts. We recognize the fact that men and women, restricted by upbringing or circumstance to the exclusive company of their own sex, often will substitute members of their own sex for the opposite sex. Or we see such same-sex liaisons as a form of promiscuity in which the sex of the partner is irrelevant. Certainly we do not put such relations in the same category as choices made out of devoted love and the wish for permanent sexual companionship.

For the rest—in spite of great controversy about the causes and possible "cure" of homosexuality—it is generally assumed in our society that a few human beings reverse the expectations of heterosexual love, probably because of a trauma in childhood that made them fear or hate the opposite sex or, alternatively, deeply prefer the role of the opposite sex. And most people believe that homosexual preference as an individual's choice is no less exclusive and permanent than heterosexual preference.

Perhaps the freest development of bisexuality has come about in the past in periods and among groups in which the cultivation of individuality has been a central value. In the European Renaissance, particularly in court circles, men and women who were cultivated, leisured and deeply involved with one another experimented with a great variety of personal relationships as part of their exploration of a world in which politics, art, music, theater and intellectual concerns were complexly interwoven. In Elizabethan England, where young boys played all the feminine roles on the stage, the device of having a boy playing the romantic role of a girl disguised as a boy fall in love with a man had almost infinite possibilities of amusement for the court and the crowd alike.

At other times groups of writers, artists, musicians and men and women related to the theater have cultivated bisexuality out of a delight with personality, regardless of race or class or sex. The international clusters of artists gathered on the Left Bank in Paris before and after World War I and the Bloomsbury set in London, all of them creative, innovative men and women, were privately but quite frankly bisexual in their relationships. For many of them both the differences between men and women and differences between individuals in temperament and gift were the basis of love affairs of great intensity and meaning.

It took courage to break with Victorian prejudices and risk encounters with the savage laws against the practice of homosexuality, and the lives of these men and women, partly open to one another, were closed to the world. That many of them were married and loved and quarreled with their husbands and wives made them respectable. That many of them had passionate love affairs with the wives and husbands of others was scandalous but not outrageous. But a recognition that they also loved members of their own sex would have resulted in ostracism from the wider world in which so many of them played important roles. It is only very slowly—and often in the guise of fiction—that we have come to appreciate something of the complexity of their lives.

But times and our expectations have changed. In his recent book *Portrait of a Marriage*, Nigel Nicolson places at the center of the story of his parents' devoted marriage the diary and letters in which his mother recorded her long, passionate love affair with another woman. Vita Sackville-West, his mother, a member of a distinguished family, was a novelist and a poet; his father, Harold Nicolson, was a writer, a diplomat and for many years a Member of Parliament. Both were bisexual in their love relations. Theirs was a marriage founded on deep, abiding trust and a community of interest symbolized by the house and great garden they created together over a lifetime.

This and other biographies of creative men and women of that period are opening our eyes to a whole new aspect of our culture. For it is the first time in our English-speaking literary history that identified individuals, as opposed to fictional characters, have been treated as openly bisexual, capable of loving and relating to individuals of both sexes frankly and with the accent on both personality and sex. What is new is not bisexuality, but rather the widening of our awareness and acceptance of human capacities for sexual love.

Today the recognition of bisexuality, in oneself and in others, is part of the whole mid-20th-century movement to accord to each individual, regardless of race, class, nationality, age or sex, the right to be a person who is unique and who has a social identity that is worthy of dignity and respect.

At this time in the history of our earth there is no social

need to press any individual into parenthood. We can free men and women alike to live as persons—to elect single blessedness, to choose companionship with a member of their own or the opposite sex, to decide to live a fully communal life, to bring up children of their own or to be actively solicitous of other people's children and the children of the future. In the process, those who elect marriage and parenthood as their own fullest expression of love and concern for human life also will be freed. For they will know that they have been free to choose, and have chosen each other and a way of life together.

1. Crime: Broken Connections

MAY 1978

"That's terrible! That's a crime! Someone should do something about it!" How often have you heard that said—or said it yourself?

Heard apart from the act that triggered the reaction, these are just trite words. But like so many other well-worn phrases, they may carry a very heavy load of emotion—indignation, fear, anger. And better than many more learned definitions, they sum up people's response to crime the world over, in nations with modern, sophisticated penal codes and in tiny societies of a few hundred persons who still live by their own unwritten, customary law. A crime is something that people regard as very wrong—something terrible—that someone should do something about.

In our kind of society it is the police who should do something, and when we have reported what may be a crime to a law-enforcement officer we can, and usually do, put it out of our minds. Unless, of course, we happen to be the victim who has been robbed or assaulted or otherwise harmed. But sometimes what seems to a layperson to be a crime is not so in the law; then the police can take no action. At other times we would not consider reporting acts that every one of us knows very well are illegal, and the police too may close their eyes. During Prohibition almost every adult in town knew exactly where to buy a drink and how to contact a bootlegger. Today even young teen-agers in a city can easily find out where hard drugs are bought and sold more or less openly and with impunity.

What differs extremely around the world is the cultural

conception of what constitutes a crime, who should do something about it and what should be done. There are societies in which vulnerable persons, such as pregnant women, mourners, little children or men starting out on some large enterprise, must wear deterrent amulets or be magically charmed or ritually treated to protect them from danger—to ward off the evil eye, the angry ghost, the malicious curse, the enemy spear. Elsewhere, victims or their kin turn to the nearest sorcerer in search of vengeance. Or a malefactor may be banished from his community so that he has no one to back him up, no one to protect him in a time of need. Or the murderer may be obliged to take the place of his victim—become a husband to his victim's wife, a father to his victim's children, knowing that one day, when least expected, he too will be killed.

There seems to be no end to human ingenuity when it comes to defining what is a crime, and especially what should be done about it. In advanced civilizations the idea of some kind of penal code, clear and impersonal, is very ancient. But we only recently have begun to realize the extraordinarily arbitrary nature of both our private beliefs about crime and criminals and of our laws and to discover the depth of our emotional commitment to particular forms of punishment, legal and extralegal.

There are no societies that are totally free of crime. In every society, as far as we know, there are likely to be a very few individuals who cannot be socialized, that is, who cannot learn to control their violent, destructive impulses and who therefore are dangerous and endangered. In a very small society or in a stable, homogeneous small community where everyone knows a great deal about everyone else, the danger may be minimized by watchful awareness—not always successfully, to be sure, but most of the time.

The hazards are greater in a very populous and complex urban society. For the most part such asocial individuals are unidentifiable—unknown strangers until by some violent act they come into public view. In our society the life history of a person even with a long record of maladaptive or criminal acts may be known only superficially or in fragments, and often reform schools and penitentiaries are only too eager to rid themselves, on any pretext, of such endlessly troublesome prisoners. But the number of fundamentally violent or asocial individuals in our very large population is not great. Recently John Boone, the former Commissioner of Corrections in Massachusetts, estimated that in the whole United States there are no more than 5,000 to 6,000 such persons.

For the rest, we make our own criminals, and their crimes are congruent with the national culture we all share. It has been said that a people get the kind of political leadership they deserve. I think they also get the kinds of crime and criminals they themselves bring into being. As in every culture, it is a circular system. For instance, in a society in which people believe in sorcery, there undoubtedly will be sorcerers, and they in turn will foster effectively the practice of sorcery.

In our country white-collar crimes by educated, well-to-do and socially respected businessmen and professionals, juvenile delinquency at every social level, burglaries and armed robberies, muggings of defenseless old women and men, the prostitution of runaway teen-aged girls and boys, the drug dealing, the wife beating and child abuse, the hijackings, the senseless killing of unknown persons, the arson and vandalism that today stretch from factories and shops and public buildings to inner-city slums and suburban communities and even to the remotest rural places—all these and many other forms of crime are not simply accidental. They are the products of the way we organize the country, the way we both proclaim and reject social responsibility, the way we dichotomize our thinking about and treatment of human beings, protecting some privileged individuals from the consequences of their acts and punishing others whom from their earliest years we first neglect and then treat as expendable. Their behavior, like any-one else's, is an expression of our national culture for which all of us ultimately must take responsibility.

I believe we have concentrated too much on criminals, on the flaws in their character and the weaknesses in their back-ground, instead of asking what needs they serve and what general attitudes in our society—or in the whole of modern society—are reflected in their actions. I do not argue for the point of view that has confounded so many of our attempts at reform, namely, that because a society is ultimately re-sponsible for the behavior of its members, the individual crim-inal has been made a misfit who must not be held responsible for his acts.

Instead, I am asking what we are doing that is encouraging a rising tide of violence and crime and that has permitted men at the very top of national law-enforcement agencies— an attorney general of the United States and the long-time head of the FBI—to believe that it is right to deal harshly with criminals and at the same time that it is all right for them, and other men like them, to commit highly illegal acts.

I am asking also what has led us to avoid responsible action to bring about change. For there is a great deal of evidence that this is what we are doing. Consider, for example, the vast contemporary proliferation of insurance as a principal method of coping not only, very legitimately, with natural disasters, with illness, accident and death and with the needs of young families, but also with almost every form of delinquency and crime—including the damage our own children may inflict on the property of others.

Today insurance has become a highly organized, profitable way of accepting the existence of carelessness, irresponsibility, delinquency and almost every form of crime, from the de-struction or loss of property to the loss of life. Insurance pro-tects each of us individually—or at least those of us who can afford to buy this protection—from loss. In addition there are hidden costs, for businesses simply pass on to their customers the rising cost of insurance against shoplifting, hijacking, vandalism and other kinds of crime to which they are subject. But this still appears to be cheaper and easier for us than it would be to make the moral effort to alter attitudes and the conditions of living in which crime flourishes.

Would making such a moral effort be too high a price to pay?

I do not think so. But I believe the problem lies elsewhere.

What we are suffering from—and I do mean suffering—is a whole series of broken connections between different aspects of our behavior, our thinking and feeling. Changes, including vast changes in scale as our society has grown and become technologically sophisticated, have obscured the connections between our beliefs and our actions, have fragmented our awareness of one another. Consequently our response has been to turn away from the hard problems we have solved badly or left unsolved.

We value human rights, for example, but we do not see the connection between our rejection of the elderly and the handicapped and whatever of value they have to offer us, on the one hand, and on the other the mugging of the old by street children and the scandalous exploitation of the elderly in lonely rooms or frightening welfare "hotels" or nursing homes. We believe that the nation's children are the keepers of the future, but we do not see the connection between juvenile crime and living conditions of families in inner cities or the poverty-stricken countryside, between such crime and our deteriorating schools in which children are demeaned and punished because we have failed them as teachers and interpreters of our culture. We do not see the connection between the very high rates of joblessness among young people who have few skills and no resources and who have lost their readiness to learn and the extremely high rate of crime, especially violent crime, among these adolescents and young adults.

The right to a second—or a third or fourth—new chance is central in our culture. But we have lost the connection between our perceptions of whole groups in our population—particularly those whom we have already put down, ripped off and denigrated as human beings by the conditions of life to which they are condemned because they are poor, members of minority groups or illegal immigrants, young, unskilled and feared—and our handling of criminals. We have lost the connection between the conditions in the places of detention for young offenders (among whom are the runaways, so often children already offended against) and in the reformatories and penitentiaries, where once optimistic reformers hoped that prisoners would be treated as penitents, and the increasing number of persons, today women as well as men, who have become hopelessly addicted to a life of crime.

But there is still another, a further and final step. We have lost the connection between our ambiguous apparent admiration for and rejection of criminals whom we believe to be irreparably violent and our increasingly loud insistence that the only legitimate response to violence is violence.

In our private lives we insist that citizens must retain the right to be armed and to have at hand the lethal weapons that threaten the lives not only of intruders but also of members of their families and, indeed, anyone against whom an individual may turn in a temporary excess of rage or fear. In parts of the country where hunting still is a sanctioned traditional sport, the young may be instructed in the care of guns and taught to respect them as dangerous. But not so in cities.

And almost everywhere, law-enforcement officers have spent millions of dollars on sophisticated weapons. But what has happened is that individual policemen have become correspondingly warier of being attacked and more trigger-ready to shoot to kill before they know whether the suspected wrongdoer is also armed and about to attack.

When the Supreme Court effectively abolished the death

sentence for crime, it seemed possible that we might now reconsider the whole connection between violent crime and violent retribution. Instead, the legislatures of many states are attempting to draft new state laws that will permit us, after all, to go on legally killing members of our own society, members of our own human species, whom we have utterly rejected.

Can we do this now without also strengthening the belief that lethal violence can be legitimate? I do not believe so. Far from providing a deterrent, the reinstated death penalty—for different crimes in different states—will increase the belief in violence not only among ordinary criminals but also among those disturbed and distorted persons who seek some highly publicized goal by means of arson, kidnapping or hijacking and killing well-known individuals or groups of helpless, uninvolved persons, children and adults.

Is there no alternative?

I believe there is, providing we will accept the responsibility for our decisions and our subsequent actions.

2. *Crime: A Life for a Life*

JUNE 1978

As Americans we have declared ourselves to be champions of human rights in the world at large. But at home . . .

At home the Congress and the majority of our state legislatures have been hurrying to pass new laws to ensure that persons convicted of various violent crimes (but not the same ones in all states) may be—or must be—executed.

In my view, it is a sorry spectacle to see a great nation publicly proclaiming efforts to modify violence and to protect human rights in distant parts of the world and at the same time devoting an inordinate amount of time and energy at every level of government to ensure that those men and women convicted of capital offenses will be condemned to death and executed. Decisions to carry out such vengeful, punitive measures against our own people would reverberate around the world, making a cold mockery of our very real concern for human rights and our serious efforts to bring about peace and controlled disarmament among nations.

If we do in fact take seriously our chosen role as champions of human rights, then certainly we must also reinterpret drastically the very ancient law of "a life for a life" as it affects human beings in our own society today. I see this as a major challenge, especially for modern women.

But first we must understand where we are now.

In the late 1960s we lived through a kind of twilight period when, without any changes in our laws, men and women were condemned to death but the sentences were not carried out. Those who had been condemned were left to sit and wait—often for years.

In 1972 there was a brief period when it seemed that capital punishment had finally been abolished in the whole United States, as it has been in most of the modern countries of western Europe and in many other countries. For then, in the case of *Furman v. Georgia*, the Supreme Court of the United States ruled that existing laws whereby certain convicted criminals were condemned to death were haphazard and arbitrary in their application and constituted cruel and unusual punishment, which is prohibited by the Eighth Amendment to the Constitution. True, the Court was divided; even the five justices who supported the ruling were quite sharply divided in their reasoning. Nevertheless, *Furman v. Georgia* saved the lives of 631 persons in prisons across the country who were under sentence of death.

It seemed that we had passed a watershed.

But we were quickly disillusioned. The Supreme Court had not yet abolished capital punishment; the justices merely had ruled out the discriminatory manner in which the current laws were applied. As Justice William O. Douglas pointed out in his concurring opinion, the existing system allowed "the penalty to be discriminatorily and disproportionately applied to the poor, the Blacks and the members of unpopular groups."

In response, lawmakers in many states—often pushed by their constituents and by law-enforcement agencies—tried to meet the objections by means of new and contrasting laws. Some of these laws made the death penalty mandatory; no exceptions or mitigating circumstances were possible. Others made the death penalty discretionary, that is, they provided very specific guidelines for defining mitigating circumstances that should be taken into account. The reason was that experts differed radically in their opinions as to what the justices of the Supreme Court would find acceptable in revised laws.

In their haste, these lawmakers missed their chance to think in quite other terms.

Meanwhile, of course, cases were tried and a few women and many men were once more condemned. In July, 1976, the principles underlying the new laws were tested as the Supreme Court of the United States announced rulings in five of these cases, upholding three discretionary death-penalty statutes and ruling against two that imposed mandatory capital punishment. As a result, the death sentences of 389 persons in 19 states were later reduced to life imprisonment.

But the lawmaking and the convictions have continued. At the end of 1977, the number of condemned prisoners in the death rows of penitentiaries in the 33 states that then had capital-punishment laws amounted to 407—five women and 402 men—divided almost evenly between white Americans and Black or Hispanic Americans. Two were Native Americans—Indians—and concerning six, even this meager background information was lacking. Most were poor and ill educated, too unimportant to be permitted to enter into plea bargaining and too poor to hire the expensive legal talent that makes possible very different treatment in the courts for more affluent and protected individuals.

In early 1977 one man, Gary Gilmore, whose two attempts at suicide were given extravagant publicity, finally was executed in the midst of glaring national publicity in the mass media. Looking back at this one sordidly exploited event, can anyone picture how we would react if, without discussion, it were suddenly decided to execute *all* the death row prisoners who were without resources to prolong their lives?

What we are much more likely to do, I think, is to seesaw between the old, old demand for drastic retribution for crimes against human beings that very rightly rouse us to anger, fear and disgust and our rather special American belief that almost everyone (except the suspected criminal we catch on the run and kill forthwith) is entitled to a second chance. So we make harsh laws, convict some of the people who break them—and then hesitate. What next?

Every month the number of those convicted, sentenced and waiting grows. Violent criminals, they become the victims of our very ambiguous attitudes toward violence and our unwillingness to face the true issues.

The struggle for and against the abolition of capital punishment has been going on in our country and among enlightened peoples everywhere for well over a century. In the year before the Civil War the fight to end the death penalty was led in America by men like Horace Greeley, who also was fighting strongly to abolish slavery, and by a tiny handful of active women like New England's Dorothea Dix, who was fighting for prison reform. In those years three states—Michigan in 1847, Rhode Island in 1852 and Wisconsin in 1853—renounced the use of capital punishment, the first jurisdictions in the modern world to do so.

Both sides claim a primary concern for human rights. Those who demand that we keep—and carry out—the death penalty speak for the victims of capital crimes, holding that it is only just that murderers, kidnappers, rapists, hijackers and other violent criminals should suffer for the harm they have done and so deter others from committing atrocious crimes.

In contrast, those who demand that we abolish capital punishment altogether are convinced that violence breeds violence—that the death penalty carried out by the State against its own citizens in effect legitimizes willful killing. Over time, their concern has been part of a much more inclusive struggle for human rights and human dignity. They were among those who fought against slavery and they have been among those who have fought for the civil rights of Black Americans, of immigrants and of ethnic minorities and Native Americans, for the rights of prisoners of war as well as for the prisoners in penitentiaries, for the rights of the poor, the unemployed and the unemployable, for women's rights and for the rights of the elderly and of children.

Now, I believe, we can—if we will—put this all together

and realize that in our kind of civilization "a life for a life" need not mean destructive retribution, but instead the development of new forms of community in which, because all lives are valuable, what is emphasized is the prevention of crime and the protection of all those who are vulnerable.

The first step is to realize that in our society we have permitted the kinds of vulnerability that characterize the victims of violent crime and have ignored, where we could, the hostility and alienation that enter into the making of violent criminals. No rational person condones violent crime, and I have no patience with sentimental attitudes toward violent criminals. But it is time that we open our eyes to the conditions that foster violence and that ensure the existence of easily recognizable victims.

Americans respond generously—if not always wisely—to the occurrence of natural catastrophes. But except where we are brought face to face with an unhappy individual or a family in trouble, we are turned off by the humanly far more desperate social catastrophes of children who are trashed by the schools—and the local community—where they should be learning for themselves what it means and how it feels to be a valued human being. We demean the men and women who are overwhelmed by their inability to meet their responsibilities to one another or even to go it alone, and we shut out awareness of the fate of the unskilled, the handicapped and the barely tolerated elderly. As our own lives have become so much more complex and our social ties extraordinarily fragile, we have lost any sense of community with others whose problems and difficulties and catastrophes are not our own.

We do know that human lives are being violated—and not only by criminals. But at least we can punish criminals. That is a stopgap way. But it is not the way out of our dilemma.

We also know that in any society, however organized, security rests on accepted participation—on what I have called here a sense of community in which everyone shares.

Up to the present, the responsibility for working out and maintaining the principles on which any code of law must depend and for the practical administration of justice has been primarily a male preoccupation. At best, women working within this framework have been able sometimes to modify and sometimes to mitigate the working of the system of law.

Now, however, if the way out is for us to place the occurrence of crime and the fate of the victim and of the criminal consciously within the context of our way of living and our view of human values, then I believe liberated women have a major part to play and a wholly new place to create for themselves in public life as professional women, as volunteers and as private citizens concerned with the quality of life in our nation. For it is women who have constantly had to visualize in personal, human terms the relationships between the intimate details of living and the setting in which living takes place. And it is this kind of experience that we shall need in creating new kinds of community.

Women working in new kinds of partnership with men should be able to bring fresh thinking into law and the administration of justice with a greater awareness of the needs of individuals at different stages of life and the potentialities of social institutions in meeting those needs. What we shall be working toward is a form of deterrence based not on fear of punishment—which we know is ineffective, even when the punishment is the threat of death—but on a shared way of living.

It will be a slow process at best to convince our fellow citizens that justice and a decline in violence can be attained only by the development of communities in which the elderly and children, families and single persons, the gifted, the slow and the handicapped can have a meaningful place and live with dignity and in which rights and responsibilities are aspects of each other. And I believe that we can make a start only if we have a long view, but know very well that what we can do today and tomorrow and next year will not bring us to utopia. We cannot establish instant security; we can only build for it step by step.

We must also face the reality that as far as we can foresee there will always be a need for places of confinement—prisons of different kinds, to be frank—where individuals will have to be segregated for short periods, for longer periods or even, for some, for a whole lifetime. The fear that the violent person will be set free in our communities (as we all know happens all too often under our present system of law) is an important component in the drive to strengthen—certainly not to abolish —the death penalty. For their own protection as well as that of others, the few who cannot control their violent impulses and, for the time being, the larger number who have become hopelessly violent must be sequestered.

But we shall have to reconsider the whole question of what it means to be confined under some form of restraint, whether for a short period or for a lifetime. Clearly, prisons can no longer be set apart from the world. Prisoners must have some real and enduring relationship to a wider community if they are to have and exercise human rights. Whether as a way station or as a permanent way of living for a few persons, prison life must in some way be made meaningful.

There is today a Prisoners Union, organized by former prisoners, as well as a variety of local unions within many prisons. We shall have to draw on the knowledge and experience of groups of this kind. Here again I believe that women, who have not been regularly and professionally involved in traditional prison practices, may be freer to think about and construct new practices than male experts working alone.

The tasks are urgent and difficult. Realistically we know we cannot abolish crime. But we can abolish crude and vengeful treatment of crime. We can abolish—as a nation, not just state by state—capital punishment. We can accept the fact that prisoners, convicted criminals, are hostages to our own human failures to develop and support a decent way of living. And we can accept the fact that we are responsible to them, as to all living beings, for the protection of society, and especially responsible for those among us who need protection for the sake of society.

Many Rights to Life

JULY 1978

Everywhere in the United States—indeed, I believe, in every part of the world—thinking women and men are struggling with the problems of their own new awareness of emerging rights to life and the responsibilities they must entail. As always in the past, these new rights are related both to the present state of our knowledge and to our ongoing way of living, that is, our culture. They are affirmed and must be supported by a shared social ethic—and there lies the most difficult problem.

Clean air and safe water have become rights to life for every person in the world almost within our own living memory. Lakes and rivers and the oceans touch many shores; the circulating winds know no bounds of countries or continents; and people far from some source of pollution may still come to harm. In the past, privileged persons could flee from a danger spot of plague or yellow fever. Today we have created far more insidious pollutants; but we also know what must be done to control them. And so clean air and safe water have become rights to life for all living things, not only for human beings.

But there are also certain rights to life that are so very ancient, so universally human too, that we do not even think of them as "rights." For who within any cultural group would deny them?

There is, for example, the right of young, dependent beings to receive nurturing care—safety, shelter, warmth, food and, above all, love and comfort and instruction. Reciprocally, there is the right of full-grown adults to give and to share nurturing care—to have the means of providing others with safety and shelter, warmth and food, affection and comfort and instruction, in full measure. There is also the right of every individual to a recognized place to live in privacy as well as in communication with a family, a neighborhood and a community.

In addition, in every society I know of, rights to life have included rights to die—the right, for example, to die in accordance with the customs of one's own society, to be mourned and remembered and then, in time, to be incorporated into myth or history or, as an individual, to vanish into the unremembered past. So the outcast from his own society —the extreme maverick and the unreliable, uncontrollable person—lost not only the right to a good life but also the right to a good death. Rights to life and rights to death always have been bound up together.

But now we are witnessing a bitter struggle between those Americans who, however reluctantly, accept the present necessity for allowing abortions and others who would deny the right of decision about an abortion to all women—or, in any case, to women who cannot back up their decision with their own money. What is significant is that those who support the Right to Life movement would have us believe that there is but one overriding right to life, which is simple, indivisible and absolute. This is specifically the right of the conceived but unborn infant to emerge alive from the womb.

Many Right to Life adherents also would like to prevent a pregnant woman from learning by such methods as amniocentesis—a medical process, not without risk, in which the amniotic fluid is tapped and analyzed—whether a fetus has been harmed by the mother's German measles infection, for instance, or has (or has not) been spared one of several severe heritable defects. A generation ago we knew only enough to counsel a high-risk couple not to have children. Today, knowing more, such a couple can try for a normal baby, but need not face the tragedy of having predestined a living being to defective survival.

Where it can be made, I believe, this is a responsible choice. But members of the Right to Life movement will not accept this solution as evidence of prenatal nurturing care. And at the extreme they will not even acknowledge the right of a woman—or a man and a woman, as a responsible couple—to prevent conception.

Their propaganda has also touched off, perhaps only indirectly, a kind of irresponsible, lunatic violence. Leaders of the National Right to Life Committee and of related groups insist that they do not condone illegal, especially violent, activities and have disclaimed any responsibility. Nevertheless, over the last 18 months or so there have been many attacks on women's clinics where abortions may be obtained and counseling is given. At least five clinics have been forced to close or move because of severe and costly damage caused by fire bombs, chemical bombs and fires. Elsewhere unruly demonstrators have broken into clinics where they have harassed the staff and patients. Until early this year damage was confined to property—to buildings and valuable equipment. But in mid-February, 1978, an employee of a clinic in Cleveland was temporarily blinded in such an assault.

How are we to understand the blind anger—anger that may at any time explode into violence—that characterizes the behavior of many individuals on the opposing sides of this conflict? It is not enough to say that though they are irrevocably opposed to each other's point of view, people on both sides believe deeply and sincerely that they are acting in good conscience to protect the sanctity of life. It is true, but certainly not enough!

It seems to me that in debating this one conspicuous issue, people everywhere are indirectly trying to clarify for themselves and for one another a whole series of issues that represent emergent rights to life, not just for ourselves as Americans, but for all human beings anywhere. I have already spoken of the right of every person to have access to clean air and safe water. But there are many other rights. There is the right also not merely to have access to food—or to ways of obtaining it, as in the most distant past—but to have food that is good and preserved in safe ways.

There is the right to decent shelter within a sheltering community. Once human communities were formed to protect their members not only against hostile strangers but also against the isolation of unpopulated space. Today human beings have to be protected against the hostility and isolation of vastly overcrowded space, within which it is virtually impossible to form any kind of community.

There is the right to have access to preventive medicine and the related right to rehabilitation after injury arising from accident or illness. These rights build upon very ancient rights to care, using our most modern knowledge of medicine and our growing understanding of human adaptive capacities.

Yet there are children in our cities, living close to clinics, who are not being given the most elementary preventive medical care. Equally, in the most faraway places—for example, on the upper reaches of the Sepik River in the new country of Papua New Guinea—children have been attacked by "modern" diseases like polio, from which they once were protected by geographical isolation. Now they require access to the same preventive and rehabilitative care as children living in urban civilizations.

There is the right to a chosen sexual identity. This is truly an emerging right to life, and one that we must expect will lead to deep conflict. Historically many societies have recognized one or another variation in sexual identification and have expressed this by institutionalizing a variant cluster of behavior, as Plains Indians institutionalized in different ways the role of the *berdache*, a strong man who chose to assume the role of a woman. But no society that I know of has as yet institutionalized the right of *all* individuals to choose and live out a chosen sexual preference.

You yourself will surely identify other rights to life that are at risk because they are new or because we need to re-think and reinterpret them as, increasingly, we have to think of belonging to a world society as well as to our own national culture.

And I believe that, as you think about these rights to life, for which each of us must take some responsibility, you will see that our greatest difficulties lie, not in recognizing them, but in articulating an ethic within which we can carry out our responsibilities, and in developing an approach that will strengthen and reinforce the openness of our plural society so that we and all people can enjoy our human rights to life.

In Western countries we have long accepted the Judeo-Christian commandment "Thou shalt do no murder," the meaning of which we are beginning to alter and amplify in our everyday life with the Biblical paraphrase "Thou shalt not kill."

This also has long been amplified, in the Old Testament and especially in the New Testament, by the command-ment "Thou shalt love thy neighbor as thyself." What is changing in our understanding of this commandment is our awareness that only some of our neighbors live next door and include a few people who have known us from the day of our birth—or even "from the day your mother told me you were coming," as an elderly neighbor once said to me, a small child. We know now that other neigh-bors are strangers living half the world away, people of different races and cultures whom we shall never know in person, but with whom we necessarily share concern and re-sponsibility for children not yet conceived, our heirs in later centuries.

I believe we can create a viable ethic based on these com-mandments.

The danger lies elsewhere, and almost equally with absolutists who want to hold on to the past and absolutists who want to bring the future into being now, immediately. And it is this conflict between absolutists who take opposing stands—and into whose arena we all inevitably are drawn from time to time—that generates passionate and implacable anger and hatred, the will to destroy the "enemy," the will to violence that could destroy us all.

This brings me back to the conflict between those who support the Right to Life movement and the many groups that try to support a woman's right to have an abortion—to choose for herself whether and when she will carry and bear a child. The Right to Life people, it seems to me, are tied to a past when, because women died so young their reproductive period was very short (only about 15 years in the late Middle Ages) and because so many children could not survive, there was always the danger that there might not be enough people to carry on the world's work.

Looking around them at an overcrowded world in which there are so many children who are in terrible need, so many who are unwanted, neglected and abused, so many who seem to have no chance, those who favor abortion want to hurry the day into the present when every child will be well born.

This is not the way. We cannot hold on to the past and we cannot bring about any future in which we can take pride and joy simply by fiat. We can only bring about conflict, and this, at the very least, distracts us from our good purposes, namely to implement rights to life in a whole world of plural societies.

There is another way. We can rescind—and stop making—laws that prevent freedom of choice: the right of each individual to make free choices and the right to let others make theirs, different from yours and mine. Our ancestors' earliest experience in the New World—the kind of experience we celebrate each glorious July Fourth—became the basis for an ethic that protects freedom of conscience, freedom to speak out and freedom to listen, and freedom to act according to one's conscience. As we learn to take action in support of these freedoms, we can, I believe, take the first steps toward the 21st-century task of bringing the rights to life together in some coherent whole.

1. Adoption: Adopting Parents, Adopted Children— a Real Family?

SEPTEMBER 1978

How many families do you know, among your own relatives and close friends, in which there is an adopted child—a child who has completely become a member of her new family but who has no kinship ties at all to her adoptive parents? Probably you can think of several families, some of them with more than one adopted daughter or son. Most Americans think adoption is a good thing.

Recently it has also become quite common for a husband to adopt his wife's children born of an earlier marriage, especially if they are still small. They know who their birth father is, but usually they carry their adoptive father's name. Far more rarely, as yet, a wife may adopt her husband's children born of another marriage. In one such case the judge hearing the woman's petition to adopt was frankly puzzled. "Why are you doing this?" he inquired. "It isn't necessary. It doesn't change anything."

"Oh, but it does," the adopting mother insisted. "It makes us all one family—a *real* family!"

For us, as Americans, this—making a real family—is at the heart of adoptions, particularly those about which we hear most often in which the birth parents are neither relatives nor friends of the adopting family, but strangers unknown to the adopting parents and the adopted children alike. Taking these children, often as young infants, to become our own children, we pray that they in turn will accept us as their true parents. We want to create a real family, and one, we

298

hope, that will be less troubled than are so many real—that is, birth—families.

Nowadays adoptive parents are counseled to explain to the child as early as possible that she was adopted and for this very reason is especially precious. However, not so long ago the fact of adoption was one of the best-kept social secrets—until the day the tale was told. Naturally, every adult close to the family and almost every neighbor knew the truth. But they honored the illusion and tacitly conspired with the new parents to keep the secret. Then all too often it was another child—a taunting child who had heard whispered gossip—who broke the news: "You don't really belong. You're adopted!" And all too often this news shattered the fragile identity of the family and traumatized everyone—parents and children—who had believed that their family was "real." Only a fortunate few ever recovered completely.

Partly in rebellion against painful experiences of this kind, many young couples over the last generation have deliberately adopted children who are so startlingly unlike each other and the adoptive parents that there can be no possible doubt that theirs is a family formed by choice, not by birth. It is a practice that has distressed social workers in adoption agencies, who had been trained to believe that a good match between parents and children was necessary for the adoptive relationship to work out successfully. Disregarding this, many prospective parents sought out not only American-born Black or Hispanic babies for adoption, but also Japanese, Korean, Chinese or Vietnamese infants or the mixed-race children fathered and abandoned by our soldiers during foreign wars.

The obvious physical difference certainly did away with one kind of secrecy. But the aim remained the same. The child's birth parents were even more remote, strange and untraceable. And the new parents hoped that with so much out in the open, the adults who chose and the infants who were chosen—because they were *not* required to match physically—

would be joined together through shared love as a real family.

This is a daydream it would be very easy for almost any of us to share. What very few of us realize is that it is a very American daydream. The dilemma of wanting and not having a child—or of lacking many healthy children—is virtually universal. But in different societies people have found the most various solutions. Ours is only one, and it is a rare and unusual solution at that.

In general, it provided a humane and workable answer to the problems of a great many married couples who have longed for children, and to the problems of children in desperate need of a family. However, even good social institutions are open to criticism, and adoption as we have institutionalized it is no exception.

From the beginning, many prospective parents who have been rejected by placement agencies, for whatever reason, have looked for black-market babies, a practice that has often fostered corruption and sometimes has led to blackmail. Other prospective parents have objected strenuously because they have been refused a child of another race or ethnic background or even of a religion other than their own. In still other cases the rigid separation of foster care and adoption, as we all know, has led to tragedies for caring adults and the children they love. And finally, today there are many adults adopted as babies who want to know something about their origins: who their birth parents were, why they were given up for adoption, whether they have sisters and brothers. Yet our present laws forbid the breaking of silence on this whole subject.

Have we become too rigid? Can we learn from the solutions others have devised?

Everywhere in the world, societies are built on the expectation that men and women will marry and have children of both sexes. The preference for a son (or many sons) or for a daughter (or many daughters) varies widely, but the desire and the need for daughters and sons are taken for granted.

Some Balinese villages retired a man from citizenship—that is, from active participation in village affairs—if he produced four daughters in succession and then, after another four years, still had produced no son. In traditional China, a young wife felt secure as a new member of her husband's family only after she had borne a healthy son. But at the same time in China, daughters who married out and wives who married in gave a family access to a double network of relationships that might extend far across the country. And in societies in which the preferred marriage form is an exchange of sisters, a father who has no daughter to give in exchange for a wife for his son may have to pay very heavily to make up for the deficiency.

In many societies a woman or a man who has never borne or begotten a child is regarded as an incomplete or permanently immature human being. But societies also may deny marriage and parenthood to certain people. For example, among the Iatmul of Papua New Guinea, a deaf-mute girl often followed an older sister into marriage and was warmly regarded as a good wife and mother. But a deaf-mute man, however handsome and hard-working, could not find a sexual partner; however skilled as a craftsman, he was denied recognition as an artist by other men. In older Manus, the situation was reversed. No man wanted a deaf-mute wife, since she would be unable to hear and respond to his verbal ranting, but a deaf-mute man who wanted to marry had no difficulty in winning an able wife.

Given the omnipresent need for descendants and the rejection of some individuals as inadequate, it is not surprising that people everywhere have worked out some form of adoption to obtain a longed-for daughter or son and that some societies have greatly elaborated on the possibilities of adoption.

In many Western societies, godparents are familiar parental surrogates. Children know that they will be taken care of should their parents die—always a terrifying possibility where epidemics can devastate a community. In peasant Haiti, godparents must back up their godchildren, and it is said that godchildren in turn must serve their godparents in heaven as they served their parents on earth.

Adoption stresses election. In most situations adults elect to adopt a child, and children have little to say in the matter. However, although contemporary discussions ignore the possibility, sometimes a child may initiate an adoption. In some societies, as in Polynesia, where there are large kin groups —and sometimes in our own society—children in village communities may choose a home other than their own and obstinately insist on living there until at last the adults give in. I also remember how in Bali, in the 1930s, a small boy in Sanur found favor in the eyes of an American dancer; soon afterward he arrived at her nearby home, accompanied by relatives bearing handsome gifts, and announced that he wished to become the woman's adopted son.

This kind of junior selection shades into the many kinds of apprenticeship found in societies without formal schooling for children. There a boy—or a girl, for that matter—who wants to learn some specialized skill tries to become an apprentice to an expert and, once accepted, becomes in many respects that person's child.

In older, traditional France, adoption was, in an important sense, a contract between a whole family—not merely the childless couple—and the person who was to be adopted. Family members had to agree to the adoption, which affected their rights to inheritance, and the arrangement could be formally completed only when the adopted child reached legal maturity and consented to become a member of that family.

Adoption may also be a desperate measure taken for entirely different reasons. Formerly in certain parts of China, poverty-stricken parents sometimes adopted a daughter from an equally poor family to become the child-nurse and playmate of their son and eventually his wife. Or well-to-do parents mindful of their responsibilities for a son who was simple, mildly disturbed or physically incapacitated, sometimes chose to adopt a strong and able girl who would later, as a wife, take over responsibility for her less able husband. In traditional China a woman at marriage ceased to be a member of her birth family; adoption into her future husband's family was one step in a predestined direction.

Nevertheless, in spite of great diversity in the forms of adoption and the satisfactions people have sought through adoption, the commonest formal and articulate reasons for initiating adoption have arisen from the needs and aspirations of adults—the wish for an heir to carry on the family name and the family business, the need for young people to work the land and to provide for the elderly, the need for someone to tend the graves of the dead and to carry out the rituals of mourning on behalf of the living and the dead.

But until recently children without families, like old people without families, had no rights. Response to the desperate needs of the foundling, the orphan without close relatives, the abandoned and the grossly neglected child was left to the charity of religious orders, to the usually unsympathetic authority of local governments and to various exploitative interests.

Few people today realize that Americans had no tradition in English law to provide precedents on which we could draw in developing our own system of adoption. Adoption was not practiced in England. And, curiously, it was out of the anarchy in the treatment of dependent children that we developed our very special attitudes toward adoption and laws supporting our beliefs.

Earlier in our history, children as well as men and women were shipped to the New World as indentured servants, and children were sent to live and work on plantations and farms long after the practice of adult indenture was abandoned,

304 ASPECTS OF THE PRESENT

partly because the children were helpless and there were very few resources—outside of private charity—on which to draw for the care of children without families. Some children were lucky. The families to which they were sent accepted them not just as small laborers but also as members of a family community, with rights to physical care, education and affection. A great many others, about whose fate we know relatively little even today, were simply exploited.

Children—as well as slaves and women and Native Americans and other desperately exploited groups—began to benefit by a growing sense of outrage and efforts at reform in the mid-19th century. Some of the worst practices affecting children were controlled by new laws. But the development of an ethic centering on children and practices for the protection of dependent children remained almost up to the present in the hands of private agencies.

And in this development two ideas have reinforced each other: the idea that social experience outweighs inheritance in determining a person's character and personality; and the idea that by sealing off a child's past and giving her a suitable family in the present, her future can be assured. On this foundation we have erected the complex structure of adoption, which was—and is—intended to provide parents with children and children with parents in "real" families.

Today our most basic beliefs about adoption—that children should "match" their adoptive parents, that an adopted child should not know who her birth parents were, that foster parents may not adopt their foster children—are under attack from all sides. And now we must face the question, Where do we go from here?

2. Adoption: In the Best Interests of the Child

OCTOBER 1978

In the best interests of the child . . .

This very formal phrase, so often repeated by legislators, judges, social workers and almost everyone else concerned with policies affecting the care of children in need of homes and families and loving care, expresses the intent of decisions about adoption and foster care. It reflects an ideal and a view of childhood in which Americans have long taken pride. The child herself, we believe, should be central in our thinking about how to meet the needs of children.

The reality is something else.

The most hopeful thing is that so many young people are trying to work out new ideas. But when I consider the difficulties we ourselves have created in our efforts to cope with the admittedly complex problems of adoption and foster care, I know we still have far to go. It is true that Americans pioneered earlier in this century in the development of policies and practices we hoped would genuinely protect children. But so many of us were—and still are—perfectly content to take pride in the ideal without asking about current adoption practices.

Only if you are trying to solve some actual, very pressing problem connected with adoption or foster care do you begin to discover what a long and frustrating process is involved— with very little assurance that the outcome will be what you hope. For example, if you are foster parents who passionately want to adopt the child for whom you have long since become Mom and Dad. Or if you are a social worker in an agency concerned with children and are trying to "free" a child legally—that is, break the bonds with birth parents who have deserted her—so that she will become eligible for adoption. Or if you are prospective adoptive parents who have decided to adopt children of another race, another nationality or ethnic group or even from another state or region of our own country. In all these circumstances you will find that there are serious difficulties along the way to adoption.

And you will face problems if you are a single woman or man and believe you are quite able to take responsibility for an adopted girl or boy. Or if you are a couple with a modest income and need financial assistance to pay for the adoption procedures in court or for the continuing medical and educational needs of a child. Or if you and your husband decide that you have the courage, patience and feeling for the special skills you will need to bring up an adopted youngster who is blind or deaf or spastic or angry at the whole world or, for that matter, who may perhaps be a mathematical genius. If you are in any of these situations, *then* you discover the extraordinary obstacle courses we have set up in the way of almost anyone who takes seriously our ideal of childhood and attempts to put this ideal into practice with a child who is in immediate, desperate need of parents to love her and teach her, care for her and enjoy her.

Nevertheless, within a narrow and quite rigid framework we do have a history of many successful family-oriented—rather than child-oriented—adoptions in which carefully selected childless couples, after long study, were permitted to adopt carefully selected children. Usually—but not always—the latter are infants whose parents are unmarried and are surrendered by their mothers soon after birth. And we were proud of one innovation—the legal fiction by which the adopted child was reborn to her new, adoptive parents. That is, she was given a new birth certificate that provided her with a new name and a new set of legitimate parents. The records that connected her with her earlier past—at least with her birth mother, her place of birth and her original name, as well as, perhaps, some family or medical history—were sealed, presumably forever, for everyone's (but particularly the child's) protection.

This practice, which seemed eminently safe and sensible, provided a model for handling adoption in a number of other countries. But today it has blown up a tempest. Adults who were adopted as unknowing infants now insist that it is their human right to know who they "really" are, where they came from and who their birth mother is. Curiously, few of them seem to worry about their birth father and his ancestors. They wonder whether they have brothers and sisters, and sometimes are afraid that they may unwittingly commit incest.

Nowadays many people are searching for their roots in the past. One difficulty for all adopted children who have been "reborn" is that they cannot reach out and touch their own roots anywhere. Perhaps it wouldn't help to find your birth mother—but it might. Often adopted children hesitate to start the long, weary search, or try to keep it a secret; they fear that their adoptive parents may see it as a rejection of years of loving care. But usually such fears are unfounded; in an increasing number of cases, adoptive parents have helped in the search. And adult adoptees, released from daydreams and nightmares about what may lie in the past—because they have searched the records and managed reunions—have gained the freedom to choose to belong to the family that chose them. In this they are like millions of immigrants who chose freely to become Americans and thus share the American past with every other citizen.

Fortunately, the problem of sealed records and unknown parentage is one that can be solved. The English passed their first laws regulating adoption in the 1920s, in response to the needs of war orphans of World War I. At that time they took over the practice of sealed records. But now, after some 50 years' experience, they have passed a new law that allows an

18-year-old adoptee to sit down with a special counselor and learn the facts of her past.

True, this may work hardship for some birth parents who counted on remaining unknown, but others will have the joy of knowing how a child given up long ago has fared. And certainly adoptees themselves will have a much surer sense of identity. From now on in England, under the new law birth parents and adoptive parents will be aware from the beginning that the adopted child, on reaching the age of 18, will have the right to know her own history. Incorporating this awareness of an adopted child's right to such knowledge is now an essential part of the English adoption plan.

Other countries—for example, Israel and Finland—have moved with the times and now permit disclosure of information concerning the family and past of an adopted child. After all, as women have become liberated in Western countries, people have been giving up their punitive attitudes toward single mothers and their children. I believe this is the decision we too must make. Long talks with adult adoptees who have given years of their lives to the frustrating search for their past have convinced me that we cannot continue to let the past rule the present. Surely if a young adult who has grown up with love has the strength to accept the reality of her beginnings, her birth parents and adoptive parents can do so as well!

But how shall we accomplish this?

This question brings us to the much more serious—indeed, almost overwhelmingly difficult—problems of adoption and foster care, the problems that arise from the fact that in our country child welfare is the primary responsibility of each state. This means that instead of a national plan and national regulations that can be modified for the whole country as our growing experience suggests and as our changing social attitudes are reflected in new styles of living, we have 50 disparate

sets of regulations, each tied to local preferences and prejudices and each subject to local pressures.

Everyone who has been working in the civil-rights movement and everyone who understands the need for the Equal
Rights Amendment is fully conscious of the difference between having and not having a nationally accepted frame of
reference within which people can work out their local styles
of action. It is the lack of any overarching principles that
makes people despair of ever modifying and unifying our ways
of caring for children.

It is true that when one progressive state sets a precedent,
other progressive states with enlightened views of child welfare may follow suit. In 1965 California permitted an adoption by a single adult, and other states accepted the challenge
and added their weight to this change in style. But every
change of this kind potentially has to be fought on 50 fronts
to be accepted by the country as a whole. For up to the
present the Federal Government has done almost nothing with
adoption, and only recently—through financial benefits provided by the Social Security laws—has backed up state plans
for foster-home care for homeless children.

Yet the most urgent problems of children and the kinds of
action that would be truly in their best interests—actions
breaking away from older ways of doing things and actions
incorporating contemporary hopes and demands—are essentially alike everywhere.

For example, adoption and foster care have developed
along two separate tracks, and very often persons who are professionally concerned with the one aspect of child care are out
of touch with and ill informed about the other. This is because
adoption has to do with children who have been legally released—voluntarily or involuntarily—from the care of birth
parents. A mother might have given up her child, or the court
might have removed a child from her home because of gross

neglect or child abuse or mental illness or drug addiction on the part of a parent or simply abandonment of the child by her parents—the specific reasons vary considerably from one state to the next.

In contrast, foster care has to do with children who have not been legally "freed" but whose problems may be no different from those who have been. In theory, foster care is strictly a temporary solution for children who will one day return to their birth parents. In practice, foster homes have become the principal refuge of children in limbo. They are children for whom no other solution has been found because they are Black or Hispanic or of mixed race, because they are homely or believed to be retarded or otherwise mildly or seriously incapacitated, because they are unhappy or troublesome, because they are quiet, untroublesome children who have been forgotten, because the children refuse to be separated from siblings, because they are "too old"—all reasons why caseworkers believe these children are not adoptable. Or, ironically, they remain in foster care because their foster parents, who love them, cannot support them without the monetary subsidy or the medical care not provided for adopted children.

We urgently need to unify this two-track system, for by and large, it is precisely the children who come into long-time foster care or, lacking even this, are lodged in group homes or institutions who are in most desperate need of a family to give them a viable identity and the security that will allow them to grow into mature adulthood.

We need to listen to adults who are willing—eager—to take on the responsibility of one child or several children who in no way meet the older ideal of the adoptable child. In fact, we need to draw on the experience of adoptive parents who have already fought their way through the legal and agency obstacle courses to create the most complexly organized families made up of troubled children. It is clearly a taste that grows with experience. I have heard of one set of parents and grandparents, fortunately affluent, who have 19 variously "difficult" adopted children.

But not all prospective adoptive parents who would—and could—take on the responsibility for difficult children are affluent. Like so many foster parents, they need not only a subsidy to help pay for the costs of adoption (such subsidies are available today) but also financial assistance to meet the costs of caring for and educating their adopted children, and any funds for this purpose are very hard to come by. Yet if we are really concerned for the "best interests of the child," it is crucial that we back up the hopes of troubled children and the desire on the part of adopting adults to give them a real family.

And above all, I believe, it is necessary that all those who have been working for children—as volunteers, as parents of adopted children and caring adults in charge of foster children, as members of local and national organizations concerned with child welfare and as professional people active in agencies—should now work in every possible way for a national adoption framework. Ideally, this framework should permit the smallest local group, and prospective adoptive parents anywhere in our country, to arrange adoptions and to care for children, who are our country's future.

Anyone can tell you it will not be easy. It will take time and thought and energy and an unflagging willingness to face and overcome angry frustration. But if we will not, who will look after the human rights of children who are without power to act for themselves?

International Year of the Child: A Beacon of Hope

MAY 1979

In May of 1979, when we in the United States will be celebrating Mother's Day as usual, many American mothers will be deep into another, world-wide celebration. The year 1979 has been proclaimed by the General Assembly of the United Nations as the International Year of the Child, to mark the 20th anniversary of the UN Declaration of the Rights of the Child and to assess what we have been doing for our own and the world's children.

Here at home in May, we shall have heard early reports from our own National IYC Commission, which is scheduled to make a final report to President Carter in April of 1980 on the condition of children in the United States. We shall have heard from a great many of the more than 200 nongovernmental organizations and innumerable local groups that have been meeting and talking and planning programs to honor our American version of IYC. And along the way we shall have encountered enough programs and projects about children in other parts of the world to bring home to us the fact that this year-long event concerns not only our own children but also all the children in the world, and is being celebrated by all the peoples in the 141 countries of the United Nations.

This is all very good, and it should be very exciting.

But I wonder. Have you asked yourself: What is *my* contribution to this year of the child? Have you taken a fresh, informed look at all the different children living in your neighborhood or town? Are you pleased with what you see, or are you troubled by the great needs of some—perhaps many—of the children? Are you a passive onlooker in this celebration, or are you actively working as a volunteer or a professional woman with a group that is trying to assess and meet such needs? Have you given thought to the problems of children elsewhere in the world? Have you asked your own children how they feel about growing up in the world we have made for them?

These aren't simply rhetorical questions. They are, I am convinced, questions every one of us must ask ourselves and each other, questions we must ask in our own community and every other community, wherever we can, at home and abroad. Asking questions helps one to focus one's attention, and that is the first, essential step to useful action.

But isn't it enough simply to celebrate the well-being of so many of our children?

No, it is not. It is critically important that each of us act— that we become involved. IYC has to do with something like one third of the world's total population of 4 billion people, among them about 66 million citizens of our own country. As a group they are both vulnerable and, unless we act for them, relatively helpless, for they are the world's children under 18 years of age. But potentially they are also very powerful. By the year 2000—only 21 years away—they will have become the women and men who are taking charge everywhere on earth. How they will then live together on our planet and, looking ahead, what they will then plan for their own future will depend a great deal on what we do—and on what we neglect to do—for the world's children today.

In my own childhood, English-speaking children learned Robert Louis Stevenson's verse:

> "Little Indian, Sioux or Crow,
> Little frosty Eskimo,
> Little Turk or Japanee,
> Oh, don't you wish that
> you were me?"

And thereby learned both that children around the world were very different from one another and that some—they themselves—were far more privileged.

Today this has changed profoundly. The needs of children that are crying to be met in other, poorer countries—the need for health care and education and protection—exist among our own children as well. And because radio and television have brought us closer together—at least superficially—children all over the world are not so different from one another as they once were.

Theirs is a unique generation—the first generation that has always known a world with a network of immediate communications reaching the most remote places on earth and with swift means of travel to those most distant places. Because of these international connections, this generation everywhere, not only in a few sophisticated centers, could benefit by the best understanding we have of what children need to grow in health and to realize high life expectations. Already, wherever they are, children are beginning to share some of their life experiences.

In the 1960s, when I returned to Manus, in the Admiralty Islands of Papua New Guinea, teen-aged schoolchildren were singing the Beatles' songs. And today, almost everywhere, you can hear very *little* children singing the *Sesame Street* songs. What this means is that these girls and boys, though they may never actually meet, will forever share a kind of imagery, a way of learning and a view of the world that belongs to their whole generation.

Surely this new sharing is worth celebrating! But it is no more than a beginning. So much depends on what we are willing to do—whether we will work to improve the chances of all children or will shrug off the opportunity, not caring that people who have shared some experiences must be doubly aware of the less positive circumstances in their lives that set them apart.

So many Americans have said to me: "Of course, we are a very progressive people. Children are the future and we have always put the children first!" We certainly have believed this, and not too long ago it might have been true, at least as a dream—a hope—that drove many parents to the hardest work so that their children would have fuller, more satisfying lives than they themselves had had. It was a dream that brought young people to America from the ends of the earth and was part of the adventure of opening the whole continent.

Today most parents still hope that their own children will succeed in life. But the dream that *all* children will share alike in a better, more satisfying life seems to be fading. We still speak the words, but do we share the belief? Are we willing to work for it?

In fact, the belief is embodied as an ideal for the whole world in the Declaration of Rights of the Child, adopted by the United Nations in 1959, which states that each child has the right:

to affection, love and understanding
to adequate nutrition and medical care
to a free education
to the opportunity for play and recreation
to a name and nationality
to special care, if handicapped
to have a chance to become a useful member of society and to develop individual abilities
to live in peace and universal brotherhood
to the enjoyment of these rights, regardless of race, color, sex, religion, national or social origin

But when we look at the children in our own country alone, we find that a great many of them live in circumstances that reflect something very different from the rights set forth in the Declaration. We find that in some ways we are retreating from our clear social responsibilities although we are in a better position than ever before—at least in terms of our understanding of children's needs—to implement them.

It is impossible, of course, to legislate "affection, love and understanding." But we *can* work toward communities of caring people, communities in which there are resources to which adults and children in troubled families can turn for help and on which parents and children can depend when, inevitably, some adults can't make it and some children break down in despair or rebellion.

Instead, we are faced with a growing number of single-parent families—an outcome in part of what we euphemistically call our "welfare" system. We are discovering that a vast number of small children, perhaps as many as 1 million a year, suffer from extreme neglect and from physical or emotional abuse by the very adults on whom they depend for survival. Accidents, so often related to child abuse or neglect, are now the leading cause of death of children under 14 years of age. The rate of child suicide is going up: Among boys between 10 and 14 years of age it has doubled and among boys between 15 and 19 it has tripled since 1950. And every year the number of child runaways grows, and we are discovering new forms of abuse as these children are drawn into pornographic displays and both boy and girl prostitution. How many safe places have we provided for children who fear to go home and fear for their lives in the streets?

We could, if we decided to do so, legislate shelters for abused or homeless children; we could legislate adequate health care for all our children, including preventive care for well children and the special kinds of care for handicapped children that would open the way for most of them to a mature and independent adulthood. We could supplement the diet of pregnant women, babies and children in their growing years so that they would have a good chance to do well, physically and mentally.

More than one third of our children under 14 years of age are not fully protected against preventable childhood diseases and almost one third of all children under 17 have never been treated by a dentist. And not all these children live in families that cannot afford medical care, nor are all under- and over-nourished children in families too poor or too ignorant to give them proper nourishment.

We are making some fresh beginnings, based on better knowledge, in our methods of care for children with different kinds of handicaps. In the past, too many handicapped children could receive some education and training only by leaving their homes and living for months and years in special institutions, where they were cut off from play with well children and from the everyday life of a community of families, adults and children of all kinds. Legislation has been passed. But as yet how many children with handicaps have open to them both the special help they so urgently need and education in the company of other children? How many teachers are we training to carry this additional, complex educational load?

It would be possible to go on with an analysis of this kind related to every one of the declared rights of children. We know very well, for example, that in spite of the turmoil about schools, there are many schools so inadequate and many pupils so grossly neglected that it has been demonstrated that they cannot read a want ad, fill out a job application properly, make sense of a driver's license manual or follow the simple instructions on a frozen-food package.

Too many people have come to believe that a good education for all children is too expensive for a community to provide. But how much more expensive is it to cope with the inadequacies, frustrations, depression and angry destructiveness of children growing into adults who are essentially illiterate in a world that depends on sophisticated literacy?

We know a great deal about what must be done to bring up a generation that can put the world into better order. But we also deny that it *can* be done. All around the United States,

citizens are protesting against the cost of caring for people
—adults as well as children—other than themselves. They are,
in the newest cultlike phrase, "fiscal conservatives." They
are, in fact, using this label as a mask for an ancient evil—
social irresponsibility.

I think it is true that in some respects we have been spending money—and using our most precious resources in people
and knowledge—unwisely. But the answer lies not in remov-
ing ourselves from the scene, hardening our hearts, closing
our minds and simply taking back what once was given.

The answer—or at least the first steps to some answers—
lies with every one of us. Each of us needs to commit herself
to work with intelligence and caring concern in her own community—for adequate child-care centers, particularly for the
children of working mothers, and for after-school programs
for older children; for supplemental nutritional programs for
those who need wholesome food, sponsored by local schools
and churches, hospitals and clinics; for schools that teach and
teaching that will include handicapped children as full members of the school community. We need to make sure that
there are in our communities resources for the protection of
abused children, and facilities to which teen-aged girls—expectant mothers and mothers of young babies—can turn for
care and counseling. We need to broaden the possibilities for
foster care, especially for children threatened by a family
crisis.

Where we can, each of us needs to work *in* such programs:
as teachers' aides, as helpers in hard-pressed clinics and shelters, as planners and clerks, sometimes even as envelope-stuff-
ers for those organizations that are working for the good of
children and of the community. By involving ourselves within
our communities, I believe, we shall also begin to reach out,
seeing what we do as part of a national and a world-wide
effort.

Over the last generation we have turned far too much over

to professionals with whom we are out of touch. We need those professionals—indeed, we need far more women and men who are professionally informed. But equally we need people at every level of community life who are involved because they are both caring *and* informed. We need, in fact, volunteers with energy, clear minds and strongly beating hearts. And who can they be but you yourselves?

Talk with your own children. Who better can convince you?

And then if you and your children together will agree to treat Mother's Day as a day of commitment—a commitment to be renewed each year—our thinking and working will go on *long after the end* of this International Year of the Child and there will be bright hope in the future for all the world's children—and that means for all of us.

Epigraph

"In a darkened world beset by the fear of nuclear holocaust, degradation of our soil and air and imbalance of population growth that threatens to strangle our human settlements, the Year of the Child stands like a beacon of hope. We must see that its light guides us and gives us direction for preparing a livable, sustainable, beautiful world for our children—those who have been born, those who have been conceived but not yet born, and those children of the future not yet conceived. By keeping our eyes steadily on the pressing needs of children we can determine what needs to be done, and what can be prepared for but accomplished later. For babies cannot wait."

— Margaret Mead
(1901-1978)

From the "Preliminary Report to the President," U.S. National Commission on the International Year of the Child 1979. Washington, D.C., November 30, 1978.